THE JUDICIARY

The Supreme Court in the Governmental Process

The Allyn and Bacon Series in American Government

General Editor: William M. Beaney
                    University of Denver College of Law

THE JUDICIARY

The Supreme Court
in the Governmental Process
4th edition

Henry J. Abraham

Henry L. and Grace Doherty Professor of Government and Foreign Affairs
University of Virginia

ALLYN AND BACON, INC.

Boston, London, Sydney, Toronto

To Peter

Library of Congress Cataloging in Publication Data

Abraham, Henry Julian, 1921-
    The judiciary.

    (The Allyn and Bacon series in American government)
    Bibliography: p.
    Includes index.
    1. United States. Supreme Court. I. Title.
KF8748.A2 1977   347'.73'26   76-44353

ISBN 0-205-05757-8
Third printing . . . November, 1977

Contents

Foreword

For too many years students of the American political process have been introduced to the subject through the medium of highly detailed texts that in seeking the goals of completeness and neutrality have often managed to destroy the excitement and fascination which our complex system should develop in any inquiring mind. The Allyn and Bacon Series in American Government is designed to make available a number of relatively short studies by authors of the highest reputation. Their insights into the way our political system works are based on extensive research and long teaching experience. This first volume in the series, *The Judiciary* by Professor Henry J. Abraham, is an auspicious beginning of a series that promises to be exciting in itself and a useful introduction to the wider field of political science.

William M. Beaney

Preface

To the First Edition

Despite a growing awareness by the American public of the significant role played by the judiciary, the latter is still the least known, the least understood, and the most maligned of the three branches of the United States government. That this is not a surprising state of affairs does not gainsay the need to try to provide insight and material which may help to alleviate the problem. There is some evidence of a growing body of serious commentary on the judiciary, in general, and the Supreme Court, in particular—but much of it has been produced with either little or no regard for the nonprofessional reader or student, and a good deal of it is difficult or expensive to obtain. The purpose of this little book is to avoid these problems by presenting a brief but meaningful analysis of the judicial function as seen through the role of the Supreme Court of the United States in the governmental process. It is both an explanatory and an evaluative presentation, but I have endeavored to be objective in an area where far too much reaction is still based upon the answer to the question "whose ox is being gored?" This work is by no means a wholly uncritical study of the Supreme Court and its functions, but I happen to believe strongly that, on balance, it has played not only a crucial but an indispensable role in the growth and evolution of our Republic.

Designed for use by the general public as well as by students of government and politics at all levels, the book tells its essential story in three chapters: The first treats the dual system of courts in the United States and the jurisdiction and institutional setting of the Supreme Court. The second deals extensively with what has clearly become the

Court's most important function: its role in the delineation
and preservation of basic individual freedoms in our democratic society. The chapter does this topically by an analysis
and explanation of both historical and legal aspects, in particular stressing the judicial role in the interpretation and application of constitutional mandates to the national government
and the states in such vital areas as religion, expression,
political and racial equality, with a thorough consideration of
the general problem of substantive and procedural due process of law. The third chapter, after explaining the selection
of judges and justices, concentrates on three significantly
difficult and vexatious problems in the Supreme Court's
function: its ultimate power of judicial review, its role as a
"line-drawer," and that of a public policy-maker.

My greatest debt in the writing of this work is to Profes
sor William M. Beaney . . . who, as editor of the Allyn and
Bacon Series of which this is the first publication, provided
both the essential encouragement and necessary criticism; I
am deeply grateful to him. Among the many others who
stimulated and aided in a variety of ways, I should like to
single out Professor, now Congressman from Iowa, John R.
Schmidhauser, who read the entire manuscript; Mrs. Helen
White, who typed it with her usual efficiency; Mr. John R.
DeRemigis, who conceived the Allyn and Bacon Series; the
Oxford University Press for its generously granted permission
to adapt for Chapters 1 and 3 material used in my *The
Judicial Process: An Introductory Analysis of the Courts of
the United States, England, and France* (New York, 1962);
Miss Nancy L. Schnerr and Mrs. Sylvia G. Balis of the
Statistics Department, who provided a necessary "hiding
place" for me to write in peace; my faithful and hard-work-
ing research assistants, Rocco D'Amico and Paul Lutzker;
and, *bien entendu*, my wife, Mildred, who has been loyally at
my side through many a complex writing episode.

And, like an earlier one to his older brother, the book is
cheerfully dedicated to a very young man who helped, too—
in his own manner.

March 1965   Henry J. Abraham

To the Second Edition

The happily favorable reception accorded to the first edition of this little book prompted the writing of the second. All materials have been duly brought up to date until the October 1968 term of the Supreme Court. I am profoundly grateful for the helpful criticism and suggestions of a host of colleagues and students.

November 1968   **H.J.A.**

To the Third Edition

It is a pleasure to reiterate the sentiments and actions outlined in the preface to the second edition for this third, which has not only been duly brought up to date through the 1972 labors of the Supreme Court, but has been significantly enlarged, including the addition of a second chapter on fundamental freedoms.

January 1973   **H.J.A.**

To the Fourth Edition

The evolving governmental scene and the continuing happy reception of this work have combined to prompt this latest revision and thorough updating, following the basic plan of previous editions (particularly the third). I am profoundly grateful to a host of colleagues and students for their advice and encouragement.

October 1976   **H.J.A.**

I

American Courts in Practice

Most Americans know less about the judicial branch of their government than they do its other two branches, the legislative and the executive. This is particularly regrettable because it is to the courts that Americans turn almost eagerly when they seek solutions to difficult and delicate problems of public concern that the legislative and executive branches are unable or unwilling to handle. The legislative branch has been especially guilty of avoiding troublesome matters of public policy. While publicly flaying the courts—especially the Supreme Court and frequently with intemperate language if not vilification—the legislative branch has been quite willing to "pass the buck." Thus we Americans legalize our politics; a fact of governmental life Alexis de Tocqueville recognized 135 years ago when he opined that, sooner or later, in the United States every political question inexorably becomes a legal question. And so it has been.

Two illustrations of pressing and controversial public policy which thus ultimately landed in the lap of the United States Supreme Court are desegregation and legislative districting. Although the Court[1] had, and quite properly so, done its best to avoid the issues, time ran out. When these two delicate matters reached the bar of the Court, there was evidently near-unanimity among the American people in the

---

[1] Throughout this work, references to "the Court" will signify the United States Supreme Court unless specified otherwise.

1

desegregation

first matter and sizeable majority opinion in the second that a stand had to be taken by the highest tribunal in the American judicial structure. Thus came about the monumental Supreme Court decisions in *Brown* v. *Board of Education*[2] and *Baker* v. *Carr*[3]—decisions that triggered revolutionary changes in the social, economic, and political structure of America's body politic. As will be explained in Chapter III, the *Brown* decision (together with its implementation decision one year later[4]) held that state-mandated segregation by race in public schools constitutes a violation of the equal protection of the laws clause of the Fourteenth Amendment to the United States Constitution. This violation was to be eradicated "with all deliberate speed," under the banner of a "prompt and reasonable start."[5] (Earlier[6] and later[7] decisions also ruled a variety of other types of state-authorized or sanctioned racial segregation violative of the Fourteenth Amendment.)

The *Baker* case held that the question of deliberate mal-, mis-, or non-apportionment of representative districts in the several states—a matter the Court had understandably deliberately avoided as "a political question" until the 1962 decision—was a justiciable controversy in the federal courts, and that "invidious discrimination" in the drawing of district lines might well constitute a violation of the equal protection and/or due process of law clauses of the Fourteenth Amendment. *Baker* proved to be the vehicle that ultimately permitted logical extensions of the reapportionment matter in *Wesberry* v. *Sanders* (applying the "one-man-one-vote" principle to *congressional* districts)[8] and, even more dramatically,

[2] 347 U.S. 483 (1954).
[3] 369 U.S. 186 (1962).
[4] 349 U.S. 294 (1955).
[5] *Brown* v. *Board of Education of Topeka, Kansas,* 349 U.S. 294 (1955).
[6] E.g., *Sweatt* v. *Painter,* 339 U.S. 629 (1950); *Shelley* v. *Kraemer,* 334 U.S. 1 (1948); *Morgan* v. *Virginia,* 328 U.S. 373 (1946).
[7] E.g., *Cooper* v. *Aaron,* 358 U.S. 1 (1958); *Watson* v. *Memphis,* 373 U.S. 526 (1963); *Peterson* v. *Greenville,* 373 U.S. 244 (1963); *Griffin* v. *Prince Edward County School Board,* 377 U.S. 218 (1964); *Green* v. *School Board of New Kent County,* 391 U.S. 430 (1968); *Alexander* v. *Holmes County, Miss., Board of Education,* 396 U.S. 19 (1969).; *Norwood* v. *Harrison,* 413 U.S. 455 (1973).
[8] 376 U.S. 1 (1964).

in *Reynolds v. Sims* (requiring representation based on *population*, with the apportionment to reflect the principle of "approximate equality" for *both* houses of state legislatures).[9] It was extended to the county and city levels in subsequent decisions, ultimately to embrace all *elected* bodies exercising *general* governmental powers.[10]

It is probably regrettable that the desegregation and redistricting issues were not resolved by the executive or legislative branches of the government, but they had either purposely failed to act, or for a variety of reasons had been unsuccessful in acting. The responsibility fell to the judiciary of the United States, with the Supreme Court at its zenith— that institution which, in the 1963 words of its chief justice, "must always stand ready to advance the rights of . . . minorities, if the executive and legislative branches falter."[11] And falter they have on sundry occasions. Let us now briefly examine the structure and operation of the judiciary in the United States, with particular emphasis on the federal bench.

THE DUAL SYSTEM OF COURTS IN THE UNITED STATES

Because we are governed by a *federal* system in the United States, the fifty state governments, as well as the national government, make and enforce law. Consequently, there exist, side by side, either two separate systems of courts or fifty-one, depending upon one's view of how separate and distinct the several state systems are. For present purposes, however, we will adopt the concept of two distinct judicial systems that are created by the two major basic authorities under our federal structure, the national and state constitutions. Although these two systems may, and often do, come

---

[9] 377 U.S. 533 (1964).

[10] E.g., *Avery* v. *Midland County*, 390 U.S. 474 (1968) and *Hadley* v. *Junior College District of Metropolitan Kansas City*, 397 U.S. 50 (1970). But elected *judicial* bodies were exempt (*Wells* v. *Edwards*, 409 U.S. 1095, 1973) and so were certain but not all special purpose governmental bodies, such as some school boards (*Rosenthal* v. *Board of Education of Central High School*, 420 U.S. 985, 1975).

[11] As quoted in *The Philadelphia Inquirer*, October 4, 1968, p. 1.

together at the bar of the finite interpretative authority of
the federal Supreme Court, they are nonetheless wholly distinct bodies, each applying its own basic document and laws
and actions based thereon.

Legal procedures from offense to trial and appeal vary
not only between civil and criminal cases, but also among the
various jurisdictions. Generally, however, the following represent typical procedural steps:

Civil Cases	Criminal Cases
1. Plaintiff brings suit against defendant.	1. Apprehension by agents of government.
2. Summons.	2. Preliminary Examination.
3. Pleadings.	3. Grand Jury or Information."
4. Trial.	
5. Verdict.	4. Arraignment and Pleading.
6. Judgment and Sentencing.	5. Trial.
	6. Verdict.
7. Appeal.	7. Judgment and Sentencing.
8. Enforcement.	8. Appeal.
	9. Execution of Sentence.

When the two judicial systems do "converge" at the level
of the United States Supreme Court, they do so only because
litigants have been able to raise a substantial federal question
in the state courts below. (The Supreme Court itself determines what is "substantial.") Moreover, they must have
exhausted all proper remedies at the state level in order to
have proper "standing" before the Supreme Court. In all but
a handful of cases, the Supreme Court has complete discretionary authority to accept or reject a petition for review.
With the exception of this appellate pathway to the Court,
and the technical and confusing matters of injunctive relief
and habeas corpus proceedings, the two systems constitute
separate entities that must, and almost invariably do, respect
each other's jurisdictional lines. These lines may be, but only
infrequently are, reinforced by Congress in accordance with
its constitutionally granted power to establish "inferior
courts."[12]

---

[12] Article III, Section, 1, Paragraph 1.

The State Judiciary

Each and every state constitution either establishes a judicial branch, wholly or partly, or it authorizes its legislature to provide for it. However, so much variation in nomenclature as well as structure exists among the judicial systems of the fifty states that is is necessary to create a composite that will give a picture of the typical state system. The newly constituted unified court system of Florida might well serve as a commendable "model" state court system.

At the bottom of the typical state judicial hierarchy is the legendary "J.P.," the *Justice of the Peace*, also known as *Magistrate* or *Squire*. Although usually he is elected, he may be appointed, and he generally serves for a term of two to six years in his jurisdiction, normally a county, city, township, or town. He is judicial "jack-of-all-trades" who handles a host of minor civil matters and criminal misdemeanors. Since much, if not all, of his income more often than not depends upon the fees he receives for his labors, the average Justice of the Peace, who is not necessarily always trained in the law, has demonstrated a remarkable tendency toward convictions. For example, in Pennsylvania, convictions in 1968 averaged 93 percent in civil and 83 percent in criminal cases, by no means atypical percentages.[13] There are some signs that indicate the existence of genuine concern with the current state of this minor court,[14] and reforms have been effected in a number of states, but it is doubtful that it will soon take place on a general scale. Like so many "time-honored" traditions, that of the *J.P.* has been able to survive as much because of inertia as tradition.

At the next higher level in the state judiciary hierarchy is the *Municipal Court*, sometimes called *Traffic Court*, *Court of Small Claims*, *Night Court*, or *Police Court*. Whatever it is

---

[13] See my *The Judicial Process: An Introductory Analysis of the Courts of the United States, England, and France*, 3rd ed. (New York: Oxford University, 1975), pp. 139–141.

[14] In 1975 the Court granted review on the question of whether a non-lawyer jurist could constitutionally sit in a jail-carrying criminal case. (*North* v. *Russell*, 422 U.S. 1040.) Yes, it ruled some months later, 6:2—provided that the defendant have an opportunity through an appeal to obtain a second trial before a judge who is a lawyer. (*North* v. *Russell*, 44 LW 5085, 1976.)

called, the Municipal Court is generally a court of original, rather than appellate, jurisdiction, and is the first official state "court of record" (a term designed to identify those tribunals presided over by judges rather than magistrates). Its jurisdiction is relatively restricted, often with a ceiling of $500 to $1,000 in civil cases and minor criminal cases, but this varies from state to state. Its judges are almost always trained lawyers.

Third in ascending order in the judicial hierarchy lies a court of fairly general jurisdiction, more often than not known as the *County Court,* because its broad original civil and criminal jurisdiction is customarily limited to one or more counties. Juries are usually present in this court. Some of the host of associated tribunals at the County Court level are: *Quarter Sessions; Common Pleas; Oyer and Terminer; Orphans; Probate; Domestic Relations; Juvenile; Equity; Surrogate;* and *Chancery.* All these courts at the county level have original jurisdiction in the various areas roughly indicated by their names.[15]

Although in most states appeals from the County Court go directly to the State Supreme Court, the pressure of work at the latter tribunal's level has often necessitated the creation of an intermediate court of appeals. That court is frequently known as the *Appellate Division* (New York) or the *Superior Court* (Pennsylvania). Very much in the fashion of the United States Court of Appeals, it is the first, and usually final, stop for appeals that come up from the courts below in accordance with statutory requirements. In the larger states, such as the two mentioned above plus California, it performs a valuable job of disposing of appeals with considerable dispatch.[16]

In almost all of the states the highest court in the judicial hierarchy is known as the *Supreme Court.* In New York, Kentucky, and Maryland, however, it is called the *Court of*

---

[15] Oyer and Terminer is a criminal court with jurisdiction over capital crimes and other felonies; Quarter Sessions is a court that meets four times a year for criminal cases below the felony level; Chancery specializes in equity matters; and Surrogate is a court similar to Probate, which adjudicates matters involving wills, deeds, and estates.

[16] Some states use certain specialty courts which sit astride the overall system, e.g., Pennsylvania's *Commonwealth Court.* Created in

Appeals; in Maine it is known as the *Supreme Judicial Court,* and in West Virginia as the *Supreme Court of Appeals.* Whatever its name, its decisions constitute the law of the state and are thus final and binding on the hierarchy below, which is comprised of local as well as statewide tribunals. Only if all these remedies have been exhausted, and provided that a *substantial federal* question is present, do litigants now have an opportunity to hope for, but certainly not to count upon, review by the highest court of the land. The pathway of appeals from the state courts to the federal courts omits any way station in the lower federal hierarchy (except in a very few complicated jurisdictional situations which need not concern us here). If the United States Supreme Court is willing to hear a case, or, in those very rare instances, when it must, that case will move directly from the highest state court—all remedies below having been duly exhausted—to the highest federal court.

The Federal Judiciary

Two Types. There are two types of federal courts, the *constitutional* courts and the *legislative* courts. Our chief concern is with the former, and particularly with the three original[17] constitutional courts, the *United States District Courts,* the *United States Courts of Appeals,* and the *United States Supreme Court.*

The distinction between the two types of federal courts is in their functions as well as in the constitutional authority under which they were or are created. Broadly speaking, the constitutional courts are established under the judiciary article of the United States Constitution, Article III; the legislative courts, on the other hand, owe their existence to Article I, the legislative article of the Constitution. What, then, are the several significant differences between these two types of tribunals?

1970, its sole function is to hear cases relating to the tasks of government agencies.

[17]The Supreme Court is stipulated in Article III of the U.S. Constitution. The other two courts were established by the Judiciary Act of 1789.

Distinctions. One key difference is that the legislative courts possess certain functions of a "non-judicial" or at least "quasi-judicial" nature, such as administrative and/or quasi-legislative as well as judicial tasks, whereas the constitutional courts are presumably confined to strictly judicial roles. A second is that although the legislative courts are part and parcel of the constitutional appellate structure for certain specific purposes, their *raison d'être* is to aid in the administration of particular congressional statutes.

A third difference between the two types of courts is that unlike the constitutional courts, the legislative tribunals are empowered to render *advisory opinions*, i.e., rulings upon the propriety or constitutionality of governmental action in the absence of a bona fide case or controversy requiring such a ruling for its disposition. In effect, this function was established as early as 1793, when President George Washington addressed a letter to the members of the Supreme Court asking them for an opinion on the authority given to him by the Constitution to decide certain questions involving the United States's policy of neutrality in the war then in progress in Europe. Chief Justice John Jay, the Court's first, and rather reluctant, head, responded for his Court that not only would it not, *it could not*, tender legal advice, and that its role was confined to the decision of cases that arose in the course of bona fide litigation. However, both types of courts (the constitutional courts only since 1934) are statutorily empowered to render so-called *declaratory judgments.* These rulings differ from advisory opinions because of the presence of an actual controversy in the case of declaratory judgment, whereas an advisory opinion deals with an abstract or hypothetical question. In other words, a declaratory judgment enables courts of all types to enter a final judgment between litigants in an *actual controversy*, and defines their respective rights under a law, contract, will, or any other official document, *without*, however, attaching any consequential or coercive relief to that otherwise binding judgment.[18]

---

[18] For examples of declaratory judgment action by constitutional courts, see *Nashville, Chicago & St. Louis Railway* v. *Wallace*, 288 U.S. 249 (1933); *Tileston* v. *Ullman*, 318 U.S. 44 (1943); and *Steffel* v. *Thompson*, 415 U.S. 452 (1974).

Constitutional, yes

A fourth, and at least theoretically the most crucial, difference between constitutional and legislative courts, relates to the constitutionally expressed safeguards of tenure, salary, and—by implication and effect—independence that accrue to the constitutional courts by virtue of the provisions of the second sentence in Article III, Section I of the Constitution, which reads:

> The judges, both of the Supreme and inferior courts, shall hold their offices during good behavior, and shall, at stated times, receive for their services, a compensation, which shall not be diminished during their continuance in office.

Legislative, no

No such safeguards exist for the courts created under the legislative article of the Constitution, which simply says in Article I, Section 8, Clause 9 that Congress shall have power "To constitute tribunals inferior to the Supreme Court." The distinction signifies that judges of the constitutional courts are removable only when they no longer "behave well," which, in effect, clothes them with life tenure. Removal, other than by death, resignation, or retirement, can thus come about solely via the impeachment and conviction process, an unlikely but certainly not unheard-of or unresorted-to procedure. To date, as a result of bills of impeachment duly voted by the House of Representatives and sent on to the Senate for trial, nine impeachment trials have been held involving federal judges. Seven of these were against judges on the United States District Court, one against a judge on the now-defunct United States Commerce Court (a legislative court), and one, in 1804–1805, against an associate justice of the Supreme Court of the United States, Justice Samuel Chase. Of these, five resulted in acquittals, four in convictions; of the latter probably only two were justified legally.[19] If Congress chooses to do so, as indeed it has

---

[19] For a fuller description and discussion, see my *The Judicial Process*, op. cit., pp. 40–46. To convict, a two-thirds majority of the members of the Senate present and voting (there being a quorum on the floor) must find the accused guilty on at least one count of the offense(s) charged. But only a majority of members of the House is needed to vote a bill of impeachment for subsequent Senate trial.

frequently seen fit, it may extend "good behavior" tenure to legislative court judges as well, but it is under no constitutional obligation to do so.

The latter consideration also applies in the case of the constitutional injunction against reduction of judicial salaries while in office, but Congress would hardly be likely to reduce these in any case. An intriguing development in this connection was the suit by 142 lower federal judges in 1976, charging that due to inflation, their constitutional safeguard against salary reduction during their tenure had been violated! Their appeal was rejected by the U.S. Court of Claims in May 1977. Although not by any means miniscule, the 1976 salaries of federal judges (tied to the cost-of-living index as of 1975, but limited to an annual increment of 5 percent) were all too often less than those of certain state judges (e.g., New York's highest court jurist—$58,622); they ranged from $42,000 for judges of the United States Customs Court to $68,600 for the Chief Justice of the United States. His associates on the Supreme Court received $2,625 less. Raises to $54,500, $75,000, and $72,000, respectively, came in 1977.

In view of the constitutional prohibition against "diminishing compensation" during their term in office, an intriguing problem by implication soon faced the justices of the highest constitutional court in the land in connection with the matter of intergovernmental tax immunity, i.e., the problem of clarifying the extent of implied restrictions upon the taxing power which derive from the nature of our federal system of government. In other words, did the Constitution place limitations upon the power of the two prongs of the federal system, the national (federal) government and the several states, to tax each other's instrumentalities, property, and activities? This is not the place to go into the details of this complicated problem, but as the immunity doctrine began to develop (its initial and great pronunciamento came in Chief Justice Marshall's decision in the monumental case of *McCulloch* v. *Maryland*[20]), it became quite clear that the jurists would not only *not* view with favor the taxation of federal officials by the states, nor that of state officials by

---

[20] 4 Wheaton 316 (1819).

the federal government,[21] but not even that by the federal government of *its own* officials! This immunity doctrine was continued, and even enlarged, until the third decade of this century. But by then the long and strong protests by Justice Oliver Wendell Holmes, Jr. and Justice Louis D. Brandeis—who had *voluntarily* paid to the federal government what they would have to pay had their salaries been considered taxable—later joined by Justice Harlan F. Stone, coupled with new congressional legislation and new personnel on the Court, brought about the cessation of intergovernmental tax immunity for the salaries of both federal and state employees.[22]

Federal Legislative Courts

As indicated earlier, all of these courts are created under the legislative article of the Constitution, which expressly extends that power to Congress (Article I, Section 8, Clause 9). Utilizing that enabling power, Congress has thus seen fit from time to time to establish sundry legislative courts. These were established partly in order to have "more flexible" tribunals than the three leading constitutional courts—the United States Supreme Court, the Courts of Appeals, and the District Courts; partly to remove some of the crushing work load of cases from the latter tribunals; and partly as a result of technical needs in particular areas of public life—the rationale for the *United States Court of Military Appeals*, for example. What Congress does, then, is to combine this basic legislative power to establish tribunals inferior to the Supreme Court with the famous "implied powers" or "elastic clause" (I–8–18) of the Constitution *and* the specific congressional authority in which it may wish to establish the legislative court. For example, in the case of the aforementioned Court of Military Appeals, it could have used any one of the half-dozen of its overall war powers (I–8–11 through 16), but it chose to rely predominantly upon its power "To make rules for the government and regulation of

---

[21] *The Collector* v. *Day*, 11 Wallace 113 (1871).
[22] See *Helvering* v. *Gerhardt*, 304 U.S. 405 (1938) and *Graves* v. *New York ex rel O'Keefe*, 306 U.S. 466 (1939).

the land and naval forces" (I–8–14). It employed its power "To regulate commerce with foreign nations, and among the several States, and with the Indian tribes" (I–8–3) to create the now-defunct *United States Commerce Court;* the taxing power (I—8—1) for the *United States Customs Court,* the status of which it changed in 1956 to that of a constitutional court, and for the *United States Tax Court,* which it transformed from an administrative agency under I.R.S. to a legislative court in 1969; and its special power over territories and other property belonging to the United States (found in IV–3–2) to establish the various territorial courts.[23]

Federal Constitutional Courts

The three most important, and presumably best-known, federal courts are the three original *constitutional* courts, the United States District Courts, the United States Courts of Appeals, and the United States Supreme Court. Created under Article III of the Constitution (the Supreme Court is the only one expressly mentioned in the basic document), the three remained the sole constitutional courts in the American judicial hierarchy until the "transformation" of the three erstwhile legislative courts, as noted above.[24] The

---

[23] As will have become apparent, the number of legislative courts has declined with the passing of the years: some have been discontinued (the Commerce Court in 1915); some have been transformed into United States District Courts on attaining statehood (Alaska and Hawaii in 1958 and 1959, respectively); others have been transformed into constitutional courts (in addition to the already mentioned Customs Court, the *United States Court of Claims* and the *United States Court of Customs and Patent Appeals,* in 1953 and 1958, respectively). A point of additional interest here is that in 1933 the Supreme Court ruled that the United States District Court for the District of Columbia *and* the United States Court of Appeals for that District are to be regarded "at the same time" constitutional *and* legislative courts (*O'Donoghue* v. *United States,* 289 U.S. 516)—but our analysis will, for the sake of order and clarity, treat them as components of the constitutional hierarchy. In effect, the *Territorial Courts* might also be regarded as a combination of the two types of courts; but they are commonly viewed as legislative courts because of their diversified yet specific jurisdiction. They were created for, and are located in, such diverse areas as the Canal Zone (1912), Guam (1900), Puerto Rico (1900), and the Virgin Islands (1917). For additional data on legislative courts see my *The Judicial Process,* op. cit., pp. 144–153.

[24] See pp. 11–12 and fn. 23, *supra.*

federal constitutional courts still remain *the* basic courts in our system, and they adjudicate by far the major proportion of cases arising under the Constitution. The Supreme Court was established by the verbiage of the Constitution; it remained for Congress to create the balance of the basic hierarchy. It did this in one of the first pieces of legislation of the First Congress, the Judiciary Act of 1789. It was passed under the leadership of Senator Oliver Ellsworth, who had been a delegate to the Constitutional Convention from Connecticut and who was destined to succeed Chief Justice Jay as the second Chief Justice of the United States.

Overall Jurisdiction.   It is a tribute to the succinctness and comprehensiveness of the Constitution, in general, and Article III, in particular, that the general jurisdiction of the federal judiciary is spelled out in considerable detail in direct and understandable language. Its second section makes clear that the judicial power of the United States ". . . shall extend to *all Cases* [italics mine], in Law[25] and Equity,[26] arising under this Constitution, the Laws of the United States, and Treaties made, or which shall be made under their Authority. . . ." The italicized portion emphasizes one of the most significant aspects of the judicial process—already alluded to in connection with the discussion of advisory opinions[27] — namely, that federal constitutional court jurisdiction is limited to bona fide "cases" and "controversies." In brief, this requirement signifies that there be a genuine case or controversy involving two or more litigants on opposite sides of a genuine legal issue characterized by a true clash of interests. In the absence of these fundamental requirements, there can be no resort to the federal constitutional courts.

---

[25] *Law*—broadly speaking—represents the rules of conduct that pertain to a given political order of society, rules that are backed by the organized force of the community. As it has evolved through the centuries, law has been made either by the political representatives of the people or by jurists. The former type of law is generally known as *statutory law*, the latter as *common law*. The crucial distinction between them is that between codified, written (*statutory*) law and unwritten (*common*) law based on custom and tradition.

[26] *Equity* is a supplement to the common law. It begins where the law ends, taking the form of a judicial decree (not a judgment of "yes" or "no").

[27] See p. 8, *supra*.

With its decision in *Hayburn's Case*[28] in 1792, the Supreme
Court wasted little time in officially apprising the government of this significant judicial fact of life—one that applies
equally to "private" as well as "official" claimants. In that
case the Court held unanimously that it could not legally
carry out a congressional statute that it deemed not "judicial
in nature," although the justices did readily explain to a
displeased Congress how its intent could be effectuated: by
having President Washington's cabinet, rather than the judiciary, pass on disputed pension claims of invalid war veterans.

Having spelled out the basic jurisdictional case or controversy requirement, the judiciary article then explains the
various kinds of jurisdiction available to the courts. Broadly
speaking, these may be grouped under two major headings:
one, according to the nature or character of the *subject
matter* of the case; the other, according to the nature or
character of the *parties* to the suit. Under the first category
the courts are empowered to adjudicate cases and controversies in law and equity arising under: (1) the Constitution,
a federal law, or a treaty; (2) admiralty and maritime laws.
Under the second category—a considerably larger and more
complex group—they may adjudicate cases and controversies
in law and equity if: (1) the United States is party to the
suit; (2) one of the fifty states is a party to the suit (unless, in
accordance with the injunctions of the Eleventh Amendment,
the suit was commenced or prosecuted *against* a state by *any*
individual or even a foreign country); (3) they are between
citizens of *different* states (known as "diversity of citizenship" cases); (4) they affect *foreign* ambassadors and other
duly accredited representatives of a foreign land; and (5) they
arise between citizens of the *same* state because of a dispute
involving land grants claimed under title of two or more
states.

These seven grants or mandates of power do not necessarily signify their execution exclusively by the federal constitutional courts. Congress has implied authority to delegate
or assign certain aspects of them to the several states of the
Union, either on a *concurrent* or even an *exclusive* basis. An

---

[28] 2 Dallas 409. See the opinions of Associate Justices John Blair
and James Wilson.

example of this is the congressional requirement that a civil diversity of citizenship suit—a suit between two or more citizens of different states—must encompass at least $10,000 in value in order to qualify for original federal constitutional court jurisdiction. If it falls below that figure, it must go to the state tribunals. Even when it *does* meet the stated amount, Congress has seen fit to permit *concurrent* state and federal jurisdiction at the parties' discretion—although this does not, of course, remove the superior claim to federal jurisdiction should the parties disagree.

Also, Congress has deemed it advisable to distribute areas of federal jurisdiction among the several courts, a commendably orderly arrangement that began with the creation of the judicial system itself in the Judiciary Act of 1789. Obvious illustrations would be the statutory assignment of almost all federal cases of original jurisdiction (other than those involving two or more states as litigants, where the Supreme Court retains *original* jurisdiction) to the United States Direct Courts, whereas *appellate* jurisdiction from practically all District Court adjudications lies with the United States Court of Appeals. Moreover, there are certain areas where the "sovereignty" of the federal and state systems overlap. In that event, such as in cases dealing with theft involving flight in interstate commerce or those concerning embezzlement in or robbery of federally insured banks, *both* federal and state jurisdiction may exist. As of late 1977 the United States Supreme Court had resolutely declined to view the inherent possibilities of prosecution and punishment by *both* as constituting a violation of the "double jeopardy" safeguards of the Fifth Amendment or those of "due process of law" under the Fourteenth, regardless of which sovereignty might have commenced the action, and regardless of whether it resulted in an initial acquittal.[29] But, by and large, the federal government makes it a practice not to try a case where there has already been a state prosecution for "substantially the same act or acts." (Chart A below outlines the jurisdiction of the three federal constitutional courts under discussion.)

---

[29] *Bartkus* v. *Illinois*, 359 U.S. 121 (1959) and *Abbate* v. *United States*, 359 U.S. 187 (1959).

CHART A. The Jurisdiction of the Three Major Federal Constitutional Courts of the United States (Courts Created Under Article III of the Federal Constitution).†

1 *Supreme Court of the United States,* 9 judges, has:
Original jurisdiction in actions or controversies:
 *1. Between the United States and a state.
  2. Between two or more states.
 *3. Involving *foreign* ambassadors, other *foreign* public ministers, and *foreign* consuls or their "domestics or domestic servants, not inconsistent with the law of nations."
 *4. *Commenced by a state against* citizens of another state or aliens, or *against* a foreign country. (N.B.: if these actions are *commenced by the citizen or alien against a state,* or by a foreign country *against* a state, the suit must *begin in state court,* according to the provisions of Amendment Eleven.)

Appellate Jurisdiction from:
  1. All lower federal *constitutional* courts; most, but not all, federal *legislative* courts; and the *territorial* courts.
  2. The highest state courts having jurisdiction, when a "substantial federal question" is involved.

11 *United States (Circuit) Courts of Appeals,* 97 judges, have:
Appellate Jurisdiction *only* from:
  1. U.S. District Courts.
  2. U.S. Territorial Courts, the U.S. Tax Court, and some District of Columbia Courts.
  3. The U.S. Independent Regulatory Commissions.
  4. Certain federal administrative agencies and Departments (for review, but also for *enforcement* of certain of their actions and orders).

94 *United States District Courts,* approximately 400 judges, have:
Original Jurisdiction *only*** over:
  1. All crimes against the United States.
  2. All civil actions arising under the Constitution, laws, or treaties of the United States, wherein the matter in controversy exceeds $10,000 (unless the U.S. Supreme Court has jurisdiction as outlined above).

*3. Cases involving citizens of different states or citizens and aliens, provided the value of the controversy is in excess of $10,000.

4. Admiralty, maritime, and prize cases.

*5. Review and *enforcement* of orders and actions of certain federal administrative agencies and Departments.

6. All such other cases as Congress may validly prescribe by law.

---

†For the purposes of this chart, the three "special" courts (U.S. Court of Claims, U.S. Court of Customs, and U.S. Court of Customs and Patent Appeals) are omitted.

Jurisdiction not exclusive—i.e., while cases, according to Article III of the Constitution, are to originate here, legal arrangements may be made to have them handled by a different level court. For example, Congress has the power to give the federal District Courts *concurrent original jurisdiction* over cases affecting foreign ambassadors and *some* cases in which a state is a party to the suit. See *United States* v. *Ravara,* 2 Dallas 297 (1793); *Bors* v. *Preston,* 111 U.S. 252 (1884); and *Ames* v. *Kansas,* 111 U.S. 449 (1884). And in 1964, the Supreme Court declined to review a Ninth Circuit Court decision that federal District Courts have jurisdiction over suits *by the United States against a state.* (*California* v. *United States,* 379 U.S. 817.)

**A case can be made for the contention that it also has a measure of *appellate* jurisdiction, involving certain actions tried before U.S. Commissioners (one of whom is authorized for each federal district).

The ninety-four United States District Courts, staffed by about 400 judges, are the basic trial courts of the federal judiciary. In that role they are the busiest of the three court layers. From some points of view the work of a trial court is both more interesting and more creative than that found in the two appellate tiers. The battle of opposing platoons of counsel—unfortunately and frequently viewed as a legal game by some practitioners as well as laymen—takes place here. And it is here that we find the jury, that intriguing, albeit controversial, institution of citizen participation in the judicial process. Thus it is not surprising that some district judges have refused the honor of promotion to one of the two higher levels of the federal judiciary in favor of continued presence at the combatants' level below, e.g., United States Massachusetts District Judge Charles E. Wyzanski, Jr. In

recent years over 330,000 civil, criminal, and bankruptcy
cases are decided annually by the District Courts.[30] No
wonder that delays averaging from four to forty months have
plagued courts and litigants at this level, where almost all
federal civil and criminal cases necessarily commence! And it
is here that the federal government brings suit to prosecute
violations of federal laws. Typical examples of this would be
tampering with the United States mails, contempt of Congress, and conspiracy to violate the Internal Revenue Code.
United States District Courts function in one or more deline-
ated districts in each of the fifty states, the District of
Columbia, the Canal Zone, Guam, Puerto Rico, and the
Virgin Islands, and have one or more judges. New York State,
for example, has four districts (Western, Northern, Southern,
and Eastern). The Southern District, encompassing Man-
hattan, the Bronx, and adjacent counties to the north, had
the largest total of judges (twenty-seven) in a single district in
1976. Wyoming, on the other hand, had just a single judge
for its single district. (Chart B, on the following page, shows
their various locations within the eleven circuits.)

The eleven United States Courts of Appeals are essentially *appellate* courts; they stand directly above the United
States District Courts in the federal constitutional judicial
hierarchy. (They are also referred to as "Circuit Courts"—a
vestige of the days when individual justices, including those
of the Supreme Court, would literally "ride circuit" in pursuit of their judicial tasks, and as a reference to the eleven
judicial "circuits" into which the United States is divided for
purposes of these tribunals.) As Chart A indicates, they also
have certain statutory authority regarding review and enforcement of numerous federal administrative agencies.
Appeals from the highest state courts bypass both District
and Circuit Courts, assuming that appellants have properly
exhausted all remedies at the state level below, and go directly to the United States Supreme Court, which has all but

---

[30] In 1974 they received 103,530 civil, 37,667 criminal, and
189,500 bankruptcy cases, for a total of 330,697. (Bankruptcy actions
are routine, however—the judge normally accepts the findings of special
"referees.") See *Annual Report(s) of the Administrative Office of the
United States Courts.*

CHART B. *The United States Courts of Appeals and the United States District Courts.*
The large numerals indicate the various Courts of Appeals and the heavy lines represent the jurisdictional boundaries of each circuit. The broken lines represent jurisdictional boundaries of District Courts in states having more than one District.

Source: Administrative Office of the United States Courts.

D.C. indicates the "eleventh" circuit court, situated in the District of Columbia and titled "United States District Court for the District of Columbia."

complete discretion to accept or reject a petition for review. There are also some instances in which it is possible to bypass the level of the Court of Appeals and go directly to the Supreme Court from a District Court.[31]

Nonetheless, the usual appellate path of the judicial process begins in the Courts of Appeals. About 6,500 cases annually now reach that level from the several District Courts. A well-known example is the famous case of *Dennis* v. *United States*,[32] in which Eugene Dennis and his ten fellow leaders of the United States Communist Party appealed their lower court convictions to the Court of Appeals for the Second Circuit. Unsuccessful in their appeal there, the eleven then appealed to the last tribunal, the United States Supreme Court, which sustained their conviction by a 6:2 vote.[33]

The eleven circuits illustrated in Chart B, together with the districts that lie in each circuit, have a total of ninety-seven judges. Sitting *en banc*, customarily groups of three judges hear cases, although there may be as many as nine judges. There is a chief judge for each Court of Appeals. Like the District Court judges below but unlike the Supreme Court justices above, he must relinquish his chief judgeship upon reaching the voluntary retirement age of 70, but is permitted to remain as an otherwise full-fledged member of the tribunal. Each of the eleven circuits is theoretically "headed" by a justice of the United States Supreme Court, a throwback to the original days of "circuit-riding"; the two junior members in service of the Court are usually, although not always, assigned the two "extra" circuits. The role of the

---

[31] Three, to be exact: (1) in decisions by special three-judge United States District Courts, which are convened in certain statutorily provided cases, frequently involving questions of unconstitutionality; (2) where a direct appeal is statutorily authorized to the Supreme Court from a limited number of ordinary District Court cases; and (3) upon a showing that a case is "of such imperative public importance . . . as to require immediate settlement"—e.g., the 1952 *Steel Seizure* case (*Youngstown Sheet and Tube Co.* v. *Sawyer*, 343 U.S. 579); the *Amchitka Nuclear Test* case of 1971 (*Committee for Nuclear Responsibility* v. *Schlesinger*, 404 U.S. 917); and the dramatic 1974 "*Nixon Tapes*" case (*United States* v. *Nixon*, 417 U.S. 683).
[32] 183 F. 2d (1950).
[33] 341 U.S. 494 (1951).

Supreme Court justices assigned to the various circuits is today little more than a token in view of the demands of time, but the role does become a real one in instances such as petitions for extraordinary procedures in appeals and pleas for stays of execution. Thus Justice Charles Evans Whittaker was involved in the procedural "speed-up" in the *Little Rock Case*,[34] and Justice Douglas in the delays in the case of the convicted atom spies, Ethel and Julius Rosenberg.[35]

In the normal course of events, appeals from the United States District Courts are duly heard and adjudicated finally at the bar of the Circuit Courts of Appeals. Here no new *factual* evidence may be presented, as the record in the courts below constitutes the basis for judgment. But in some instances it is possible to reach the ultimate appellate tribunal, the United States Supreme Court.

THE SUPREME COURT OF THE UNITED STATES

There is no gainsaying the importance and the majesty of this most powerful of courts, not only in the United States, but in the entire free world. In the United States there is no appeal from the Supreme Court's "No," other than an appeal to the public and/or its representatives in Congress. Congress has the power and ability, within the limits of the Constitution and the realities of the political process, to reverse the Court by remedial legislation[36] or, joining with the states, by constitutional amendment.[37] But these are difficult and uncertain pathways, at least in the *short* run. In the *long* run, however, change is not only possible, but may well get a hand from the Court itself. Moreover, as a great student of the

[34] *Cooper* v. *Aaron*, 358 U.S. 1 (1958).

[35] *Rosenberg* v. *United States*, 346 U.S. 273 (1953).

[36] E.g., certain provisions of the Omnibus Crime Control and Safe Streets Act of 1968 and the Organized Crime Control Act of 1970.

[37] E.g., the enactment of the Twenty-sixth Amendment, ratified in record time in 1971, which enfranchised 18-year-olds at the *state* level—after the Court had struck down that portion of the Voting Rights Act of 1970 (*Oregon* v. *Mitchell*, 400 U.S. 112) while upholding their enfranchisement at the *federal* level.

Constitution, the late Edward S. Corwin, was fond of putting it: "[T]he run must not be too long a run either!"[38] In the long run, the Supreme Court of the United States is "the child of its time." It does, indeed, possess considerable educational power but, as Alexis de Tocqueville observed five generations ago, ultimately "it is the power of public opinion." Decisions running counter to the broad consensus simply do not last in the *long* run. Still, the Court must be, and often has been the leader of public opinion, not merely its register—as was true, in considerable degree, of the Warren Court. Finally, as Justice Robert H. Jackson observed so well in the 1955 Godkin Lectures: "The people have seemed to feel that the Supreme Court, whatever its defects, is still the most detached, dispassionate, and trustworthy custodian that our system affords for the translation of abstract into constitutional commands."[39] And so, in the final analysis, as they did so notably in *United States* v. *Nixon* in the troubled days of 1974,[40] the people ultimately turn to it for constitutional resolution and sustenance.

The public does, in the final analysis, look to the Court to be its guide, no matter how major or minor the constitutional or statutory issue involved. Thus, there appeared in a prominent spot in *The New York Times* in the summer of 1959 the following breathless advertisement:

STARTS FRIDAY AT THE LITTLE CARNEGIE
By Decision of
The United States Supreme Court:
D. H. Lawrence's
controversial masterpiece
Lady Chatterley's Lover
The motion picture
version of the most talked
about book of the year.[41]

---

[38] *Court Over Constitution* (Princeton, N.J.: Princeton University Press, 1938), p. 127.

[39] *The Supreme Court in the American System of Government* (Cambridge: Harvard University Press, 1955), p. 23.

[40] 417 U.S. 683.

[41] *The New York Times*, July 5, 1959, referring to the decision in *Kingsley Corporation* v. *Regents of the University of New York*, 360 U.S. 684 (1959).

—*or*, to cite a different kind of adjudication:

> Leo F.Koch, biology teacher at the University of Illinois, was denied today a Supreme Court hearing on his protest against dismissal for advocating [premarital] sexual intercourse among students.[42]

—*or*, to point to a delicate problem of societal morals:

> The principle that sustains compulsory vaccination is broad enough to cover cutting Fallopian tubes. . . . Three generations of imbeciles are enough.[43]

—*or*, to adjudicate the most pressing social issue of our time:

> We conclude that in the field of public education the doctrine of "separate but equal" has no place. Separate educational facilities are inherently unequal.[44]

—*or*, to embark upon the most sensitive of matters of conscience:

> It is neither sacrilegious nor antireligious to say that each separate government in this country should stay out of the business of writing or sanctioning official prayers and leave that purely religious function to the people themselves and to those the people choose to look to for religious guidance.[45]

—*or*, this front-page headline in newspapers all over the land on January 16, 1968:

> "Supreme Court Authorizes Pennsylvania and New York Central Railroads to Carry out Merger."[46]

---

[42] *The New York Times*, January 14, 1964. *Koch* v. *Board of Trustees of the University of Illinois*, 375 U.S. 989 (1964).

[43] Justice Holmes, delivering the majority opinion in *Buck* v. *Bell*, 247 U.S. 200 (1927).

[44] Chief Justice Earl Warren, for the unanimous Court in *Brown* v. *Board of Education of Topeka, Kansas*, 347 U.S. 483 (1954).

[45] Justice Black, delivering the majority opinion in *Engel* v. *Vitale*, 370 U.S. 421 (1962).

[46] E.g., *The Philadelphia Inquirer* and *The New York Times*, refer-

—or, the upholding of the publication of the 7,000-page series of secret government documents dealing with the origins of the United States involvement in the Indochina war, evoking this 1971 front-page headline:

"Supreme Court, 6-3, Upholds Newspapers on Publication of the Pentagon Report; Times Resumes Its Series, Halted 15 Days."[47]

—or, the attempted identification *cum* resolution of one of the most contentious, most emotion-whipped issues of the century—abortion:

A state criminal abortion statute . . . that excepts from criminality only a *life saving* procedure on behalf of the mother, without regard to pregnancy stage and without recognition of the other interests involved, is violative of the Due Process Clause of the Fourteenth Amendment.[48]

Each of these decisions represents but a tiny sample of the far-reaching decisions by the tribunal, decisions which are the law of the land and which, in the absence of proper and permissible remedial action, must be obeyed. In the admonition of Justice Felix Frankfurter:

Even this court has the last say only for a time. Being composed of fallible men, it may err. But revision of its errors must be by orderly process of law.

The court may be asked to reconsider its decisions, and this has been done successfully again and again throughout our history. Or, what this court has deemed its duty to decide may be changed by legislation, as it often has been, and, on occasion, by constitutional amendment.[49]

ring to the *Penn-Central Merger* and *N & W Inclusion* cases, decided on January 15, 1968.
    [47] *The New York Times,* July 1, 1972, p. 1. *The New York Times* v. *United States* and *United States* v. *The Washington Post,* 403 U.S. 713 (1971).
    [48] Justice Harry Blackmun, rendering the 7:2 majority opinion in *Roe* v. *Wade,* 410 U.S. 113 (1973).
    [49] Concurring opinion, *Cooper* v. *Aaron,* 358 U.S. 1 (1958), quot-

There is no doubt, however, that the Court has a duty to
decide, a duty to pass judgment in issues that properly come
before it. For, to quote again from Justice Frankfurter,
". . . in the end, judgment cannot be escaped—the judgment
of this court."[50] It is simply a fact of life that in the United
States all social and political issues sooner or later seem to
become judicial!

Jurisdiction

The highest tribunal, composed of nine justices,[51] possesses
both *original* and *appellate* jurisdiction. However, it exercises
the former only rarely, in part because of the scarcity of that
type of case; in part because of its own and Congress's desire
to share its power with the lower federal judiciary; and in
part because of the strictures of the Eleventh Amendment.
Indeed, it has had occasion to adjudicate cases in its original
jurisdiction only about 145 times. An example of the Court's
refusal to hear such a case is Massachusetts's challenge in
1970 to the constitutionality of the Indochina war.[52] As
Chart A has demonstrated, in theory there are four areas of
original jurisdiction at the bar of the highest tribunal; but
because of the grants of concurrent jurisdiction to other
courts, the Supreme Court now exercises its original jurisdiction *exclusively* only in instances involving two or more
states. A relatively recent illustration is the hotly contested,
long drawn-out water dispute between California and
Arizona, which came to the Supreme Court as a matter of
jurisdictional fact and right. After lengthy litigation involving
rearguments and rehearings, and the employment by the
Court of the special services of a fact-finding "master," the
Court ruled 7:1 in favor of Arizona (the chief justice, an

---

ing himself in *United States* v. *United Mine Workers,* 330 U.S. 258
(1947).
    [50]Concurring opinion, *Sweezy* v. *New Hampshire, by Wyman,
Attorney-General,* 354 U.S. 234 (1957).
    [51]There have been as many as ten (1863) and as few as five (1801)
justices on the bench, since the number of members of the Court,
unlike the creation of the body itself, is subject to statutory discretion,
provided the various constitutional safeguards (discussed earlier in the
chapter) are observed.
    [52]*Massachusetts* v. *Laird,* 400 U.S. 886.

ex-governor of California, abstained).[53] Another, in a totally different area of concern, was Delaware's unsuccessful attempt to have the Court declare unconstitutional the electoral college count in presidential elections.[54] Another, a river boundary dispute between Louisiana and Texas.[55]

Appellate Jurisdiction. But by far the primary task of the Supreme Court is in the realm of *appellate* jurisdiction. Here the Court serves as final arbiter on the construction of the Constitution, and within the confines of the taught tradition of the law and adherence to precedent (duly modified by its judicial prerogative to change its mind), it provides us with an authoritative and uniform interpretation of the law of the land. As Chart C shows, appellate cases reach the Supreme Court from both the constitutional and the legislative lower federal courts and the highest state courts. There are three principal avenues, called *writs*, by which matters for appellate jurisdiction reach the Court: (1) on what lawyers term *appeal*, i.e., a writ issued as a matter of right; (2) on *certiorari*, i.e., a writ granted by the Court as a matter of discretion; and (3) by *certification*. (The old *writ of error* was discontinued in 1928; its place has been taken by the writ of appeal.)

Certification may be disposed of quickly: it is seldom used. Essentially an "inquiry" of or a request to a higher court by a lower one, it presumably reaches "any question of law in any civil or criminal case in which instructions are desired" by a lower court, customarily a Court of Appeals or the Court of Claims. One of the very infrequent examples of its use was that by the Fifth Circuit Court of Appeals in 1963, which "certified" the question of whether its criminal contempt citation of Mississippi's Governor Ross R. Barnett and Lieutenant Governor Paul B. Johnson, Jr., necessitated a trial by jury. The Court of Appeals was evenly divided on the delicate question, 4:4, and it eagerly turned to the Supreme Court[56] to decide the ticklish matter arising out of the federally enforced admission of James H. Meredith to the until then entirely segregated University of Mississippi at

---

[53] *Arizona* v. *California*, 373 U.S. 546 (1963).
[54] *Delaware et al.* v. *New York et al.*, 385 U.S. 895 (1966).
[55] *Texas* v. *Louisiana*, 410 U.S. 702 (1973).
[56] 375 U.S. 805 (1963).

Oxford. (The Supreme Court ultimately held 5:4 that the Constitution's jury trial requirements do not apply to contempt cases, but it indicated that any non-jury *criminal* sentence imposed must be limited to one akin to a "petty offense."[57])

Appeal is a writ theoretically granted to a duly qualified applicant, known as the *appellant*, as a matter of statutorily granted *right*, with the answering party known as the *appellee* or *respondent*. But in 1928 the Court was given the important discretionary tool of evaluating the appeal as to whether the otherwise validly raised issue is of a "substantial" federal nature; hence, if it deems the issue to lack such substantiality, it may refuse to entertain the petition. Fully 50 to 60 percent of all such petitions fall victim to the rule and related jurisdictional loopholes, thus reducing to approximately 15 percent the share of writs of appeal among all cases and controversies presented to the Supreme Court. Chart C outlines in detail the eight types of cases that may come to it on appeal, but the two most common instances are: *one,* when a state court of last resort has ruled *in favor of a state law or a provision of a state constitution against a substantial challenge that it conflicts* with a provision of the *federal* Constitution, a *federal* law, or a *federal* treaty; *two,* when a United States District Court or, more likely today, one of the special three-judge district courts (which includes at least one judge from a United States Court of Appeals) has granted or denied an injunction in any proceeding required to be heard by such tribunal.

CHART C.   United States Supreme Court Review.

Cases normally reach the U.S. Supreme Court for purposes of review *(as distinct from original jurisdiction) in one of three principal ways:*

1. on APPEAL, i.e., as a matter of right;
2. on a writ of CERTIORARI, as a matter of Court discretion.

---

[57] *United States* v. *Barnett,* 376 U.S. 681 (1964). One year later the Court of Appeals cleared the two because of "changed circumstances and conditions." (*Ibid.,* 346 F. 2d 99.)

3. by CERTIFICATION. (The old writ of ERROR, a common law process strongly akin to (1) above, was statutorily discontinued in the federal courts in 1928. It brought the entire record of a case proceeding in a lower court before the Supreme Court for its consideration for alleged "errors of law" committed below.)

N.B. Title 28 of the United States Code, formulated as a result of congressional legislation, governs the types of review available to an appellant. (See Secs. 1254 and 1257.)

I. *Cases reaching the U.S. Supreme Court on* APPEAL (i.e., the Court reviews because it *must*).

    A. *From the State Court of Last Resort* having statutory jurisdiction in any particular case (usually, but not always, the *Highest State Court*, which normally, but not always, is the State Supreme Court):

        1. When a state court has declared a federal law or a federal treaty, or provisions thereof, unconstitutional.

        2. When a state court has *upheld* a state law or a provision of the state constitution *against* the challenge that it *conflicts* with the federal Constitution, a federal law, a federal treaty, or any provision thereof.

    B. *From the U.S. (Circuit) Courts of Appeals:*

        1. When a state law or a provision of a state constitution has been *invalidated* because of a conflict with a federal law, a federal treaty, or a provision of the federal Constitution.

        2. When a federal law has been held *unconstitutional, provided* the United States, or one of its agencies, officers, or employees is a party to the suit.

    C. *From the U.S. District Courts:*

        1. When a federal statute has been held *unconstitutional, provided* the United States, or one of its agencies, officers, or employees is a party to the suit.

        2. When the United States is a party to a *civil* suit under the federal interstate-commerce, communication, or anti-trust laws.

        3. When a *special three-judge district court* (which

must include at least one circuit judge) has granted or denied an interlocutory or permanent injunction in any proceeding required to be heard by such a court. (These three-judge courts usually sit in suits brought to *restrain enforcement, operation, or execution of federal or of state statutes or orders of state administrative agencies* on the grounds of unconstitutionality; or because of an order of the Interstate Commerce Commission. Their jurisdiction was reduced in 1976.)

D. *From "Any Court of the United States"* (comprising the *constitutional, legislative,* and *territorial* courts)— and specifically including, a.o., the *Court of Claims,* the *Court of Customs and Patent Appeals,* etc.:
   1. When a federal statute has been held *unconstitutional* in any *civil* action, suit, or proceeding, *provided* the United States, or one of its agencies, officers, or employees is a party to it.

II. *Cases reaching the U.S. Supreme Court on a writ of* CERTIORARI (i.e., because a minimum of *four* Supreme Court justices have agreed to a review). Writs of *certiorari* are granted or denied at the *discretion of the Court*— subject always to the latent power of Congress to define and limit the *appellate* power of a Court.
A. *From the State Court of Last Resort having statutory jurisdiction* in any particular case (usually, but not always, the *Highest State Court,* which normally, but not always, is the State Supreme Court).
   1. In all cases, *other than* those for which the remedy is APPEAL (see I, A, 1 and 2 above), in which a *"substantial federal question"* has been properly raised. (The Court itself determines just what constitutes such a question.)

B. *From U.S. (Circuit) Courts of Appeals* (and, in all pertinent cases, from the *U.S. Court of Claims,* and the *Court of Customs and Patent Appeals):*
   1. When a decision involves the *application or interpretation* of a federal law, a federal treaty, the federal Constitution, or provisions thereof.
   2. Where the U.S. Court of Appeals has *upheld* a

state law or a provision of a state constitution *against* the challenge that it conflicts with a federal law, a federal treaty, the federal Constitution, or provisions thereof.

An illustration of the first instance is the case of *Torcaso* v. *Watkins*,[58] which came to the Supreme Court upon Roy Torcaso's successful plea for review on appeal from his losing cause at the bar of the highest court of the State of Maryland, the Court of Appeals. At issue was a provision of the Maryland Constitution that compelled all state officeholders to declare their belief in God as a condition to public employment. Torcaso, a nonbeliever, refused to take the required oath, and challenged the pertinent provision as a violation of his religious freedom under the due process of law clause of the Fourteenth Amendment, as comprehended by the freedom of religion provisions of the First Amendment of the United States Constitution. The Supreme Court unanimously upheld Torcaso's challenge on appeal, and struck down as unconstitutional the pertinent Maryland provision as a "religious test for public office." An example of the second instance of relatively frequent Supreme Court review on appeal was the 1964 decision in *Schiro* v. *Bynum*[59] in which it unanimously and summarily affirmed a three-judge District Court decision striking down a Louisiana law requiring segregation at sports events and entertainments open to the general public. The constitutional issue thus adjudicated here was the meaning of the equal protection of the laws clause of the Fourteenth Amendment.

Far more often than not, a petition for a writ of appeal is rejected by the highest tribunal of the land for "want of a substantial federal question." Examples are legion, ranging from the Court's refusal to hear the contention of the Stover family of Rye, New York, that it had a constitutional right of free expression to hang six clotheslines of laundry in its yard as a protest against taxes,[60] to that of the due process claim

---

[58] 367 U.S. 488 (1961).
[59] 375 U.S. 395.
[60] *Stover* v. *New York*, 375 U.S. 42 (1963). A local ordinance proscribed such displays.

of Pasquale Albanese of Newtown, Connecticut, who challenged a Connecticut law that allows a person injured by a
drunk to sue the man who sold the drink![61]

Certiorari, of course, is the most frequently granted writ
in the Supreme Court. A Latin term, translatable as "made
more certain" or "better informed," it signifies the willingness of the Court to review the case, but not necessarily hear
oral argument. Strictly a discretionary writ, it is granted
when *a minimum of four justices* agree that "there are special
and important reasons" (a requirement of the Court's own
famous Rule 19 of the Court's Revised Rules of 1967) that
warrant an order to the court below to "send up" the record
for review. But more than 90 percent of all petitions for writs
of certiorari are denied, and normally without any explanation for the denial, other than the terse order "petition for
writ of certiorari denied." On occasion, however, that order
will carry a note that one or more of the justices—but
necessarily less than four—believe that certiorari should have
been granted; these justices are usually identified.[62]

An intriguing and ever-contentious question is just what
denial of a writ of certiorari means. It is clear enough what it
means to the disappointed litigant: he lost. But the justices
disagree among themselves on the matter at issue. For example, Justice Jackson viewed "uncert-worthiness" as a tacit
agreement by a quorum of the justices that a decision below
is good enough to stand, and that "the fatal sentence that in
real life writes finis to many cases cannot in legal theory be a
complete blank."[63]   On the other hand, Justice Frankfurter
always insisted during his almost quarter of a century on the
Court that no significance attaches to the denial of certiorari,
that it "in no wise" implies Supreme Court approval of the
decision below. On numerous occasions he stoutly defended

---

[61] *Albanese* v. *Gilleo*, 350 U.S. 845 (1955).

[62] For example, Justices Douglas and Stewart, dissenting from the
Court's 1967 refusal to grant the writ in *Mora* v. *McNamara* (389 U.S.
934)—a Viet Nam war legality case; and Douglas, this time joined by
Brennan, did so again in another Viet Nam war legality case, one that
invoked Congressional appropriations of funds (*Sarnoff* v. *Shultz*, 409
U.S. 929 [1972]). The two had similarly lost a year earlier in *Orlando*
v. *Laird*, 404 U.S. 869.

[63] *Brown* v. *Allen*, 344 U.S. 443 (1953), at 543, concurring opinion.

his contention that all the denial means is that for reasons seldom, if ever, disclosed, four justices evidently do not believe that the case ought to be reviewed, that a denial is thus simply an avoidance of adjudication on the merits of the case.[64] Of course, it is possible, but highly improbable, to obtain a reconsideration or a rehearing by the Court.

A few examples of acceptance and rejection will indicate the diversity of petitions for certiorari (Chart C outlined the overall jurisdictional field). In recent years, among the more famous cases to come before the Court on certiorari from a lower federal court was the *Steel Seizure Case*,[65] which involved questions of separation of power. And one from a state court of last resort was the successful claim of police brutality and allied unconstitutional procedure in violation of the Fourteenth Amendment due process of law rights of one Rochin, a California citizen.[66] One instance of rejection from the state level is the unsuccessful due process plea by Hirshhorn in opposition to a New York statute that makes it illegal for a man to masquerade as a woman in public. [67] Another denial of certiorari, this one at the federal level, concerned a narcotics violation by one Beck. Beck's conviction was based in part on the testimony of an alleged accomplice, who had initially pleaded guilty but later, after Beck had appealed his sentence, was permitted to change his plea and had the charge dismissed. Beck unsuccessfully raised Fifth Amendment claims, although Justices Black and Douglas dissented from the Court's denial of certiorari.[68] Another, and one indicative of the aforementioned variety of the Court's work, is the denial of a law professor's claim that the *Rutgers Law Review*'s rejection of his manuscript for a proposed article constituted state action denying him the equal protection of the laws under the Fourteenth Amend-

---

[64] *Sheppard* v. *Ohio*, 352 U.S. 910 (1956), certiorari denied. (However the Court took up the case a decade later—ultimately resulting in Dr. Sheppard's victory, *Sheppard* v. *Maxwell*, 384 U.S. 333 (1966).)

[65] *Youngstown Sheet and Tube Co.* v. *Sawyer*, 343 U.S. 579 (1952).

[66] *Rochin* v. *California*, 342 U.S. 165 (1952).

[67] *Hirshhorn* v. *New York*, 386 U.S. 984 (1967).

[68] *Beck* v. *United States*, 375 U.S. 972 (1964).

ment! (He alleged that irrelevant personal bias had dictated the refusal.)[69]

Work Load. That the Supreme Court of the United States is a busy tribunal is axiomatic. Its case load has been growing steadily, despite the much needed and desired wide *discretionary* powers of review bestowed upon it by the so-called Judges Bill of 1925. Whether or not formal oral arguments are granted and written opinions are issued, merely to say "no" requires considerable time and energy. One of the least understood, yet most important aspects of the Court's work is that *every justice participates in each and every action of the Court,* no matter what its disposition may ultimately be. The Supreme Court is a collegial body, but it is not only a joint group of equi-powerful individuals. It is also a group of nine individual jurists who are joined together for the purpose of arriving at decisions and judgments growing out of their own judico-philosophical perspectives, perspectives that frequently do not permit agreement and thus result in concurring or even dissenting opinions. The chief justice is *primus inter pares* (first among equals), and his *primus* is confined largely to administrative aspects of the Court's work as well as the perhaps more crucial but undefinable one of "setting the tone."

Without burdening the reader with excessive statistics (these are readily available in the Annual Report(s) of the Administrative Office of the United States Courts), the 1973–1974 term of the Supreme Court saw a new high of 5,079 cases on its dockets (the Original, Appellate, and Miscellaneous), with 3,876 disposed of and the balance of 1203, largest on record, carried over to the 1974–1975 term. Of those disposed of, 468 were decided on the merits; only 147 of these with full *written opinions,* the rest by *memorandum order*—the latter featuring a terse order, such as "affirmed," "dismissed," or "reversed and remanded." The remainder of the large number of cases of which the Court disposed represented denials of review and assorted other dispositions.

---

[69] *Avins* v. *Rutgers,* 390 U.S. 920 (1968).

Again, it must be stressed that even a denial of certiorari calls for study and a position by each and every justice. Law clerks, those bright young law school products of whom each justice may now (1977) be assigned three, and the chief justice five, can be helpful indeed, but they cannot and do not act for their justices in any sense of the term. They are hardly the judicial Rasputins they are sometimes pictured to be by certain critics of the Court! It is the justice himself who must and does decide in his responsible and authoritative role, and in a capacity that, in the memorable characterization of Justice Frankfurter, calls for the combined ability and wisdom of a philosopher, historian, and prophet—to which Justice William J. Brennan, Jr., wistfully added, "inordinate patience."[70]

The Institutional Setting

Unless it is convoked into special session—as was done because of the Little Rock, Arkansas, 1957–1958 high-school desegregation crisis[71] —the United States Supreme Court is in formal session thirty-six weeks annually, normally from the first or second Monday in October until the end of June. Occasionally it meets somewhat longer, as it did to adjudicate the *Pentagon Papers* case at the end of its term in June 1971[72] and the *Nixon Tapes* case at the end of its June 1974 session.[73] (But there is more than sufficient "homework" to keep the jurists occupied on a year-round basis!) Since its construction in 1935, the home of the Court has been the magnificent Corinthian-columned, white-marbled structure at 1 First Street, N.E., Washington, D.C. 20543, fully guarded around the clock by a special thirty-three-man Supreme Court police force. The beautiful, imposing structure was patterned after the Temple of Diana at Ephesus (one of the seven wonders of the ancient world) and the noble words

---

[70] Comment to the author, Philadelphia, Pa., May 24, 1962.

[71] *Cooper* v. *Aaron*, 358 U.S. 1 (1958).

[72] *The New York Times* v. *United States* and *United States* v. *The Washington Post*, 403 U.S. 713.

[73] *United States* v. *Nixon*, 417 U.S. 683.

"Equal Justice Under Law" are carved above the majestic
entrance, which is enhanced by great bronze doors.

The Court convenes in a large and resplendent forty-four-
foot, high-ceilinged courtroom, seating 300 people. Its nine
justices are clad in black robes—those judicial vestments
Judge Jerome Frank always wanted to see banished[74] —and
are seated behind a raised bench (for 181 years a simple
straight one, but since 1972 shaped in the form of a half-hex-
agon or shallow "L"). When the Court is in session, the chief
justice is the first to enter through the draperies behind the
bench, followed by the eight associate justices in order of
seniority. The Court and the audience remain standing until
the marshal has completed his traditional introduction:
"Oyez, Oyez, Oyez! All persons having business before the
Honorable, the Supreme Court of the United States, are
admonished to draw near and give their attention, for the
Court is now sitting. God save the United States and this
Honorable Court" [a remark that has been the butt of a
number of tasteless jokes]. The seats of the nine justices are
arranged according to length of continuous service on the
bench: the chief justice in the center, flanked by the senior
associate justice on his right, the second-ranking on his left,
and continuing alternately in declining order of seniority (see
Chart D).

Oral Argument. The assembled Court hears oral argument
for the first three or four days in two weeks of each month in
those few cases—approximately 150-175—that it has agreed
to hear in this formal and impressive setting. (The other two
weeks are spent behind closed doors considering cases and
writing opinions.) For the oral arguments, forty copies of the
printed briefs—with one set going to each justice—must have
been filed with the Clerk of the Court well in advance, in
accordance with prescribed format. Bona fide paupers, however, may file handwritten or typewritten briefs. An important illustration of such an *in forma pauperis* action is the

---

[74] See his amusing "The Cult of the Robe," in his *Courts on Trial:
Myth and Reality in American Justice* (Princeton: Princeton University
Press, 1959), Ch. 18.

CHART D.   The 1976 Supreme Court.

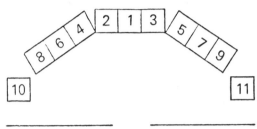

	1. Mr. Chief Justice Burger	
2. Mr. Justice Brennan		3. Mr. Justice Stewart
4. Mr. Justice White		5. Mr. Justice Marshall
6. Mr. Justice Blackmun		7. Mr. Justice Powell
8. Mr. Justice Rehnquist		9. Mr. Justice Stevens
10. Clerk of the Court		11. Marshal of the Court
	12. Counsel	

handwritten, pencilled letter that Clarence Earl Gideon used to petition the Court for a *writ of habeas corpus*—resulting in the momentous overruling of *Betts* v. *Brady*[75] in the landmark decision of *Gideon* v. *Wainright.*[76] (The latter "incorporated" the Sixth Amendment right to counsel in all criminal cases via the due process of law clause of the Fourteenth Amendment.) Briefs generally cite the facts, issues, questions presented, actions of lower courts, and all necessary legal arguments, together with the statutes and citations of cases on which they rely.

Oral argument is heard on designated days from 10:00 a.m. to noon and from 1:00 until 3:00 p.m.[77] Infinitely

[75] 316 U.S. 455 (1942).

[76] 372 U.S. 335 (1963). See Anthony Lewis's exciting account of the story of this significant case in his *Gideon's Trumpet* (New York: Random House, Inc., 1964). Observed Gideon later: "I didn't start out to do anything for anybody but myself, but the decision has done a helluva lot of good." (*Time*, December 17, 1965, p. 39.) He died six years later—a household word in the annals of criminal justice.

[77] Until 1970 there was only one-half hour for lunch; but Chief Justice Burger—cheered on by the press corps—determined that to be inhuman and altered it!

more than the "perfunctory windowdressing" it has been viewed as by some, it is both a fascinating and extremely significant aspect of the Court's public function, and it is a treat for those fortunates who have succeeded in obtaining one of the 300 available seats. (One hundred and twelve seats are allotted to the press, the justices' families, and members of the Bar, and the remaining 188 are available to the public, largely on a "first-come-first-served" basis.) Despite the carefully drawn briefs, there is at least a chance that, in supplementing the printed briefs by oral emphasis and in the give-and-take of the questioning by the justices, one or more members may take a different view of the case than the one he might have formed upon initially reading the briefs. [78] Indeed, Justice Douglas publicly stated repeatedly that "oral arguments win or lose the case."[79] This is probably too drastic a view, for we have more than one pronouncement on record in which justices made quite clear that the *loser's* argument was better than the winner's—for example, the Court's high compliment publicly paid to the then chief counsel for the A.F. of L.-C.I.O., Arthur Goldberg, on the losing end of the Taft-Hartley Act injunction test case of *United Steel Workers of America* v. *United States*[80] —but there is no doubt that oral argument may indeed prove to be both persuasive and decisive.

The lawyers who present their cases during oral argument are usually limited to one hour each for appellant and appellee, sometimes to only half an hour in those instances deemed by the Court not to require a longer presentation. There are, however, notable exceptions—the desegregation-implementation case of 1955 is an obvious and natural example—fourteen hours were allowed![81] Opposing counsel, all of whom must at some time have been admitted to practice before the Supreme Court, use a special lectern from which

---

[78] See John Marshall Harlan, "What Part Does Oral Argument Play in the Conduct of an Appeal?" 41 *Cornell Law Quarterly* 6 (1955).

[79] *The Philadelphia Inquirer*, April 9, 1963, p. 3 and The [Charlottesville, Va.] *Daily Progress*, October 7, 1972, p. 2.

[80] 361 U.S. 49 (1959).

[81] *Brown* v. *Board of Education of Topeka*, 349 U.S. 294 (1955). But the record is held by the 40 hours allotted to the water controversy case of *Arizona* v. *California* (op. cit., fn. 53).

they address the justices "on high," fully expecting, and rarely disappointed in that expectation, to be frequently interrupted with searching questions for which no "time credit" is given. Attached to the lectern are two lights, the first of which gives a white warning signal five minutes prior to time expiration; when a red light flashes, counsel must stop instantly, unless the chief justice permits him to continue. Edwin McElwain, at one time Chief Justice Charles Evans Hughes's law clerk, relates that the formidable chief justice once stopped a distinguished New York attorney in the middle of the word "if"; and that, on another occasion, when asked by the same attorney how much of his time remained, Hughes, white beard shaking, replied sternly, "Fourteen seconds, Mr. Counsel."[82] The "Government's Lawyer" at the bar of the Supreme Court is not the Attorney-General or his deputy, but the number three man in the Department of Justice, the Solicitor-General. In charge of all the federal government's litigation before the Court, litigation that comprises roughly one-half of its entire work load, he has often been a distinguished faculty member of a prestigious law school—e.g., Professor Archibald E. Cox (1961–1965) of Harvard and his Dean, Erwin N. Griswold (1967–1973).

The Conference.   The highly important weekly Friday Conference takes place, usually from 9:30 or 10:00 a.m. to 5:30 or 6:00 p.m., around a large mahogany table behind securely locked doors. (Increasingly, the Friday Conference is supplemented by post-3:00 p.m. Wednesday meetings.) Since 1910, when a "leak" was attributed to one of them, not even the page boys have been present. No record of the discussions in Conference is kept; messages from clerks are received at the door by the most junior associate justice present. We know little of what happens in Conference save what we have learned from memoirs of the justices and from their biographers. Yet it is entirely proper that such secrecy should exist—the Court cannot in good conscience open its delibera-

---

[82] "The Business of the Supreme Court as Conducted by Chief Justice Hughes," 63 *Harvard Law Review* 6 (1949).

tions to the glare of publicity, nor can it hold press con-
ferences. The Court still suffers from, and has never forgotten, the one truly disastrous leak that occurred in its
history (although allegedly there have been a half dozen or so
others): In the *Dred Scott* case, not only did the pro-slavery
Justice John Catron—aided and abetted by his colleague,
Robert C. Grier—evidently inform President-elect James
Buchanan of the probable "line-up" (7:2) of the Court in
that crucial and still-pending decision fully one month prior
to its official announcement; but also segments of the Northern press published the dissent of Justice Benjamin R. Curtis.
The secrecy of the Court's work—its "Purple Curtain"—is an
indispensable aspect of its labors and its posture.

In Conference, the justices, under the leadership of the
chief justice, discuss the several cases they have recently
heard in oral argument, as well as all pending motions and
applications for review. An average Conference agenda covers
about seventy-five items. Each member of the Court has been
advised in advance which cases will be "up" for discussion,
and each has noted his tentative stand on his copy of the
agenda. Here, too, applications for writs of certiorari are
disposed of, either with verve and controlled dispatch, as
used to be so characteristic of Chief Justice Hughes's regime,
or with much deliberation and discussion—which was the
practiced preference of Chief Justice Stone. No one can say
with finality, however, which of these two approaches is
"better" or more "just." The nine justices, who have shaken
hands with each other upon entering, are seated around a
large, rectangular conference table. The chief justice gives his
own view first in each case, followed by that of the other
justices, all of whom are prepared to "recite," in descending
order of seniority. When the time comes to take a *tentative*
vote on the case, however, the voting commences with the
junior justice, the somewhat debatable rationale being that he
will thus speak up free from the influence of his more
experienced brethren.[84] Each justice records all votes in a

---

[83] *Dred Scott* v. *Sandford*, 19 Howard 393 (1857).

[84] According to one seasoned Court observer's 1975 account, the
justices now also *vote* in order of seniority. (Warren Weaver, *The New
York Times*, February 6, 1975, p. 31m.)

hinged, lockable red-leather docket book, and the Court is now set for the next stage of its tasks—writing the opinions.

Diverse Opinions. First, however, cases must be assigned. Here the chief justice must call upon all of his powers of diplomacy, strategy, and persuasion to achieve written decisions that will be: (a) understandable; (b) understood by the public; (c) persuasive; (d) eloquent; (e) "right"; and (f) leave as few ruffled feathers as possible among the justices. Gone are the days when, partly to achieve the above aims as he saw them, Chief Justice Marshall wrote most of the opinions himself, and, more often than not, for a unanimous Court! He believed that the Court's power and prestige would be enhanced if it were to speak with but a single voice. "Judges must write down their reasons for a decision," as Dean Rostow of the Yale Law School observed, "because they are partners with us, the citizens, in an agreed procedure for reaching responsible decisions."[85] Prior to Marshall's time, decisions customarily, although not always, were rendered *seriatim*[86] —i.e., each author writing *and* delivering *his* opinion separately—a practice still prevalent with the Law Lords of Britain's House of Lords, and one that Thomas Jefferson, as president, wanted to institutionalize in the face of his political enemy Marshall's powerful influence. Today, in all cases heard on the merits, formal written opinions are rendered, save for those decided by memorandum orders, and those few in which a tie vote has resulted because of the absence or voluntary disqualification of one of the justices. (A tie vote has the effect of upholding the decision below.) [87] Except in cases of serious illness, the bench may confidently be expected to be at full strength for practically all of its

---

[85] Eugene V. Rostow, *The Sovereign Prerogative: The Supreme Court and the Quest for Law* (New Haven: Yale University Press, 1962), p. 89.
[86] A well-known illustration is the group of *seriatim* opinions by Justices Chase, Paterson, and Iredell in the early 1796 case of *Hylton* v. *United States*, 3 Dallas 171.
[87] E.g., *Bailey* v. *Richardson*, 341 U.S. 918 (1951)—4:4, a loyalty-security case, and *Grove Press* v. *Maryland State Board of Censors*, 401 U.S. 480—4:4, upholding Maryland's ban on the showing of the movie "I Am Curious Yellow" in 1971.

decisions. On occasion a judicial turnover, resulting from death or retirement, may cause the new member to abstain because he had not been present at the oral argument—e.g., Justice Byron R. White in the *New York Prayer* case. [88] Moreover, unlike members of the legislature, the justices are extremely sensitive about even the faintest possibility of a conflict of interest, and will abstain from participation rather than cause so much as a question of it—something that did not greatly trouble Chief Justice Marshall in his day, e.g., *Marbury* v. *Madison*,[89] in which he was directly and personally involved! "When in doubt, do not sit" is now a firm policy of the members of the Court. Justice Clark even *resigned* from the Court when his son, Ramsey, became U.S. Attorney-General in 1967.

The sole opinion-writing problem when the Court is unanimous is the selection of the author, who is always chosen by the chief justice in those instances. Depending on the public significance of the decision and on the nature of the subject matter, the "chief" may assign himself to write the opinion, as Chief Justice Earl Warren did in the unanimous decision of the contentious and significant *Segregation Cases of 1954*,[90] and as Chief Justice Warren Burger did in the *Nixon Tapes* case of 1974.[91] But when the chief justice is on the minority side in a case, the assignment for the writing of the majority opinion will ordinarily be made by the senior associate justice on *that* side. For example, Justice Frankfurter assigned Justice Tom C. Clark to write the majority opinion for the 5:4 Court in a dual case involving the power of congressional investigating committees.[92] The chief justice and/or the senior associate justice will also always take into account the philosophical "bent" of an assignee in cases that may be expected to evoke considerable public agitation. Thus, Chief Justice Stone assigned one of the Court's leading

---

[88] *Engel* v. *Vitale*, 370 U.S. 421 (1962).
[89] 1 Cranch 137 (1803). Nor does it necessarily seem to trouble Justice Rehnquist.
[90] *Brown* v. *Board of Education of Topeka*, 347 U.S. 483.
[91] 417 U.S. 683.
[92] *Wilkinson and Braden* v. *United States*, 365 U.S. 399 and 431 (1961).

"liberals,"[93] Justice Black, to write the majority (6:3) opinion in the highly controversial *Japanese Relocation* case.[94] Similarly, Chief Justice Warren assigned one of the Court's leading "conservatives," and a deeply religious man, Justice Clark, to write the hotly denounced opinion (8:1) outlawing the reading of the Bible and the recitation of the Lord's Prayer in public schools.[95] This does not, of course, always balm the wound or lessen the public outcry, but there is at least a chance that it might do so, and it is unquestionably sound judicial strategy.

The Supreme Court may be expected to be unanimous in about one-quarter to one-third of its decisions; hence dissenting and concurring opinions are frequent, and their length sometimes exceeds that of the majority opinion. A *concurring opinion* is one which, while concurring in the *result*, does not agree with the reasoning or the road that brought it about. It does count as a vote on the side of the majority. Thus Justice Clark agreed with the (6:2) decision in *Baker* v. *Carr*,[96] in which the Court took the momentous step, for the first time, of holding that alleged illegal or "invidiously discriminating" districting and redistricting by state legislatures was a federally justiciable controversy; but he disagreed with aspects of the rationale employed by the majority. (In that same case, Justice Frankfurter wrote a 68-page *dissenting* opinion, in which Justice John Marshall Harlan joined.) There are those who are quite critical of concurring opinions, while approving of dissenting opinions, for they believe that, essentially, a concurring opinion is meaningless: that it represents verbiage that has no effect upon the vote in the case, and hence that it is both confusing and unnecessary, and would more profitably be confined to footnotes to the majority opinion. Still, it is a demonstrable fact that many a concurring opinion has left an important mark on the course

---

[93] A *caveat* is in order regarding these labels, and this author, for one, does not approve of them, especially not in so complex a setting as the Supreme Court.
[94] *Korematsu* v. *United States*, 323 U.S. 214 (1944).
[95] *School District of Abington Township* v. *Schempp* and *Murray* v. *Curlett*, 374 U.S. 203 (1963).
[96] 369 U.S. 186 (1962).

of constitutional law—for example, Justice Clark's in the
Steel Seizure case (in which he pointed the finger at the
President's refusal to utilize available statutes) and Justice
Harlan's in *Estes* v. *Texas* (in which he limited the Court's
holding to "notorious" cases).[97]

Dissenting opinions are not normally subject to the same
criticism—although, on occasion, criticism may well be appropriate. For example, the dissenting opinion by Justice
Clark in the coerced confession case of *Rogers* v. *Richmond*,[98] in which Justice Potter Stewart joined, is a case in
point. *That* dissenting opinion was actually far more of a
concurrence with the majority, while in disagreement with
certain technical aspects, than a bona fide dissenting opinion
on the merits of the coercion. Another rather unhelpful
practice is a simple *dissent*, without any explanation, which
leaves the observer guessing as to the motives of the jurist—an
intriguing, sometimes nasty, but hardly very professional
sport! Thus, the bare announcement in the landmark case of
Palko v. *Connecticut*,[99] "Mr. Justice [Pierce] Butler dissents," is meaningless other than that it counts as a vote on
the negative side of the decision. But, whatever one's personal
appraisal of the merits of a particular dissenting opinion, it is
a practice that is frequent, and generally desirable, as a
beacon of a profoundly held conviction, Hence, it may well
strengthen rather than weaken a particular issue, although
there is no doubt that it may be an exasperating practice in
the eyes of the public and, indeed, that it may have a
tendency to muddy the judicio-political waters. Be that as it
may, there is no gainsaying the memorable evaluation of the
dissenting opinion by Charles Evans Hughes, then writing as
an ex–associate justice of the Supreme Court and soon to be
its eleventh chief justice:

A dissent [ing opinion] in a court of last resort is an
appeal to the brooding spirit of the law, to the intelli-
gence of a future day, when a later decision may pos-

---

[97] See pp. 20 and 32, *supra*, and 343 U.S. 579 (1952) and 381 U.S.
532 (1965), respectively.
[98] 365 U.S. 534 (1961).
[99] 302 U.S. 319 (1937).

sibly correct the error into which the dissenting judge believes the court to have been betrayed.[100]

Although Hughes rarely either dissented or wrote dissenting opinions, and next to Marshall, and perhaps Warren, was unquestionably the most dominant "chief" to sit on the Court, he often expressed the point of view that there is no reason to expect more unanimity on difficult problems of law than in the "higher reaches" of physics, philosophy, or theology.

Proving Roscoe Pound's wise observation that ". . . dissenting opinions may be the symptom of life in the law of time,"[101] many a memorable dissenting opinion has gone on to become, in due course, the voice of the majority of the Court or even its unanimous voice. Examples are legion; two opinions by Justice Holmes, one of the great dissenters, serve amply to illustrate this significant phenomenon. In his angry and anguished dissenting opinion in *Hammer* v. *Dagenhart*[102] (the *Child Labor* case), he vainly cried out[103] against the 5:4 majority's declaration of unconstitutionality of the Keating-Owen Child Labor Law of 1916 on grounds of its illegal interference with the powers reserved to the states under the Tenth Amendment under the guise of the congressional power over interstate commerce. This decision was unanimously and specifically overruled by the Hughes Court in *United States* v. *Darby*[104] in 1941. And there is his earlier, perhaps even better-known, dissenting opinion in the *New York Bakeshop* case, *Lochner* v. *New York*.[105] In the face of the majority's position that New York State's attempt to limit by statute the hours of bakeshop employees to ten per day and sixty per week was an unconstitutional in-

---

[100] *The Supreme Court of the United States* (New York: Columbia University Press, 1928), p. 68.

[101] "Preface," in *Justice Musmanno Dissents* (Indianapolis: Bobbs-Merrill Co., 1956).

[102] 247 U.S. 251 (1918).

[103] "It is not for this Court to pronounce when prohibition is necessary to regulation if it ever may be necessary—to say that it is permissible as against strong drink, but not as against the product of ruined lives." (*Ibid.*, at 280.)

[104] 312 U.S. 100.

[105] 198 U.S. 45 (1905).

fraction of the liberty-of-contract phase of the due process of law clause of Amendment Fourteen, he declaimed with icy majesty and scorn: "The Fourteenth Amendment does not enact Mr. Herbert Spencer's *Social Statics.*" Holmes was ninety-three years old and no longer on the Court when *Lochner's* fate was sealed with the upholding of New York's Milk Control Law in 1934, in the narrowly decided (5:4) *Nebbia* v. *New York.* [106]

No discussion of how dissenting opinions, no matter how lonely, may become majority opinions would be complete without mention of the historic, lone dissenting opinion by Justice John Marshall Harlan from the 8:1 Court decision upholding the "separate but equal" concept in *Plessy* v. *Ferguson* [107] in 1896. His solitary and moving exhortation "[O]ur Constitution is color-blind, and neither knows nor tolerates classes among citizens," had to wait fifty-eight years to become the unanimous opinion of the Court in *Brown* v. *Board of Education of Topeka.* [108] But it did!

Creating Opinions. With every justice participating at each and every stage of every opinion, the actual drafting of opinions is a laborious and time-consuming task, more often than not steeped in compromise. Aided by their clerks in research tasks, and by the private Supreme Court Library with its staff of fourteen, the justices, in general, and those who have been assigned opinions, in particular, go about this crucial stage of their work with deliberate diligence. Opinions are drafted and proof copies—printed behind locked doors by the Court's own private professional printers in the basement—are circulated among the members until such time as give-and-take (and not a little "bargaining") may produce an acceptable end result. Justice Brennan reported in a recent article that once, after an assignment by Chief Justice Warren, he circulated *ten* printed drafts before one proved to be acceptable as the opinion of the Court. [109] But, as the

---

[106] 291 U.S. 502.
[107] 163 U.S. 537.
[108] 347 U.S. 483 (1954).
[109] "Inside View of the High Court," *The New York Times Magazine,* October 6, 1963, p. 102.

same justice, on another occasion, told the world in a separate memorandum to an opinion he had written for a closely divided Court, "It cannot be suggested in cases where the author is the mere instrument of the Court he must forego expression of his own conviction."[110] On the other hand, the judicial game of persuasion *cum* bargaining may be blunt and direct, as is evidenced by a memorandum sent by the usually gentle Chief Justice Stone to the not always professionally gentle Justice Frankfurter:

> If you wish to write [the opinion] placing the case on the ground which I think tenable and desirable, I shall cheerfully join you. If not, I will add a few observations for myself.[111]

And Justice James F. Byrnes's price to his "chief" (Stone) in 1941 for refraining from dissenting in the important *California Migration* case, *Edwards* v. *California*[112] was to be permitted to write the Court's unanimous opinion in favor of Fred Edwards—but on grounds of the interstate commerce, rather than the "privileges and immunities," clause. This caused four justices to join in a concurring opinion stating a preference for the latter ground, yet it did not render the tribunal any the less unanimous in votes. In short, it is clear that although the published opinions of the Court are ostensibly the product of one person, they are, in effect, that of many minds. Whoever is charged with the writing of an opinion more often than not is obliged to add to, delete, modify, or even throw out the original draft in order to retain and/or secure the acquiescence of the necessary number of colleagues. It is essential to recognize and understand that each member of the Supreme Court of the United States takes part in each and every stage of the consideration of a case, and we see why it should not be surprising to find

---

[110]*Abbate* v. *United States*, 359 U.S. 187 (1959), at 196. Similar illustrations of this practice are Justice Jackson in *Wheeling Steel Corporation* v. *Glander*, 337 U.S. 562 (1949), at 576, and Justice Cardozo in *Helvering* v. *Davis*, 301 U.S. 619 (1937), at 639–641.

[111]Cited by Alpheus T. Mason, *Harlan Fisk Stone: Pillar of the Law* (New York: The Viking Press, 1956), p. 501.

[112]314 U.S. 160.

certain ambiguities or even contraditions in a given opinion. This fact of judicial life lends itself to the favorite parlor game of many vocal Court critics (notably the legal fraternity who ought to know better)—sticking pins and throwing darts into the end product with, of course, the delightful advantage of 20/20 hindsight.

Opinion Days. On several days during each month when the Court is in session, it formally and publicly announces its written opinions from the collegial bench. They are then duly recorded and immortalized in the series of official volumes known as the *United States Reports.*[113] (*Per curiam* opinions and the routine memorandum orders are not announced publicly on these Opinion Days, but are made a part of the permanent record in the *Reports.*) The various authors of the full opinions may read them, paraphrase them, summarize them, excerpt them, or simply state them as a matter of fact—courses of action that are left entirely to the discretion of the justices concerned. Hence a listener ought to be prepared for anything from a brief announcement or ten-minute synopsis to a word-by-word lecture, as it were, running perhaps into hours. On occasion, extemporaneous outbursts accompany the reading of a particular opinion; this may result in a warm or not-so-warm exchange between author and commentator. Thus Justice Douglas did not hesitate to charge that the 52-page *Arizona* v. *California*[114] majority opinion, written by his usually close collaborator on the Court, Justice Black, sounded "more like a Congressional committee report than a judicial opinion"—a comment he did *not write* in his dissenting opinion—and added with biting sarcasm:

> The advantage of a long opinion such as the one Justice Black has filed is that it is very difficult to see how it failed to reach the right result, because one gets lost in words.[115]

---

[113] The *Reports* and their forerunners (the latter kept by official court reporters under their names) are bound back to 1790.

[114] 373 U.S. 546 (1963).

[115] *The New York Times,* June 4, 1963, p. 22.

It is important to distinguish between the *ratio decidendi* and the *obiter dictum* of an opinion. The former becomes *res judicata*, i.e., the settled point of law, of the case. It is the legal rule to be complied with and adhered to in perpetuity, unless altered or abolished by judicial, legislative, or amendment processes. The *obiter dictum*, on the other hand, is actually a gratuitous statement, one that expresses a belief, a warning, an exhortation, a viewpoint, or simply a sentiment, not essential to the holding in the case but somehow—however vaguely—related thereto. *Obiter dicta*, or *dicta*, as they are simply called, are present frequently, and may suggest possible future developments. Chief Justice Marshall, many of whose famous opinions were replete with *dicta*, was a past master. One recent controversial *dictum* was raised in two fairly similar cases: [116] Justice Arthur J. Goldberg, joined by Justices Douglas and Brennan, suggested that the imposition of the death penalty for rape might well constitute the kind of "cruel and unusual punishment" proscribed by the Eighth Amendment to the United States Constitution (a question not raised by either petitioner in the briefs). But the *ratio decidendi* of that opinion, in which the six other justices joined, was that the doomed petitioners' due process claims did *not* warrant Supreme Court review—at least not then.[117]

Compliance and Noncompliance. Once decided and announced, the Supreme Court's decision is presumably the law of the land, and it should, consequently, automatically find ready compliance by the jurisdictions below. Normally, this is the case; indeed, *it must be* if our system of government under law means anything at all. However, compliance is by no means always automatic, and even when it seems to take place, evasions of the spirit of the decision by "reinterpretation" in the lower courts are not uncommon. Aside from the rather rare outright *defiance* of a Supreme Court order by courts below, noncompliance or snail-like compliance usually

---

[116] *Snider* v. *Cunningham* and *Rudolph* v. *Alabama*, 375 U.S. 889 (1963).

[117] But note *Furman* v. *Georgia*, 408 U.S. 238 (1972) and subsequent developments in the capital punishment realm, capped by the July 1976 decision (*Gregg* v. *Georgia*) affirming its constitutionality under carefully guarded conditions. (See p. 82, *infra.*)

takes place because of one of several reasons or peculiarities inherent in our judicial process. One is that even given the Court's unmistakably sweeping general order in a decision—such as its pronouncement against state-imposed prayers in the public schools in *Engel* v. *Vitale*[118] —the decision is in fact applicable solely to the case or controversy *in that particular case*, here the State of New York. The fact that the majority opinion by Justice Black made clear that no such limitation was either intended or implied was thus "legally" ignored by certain jurisdictions in a host of states, e.g., New Jersey and Pennsylvania, despite rulings by the two attorneys-general involved that the case did apply to *all* such practices throughout the United States. Yet a 1969 survey by *The New York Times* demonstrated that 13 percent of the nation's schools—and fully 50 percent of those in the South—continued to employ some type of devotional readings.[119] Similar noncompliance, in the absence of new suits specifically brought to cover additional jurisdictions, occurred after the Court's decision in 1948 barring the practice of "released time" in public school buildings.[120]   The most obvious illustration of all was the regionwide noncompliance and, in some cases outright defiance, of the Court's decision in the *Public School Segregation* cases of 1954 and 1955[121] and their progeny (not to mention the ingeniously and ingenuously propounded state and local legislative and executive circumventions).

Another fact of the judicial process that invites noncompliance in certain instances is that in the case of *state*, rather than federal, courts, the United States Supreme Court has no power to make a *final determination* of any cases in which it reviews judgment of *state* courts. All it can do is to decide the *federal issue* involved and *remand* the case to the state court below, usually its highest appellate court, for a final adjudication "not inconsistent with this opinion." Since the state courts may then raise new issues on remand, it is not

---

[118] 370 U.S. 421 (1962).
[119] March 26, 1969, p. 1.
[120] *McCollum* v. *Board of Education of Champagne*, 333 U.S. 203.
[121] *Brown* v. *Board of Education of Topeka*, 347 U.S. 483 (1954) and 349 U.S. 294 (1955).

terribly difficult, if the desire exists, thus to alter "legally" or even evade the substantive intent of a United States Supreme Court decision. A notorious illustration is the case of Virgil Hawkins, a Florida black who had been denied admission to the University of Florida Law School in 1949 because of his race. After lengthy legal stratagems and delays, commencing in 1950, and assorted maneuvers on all levels of the Florida State judiciary over a period of almost ten years, Hawkins was finally *ordered* admitted by the United States Supreme Court after the Florida Supreme Court continued to stall in the most patent manner; yet Hawkins never was in fact able to enter.[122]

It would be a disservice, however, to leave the impression that the Court's decisions are regularly and predictably evaded or defied. The vast majority are complied with promptly and properly—even when they are highly unpopular and contentious. This fact of judicial life is clearly illustrated by such emotional and far-reaching matters of public policy as legislative apportionment and the granting of counsel in *all* criminal cases, as a result of the Supreme Court decisions in *Baker* v. *Carr*[123] and *Reynolds* v. *Sims*,[124] and *Gideon* v. *Wainwright*[125] and *Argersinger* v. *Hamlin*,[126] respectively. These decisions witnessed prompt and meaningful compliance in most instances. Thus, as a result of *Baker*, by the end of 1966—a mere four years later—forty-one states had reapportioned one or more houses of their legislatures.[127] And this is as it should be. Informed, serious, constructive criticism of the Court is both desirable and necessary; defiance of the ultimate tribunal, however, must be barred—which does not, of course, mean that it will not be attempted.

---

[122] *Florida* ex rel *Hawkins* v. *Board of Control*, 347 U.S. 471 (1954); 350 U.S. 413 (1956); 355 U.S. 839 (1957). For an account of the Hawkins dilemma, see Walter F. Murphy and C. Herman Pritchett, *Courts, Judges, and Politics* (New York: Random House, 1961), pp. 606–618.

[123] 369 U.S. 186 (1962).

[124] 377 U.S. 533 (1964).

[125] 372 U.S. 335 (1963).

[126] 407 U.S. 25 (1972).

[127] 24 *Congressional Quarterly Weekly Report* 2055. And the 94th Congress (1975) had an average deviation from the ideal district size of less than one-half of 1 percent, whereas in the 88th (1963) it was 17 percent!

II

The Supreme Court
and Fundamental Freedoms
I: Basic Considerations

Whatever one's individual views may be regarding either the wisdom or the appropriateness of the Court's role in our democratic society, one thing is clear: the Supreme Court of the United States is beyond question *the* great and ultimate defender of the basic freedoms of the American people. Rightly or wrongly—and here again we return to the repeatedly suggested theme of "the buck stops here"—the Court, since the mid-1920's, has stepped into the vacuum created by the failure—or possibly default—of Congress and the executive branch of the government to discharge the responsibilities imposed or implied by the Constitution of the United States of America. Statistics demonstrate that the Supreme Court has been *the* steadfast guardian of the people's liberties. Its apparently mounting involvement with the basic or cultural freedoms—variously termed civil rights and/or civil liberties[1] —reflects, if it perhaps does not always do so in majoritarian terms, the obviously growing concern of

---

[1] Although some would object, the two terms are used interchangeably here. They are to be distinguished from all the other rights and freedoms individuals may enjoy under law because they are especially protected, in one manner or another, against violation *by governments*. (In Canada, the term civil *rights* refers exclusively to *private* law—the legal relationship between person and person in private life.) See J. A. Corry and Henry J. Abraham, *Elements of Democratic*

the people, both as individuals and as members of interest groups, with these freedoms and the problems that inevitably attend them.[2]

A CHANGED EMPHASIS

The development of this judicial concern and action—largely a post-1920 phenomenon—applies particularly to that area of the basic freedoms variously known as "cultural," "political," "human," or—awkwardly, but quite meaningfully— "noneconomic-proprietarian." This does not imply that there is no judicial concern with the economic-proprietarian sphere, but the vast majority of the civil rights and liberties decisions of this century have been in other areas. They are bracketed chiefly, if somewhat loosely, into five delineations: (1) due process of law in the criminal justice sector; (2) political equality in suffrage and legislative apportionment; (3) racial and other egalitarian matters; (4) freedom of religion and separation of church and state; and (5) freedom of expression.

Even a cursory glance at the Court's history proves that the economic-proprietarian sphere *was* very much in the focus of the Court's work *prior* to the arrival of the New Deal, and especially so during the chief justiceships of Melvin W. Fuller (1888–1910), Edward D. White (1910–1921), William Howard Taft (1921–1930), and Charles Evans Hughes, who became chief justice in 1930. But the Hughes Court's emphasis on the sacredness of the economic sphere in effect terminated with the legendary "switch-in-time-that-saved-nine" in 1937, four years prior to the chief justice's resignation in 1941. Both the beginning and the end of that half-century witnessed the zenith of the Court's emphasis upon economic freedom. It was Fuller's Court (with fifteen *federal* declarations of unconstitutionality alone) which "re-

---

Government, 4th ed. (New York: Oxford University Press, 1964), pp. 234–239.
    [2] On these problems, see my *Freedom and the Court: Civil Rights and Liberties in the United States,* 3rd ed. (New York: Oxford University Press, 1977), *passim.*

discovered" the tool of substantive due process—Marshall had created it with his freedom of contract decisions in the *Dartmouth College* and *Fletcher* cases[3]—in order to strike down myriad attempts by both federal and state legislatures to experiment with socioeconomic-regulatory legislation, on the grounds that these experiments violated the all but absolute liberty of contract viewed as mandated by the due process of law clauses of the Fifth and Fourteenth Amendments.[4] And it was Hughes's Court, at the end of the fifty-year period, with sixteen *federal declarations of unconstitutionality alone, which upheld the general legal philosophy of* the Fuller Court while using a somewhat different rationale: that federal legislative experimentation in the indicated economic sphere was *ultra vires*—i.e., beyond its authority—since it allegedly invaded, if it did not usurp, areas of constitutional authority reserved to the several states under the Tenth Amendment.[5] With but a few latter-day exceptions,[6] when the states *did* try to legislate in this economic-proprietarian sphere, they would find themselves slapped down by the Court in accordance with variants of the old substantive due process concept.[7]

But those days are clearly gone! Ever since the advent of the "New Deal Court" in 1937 (dating from Justice Willis Van Devanter's retirement in June of that year and his subsequent replacement by Justice Black,[8] President Roosevelt's first appointment[9]), the Court's preoccupation with, and in, the basic freedoms has been with the "noneconomic,"

---

[3] *Dartmouth College* v. *Woodward*, 4 Wheaton 518 (1819) and *Fletcher* v. *Peck*, 6 Cranch 87 (1810).
   [4] See, a.o., *Lochner* v. *New York*, 198 U.S. 45 (1905)—a state statute; *Adair* v. *United States*, 208 U.S. 161 (1908)—a federal statute.
   [5] See, a.o., *United States* v. *Butler*, 297 U.S. 1 (1936) and *Carter* v. *Carter Coal Co.*, 298 U.S. 238 (1936).
   [6] For example, *Nebbia* v. *New York*, 291 U.S. 502 (1934) and *Home Building and Loan Association* v. *Blaisdell*, 290 U.S. 398 (1934).
   [7] For example, *New State Ice Co.* v. *Liebmann*, 285 U.S. 262 and *Morehead* v. *New York* ex rel *Tipaldo*, 298 U.S. 587 (1936).
   [8] As of Black's ascent, the New Deal could usually count on, in addition to Black's, the votes of Justices Cardozo, Brandeis, Stone and—after their 1937 "conversion"—Chief Justice Hughes and/or Justice Owen J. Roberts.
   [9] Counting it, plus his elevation of Justice Stone to the chief justiceship after Hughes's retirement, F.D.R. thus appointed nine jus-

and in particular with the five areas categorized earlier. Thus, the overwhelming majority of the judicial vetoes imposed upon the states since then, and *all but two* of those against the national government—a total of forty-one by October 1976[10] —have been invoked because they infringed on personal liberties, other than economic, safeguarded under the federal Constitution.

THE "DOUBLE STANDARD"

This raises an intriguing question and/or problem: since the Court, as of a generation or so ago, has obviously been willing to strike a much stronger blow for basic freedoms and against governmental encroachment in the "cultural" or "noneconomic" realm, has it not, in fact, adopted a judicial "double

tices: Stanley F. Reed, Felix Frankfurter, William O. Douglas, Frank Murphy, Robert H. Jackson, James F. Byrnes, and Wiley B. Rutledge. Only President George Washington had appointed more: ten (actually fourteen, but four declined to serve).
[10] (1) *Tot* v. *United States*, 319 U.S. 463 (1943); (2) *United States* v. *Lovett*, 328 U.S. 303 (1946); (3) *United States* v. *Cardiff*, 344 U.S. 174 (1952); (4) *Bolling* v. *Sharpe*, 347 U.S. 497 (1954); (5) *United States* ex rel *Toth* v. *Quarles*, 350 U.S. 11 (1955); (6)–(8) *Reid* v. *Covert* and *Kinsella* v. *Kruger*, later coupled with *Kinsella* v. *Singleton* and *Grisham* v. *Hagan* and *McElroy* v. *United States*, 354 U.S. 1 (1957); 361 U.S. 234 (1960); and 361 U.S. 278 and 361 U.S. 281, respectively; (9) *Trop* v. *Dulles*, 356 U.S. 86 (1958); (10) *Kennedy* v. *Mendoza-Martinez*, 372 U.S. 144 (1963); (11) *Rusk* v. *Cort*, 372 U.S. 144 (1963); (12) *Schneider* v. *Rusk*, 377 U.S. 1963 (1964); (13) *Aptheker* v. *Secretary*, 378 U.S. 500 (1964); (14) *Lamont* v. *Postmaster General* and *Fixa* v. *Heilberg*, 381 U.S. 301 (1965); (15) *United States* v. *Brown*, 381 U.S. 437 (1965); (16) *United States* v. *Romano*, 382 U.S. 136 (1965); (17) *Afroyim* v. *Rusk*, 387 U.S. 253 (1967); (18) *United States* v. *Robel*, 389 U.S. 258 (1967); (19) *Marchetti* v. *United States*, 390 U.S. 39 (1968) and *Grosso* v. *United States*, 390 U.S. 62 (1968); (20) *Haynes* v. *United States*, 390 U.S. 85 (1968); (21) *United States* v. *Jackson*, 390 U.S. 569 (1968); (22) *Washington* v. *Legrant*, 394 U.S. 618 (1969); (23) and (24) *Leary* v. *United States*, 395 U.S. 6 (1969); (25) *Schacht* v. *United States*, 398 U.S. 58 (1970); (26) *Oregon* v. *Mitchell*, 400 U.S. 112 (1970); (27) and (28) *Blount* v. *Rizzi* and *United States* v. *The Book Bin*, 400 U.S. 410; (29) *Tilton* v. *Richardson*, 403 U.S. 672 (1971); (30) *Chief of Capitol Police* v. *Jeanette Rankin Brigade*, 409 U.S. 972 (1972); (31) *Richardson* v. *Davis* and *Richardson* v. *Griffin*, 409 U.S. 1069 (1972); (32 and 33) *U.S. Department of Agriculture* v. *Murry* and *U.S. Department of Agriculture* v.

standard"? If so, how, if at all, is such a double standard justifiable? Briefly and oversimplified—for it is never possible completely to divorce the "economic" from the "noneconomic"—the double standard detected here gives all but *carte blanche* to legislative experimentation, state as well as federal, in the realm of economic-proprietarian activities; whereas it gives minute and repeated scrutiny to complaints in litigation alleging encroachment upon the cultural basic freedoms sphere. In other words, an appellant's complaint that a state or federal wage-and-hour, child labor, or similar type of law infringes on substantive due process—a complaint that would have found an enthusiastic reception by the Fuller Court—would receive short shrift by today's Supreme Court. Indeed, it would probably not even be granted review! This posture is generally justified by the highest tribunal (and, incidentally, by those below) on the grounds of judicial self-restraint. It is based upon the contention that legislators must be given the benefit of the doubt in an area that is so peculiarly suited to their judgment as that of the economic-proprietarian sector. On the other hand, an appellant's complaint that state or federal legislation or official practices in criminal law enforcement have violated an individual's due process of law, or that a state statute or official practice has infringed on the constitutional rights of racial minorities (this is not very likely to occur on the federal level), would probably receive close judicial scrutiny. How, then, if at all, is such a double standard justifiable?

Any justification poses a fascinating moral dilemma, for in a sense it attributes political manhood to the people's representatives and other public servants in one area, while questioning their potency in the other. Basically, it is a double standard resolutely supported by both Justices

Moreno, 413 U.S. 508 and 413 U.S. 528 (1973), respectively; (34) and (35) *Frontiero* v. *Richardson*, 411 U.S. 677 (1973); (36) *Jiminez* v. *Weinberger*, 417 U.S. 628 (1974); (37) *Weinberger* v. *Wiesenfeld*, 420 U.S. 636 (1975); (38) and (39) *Buckley* v. *Valeo*, 44 LW 4127 (1976); (40) and (41) *National League of Cities* v. *Usery*, 44 LW 4974 (1976) For capsule commentaries of these through 1974, see my *The Judicial Process: An Introductory Analysis of the Courts of the United States, England, and France*, 3rd ed. (New York: Oxford University Press, 1975) pp. 281-287, followed by a tabular presentation of all declarations of unconstitutionality from *Marbury* v. *Madison* (1803) to 1975.

Holmes and Brandeis. These two great, long-term jurists, who had considerable faith in the legislative process, albeit for somewhat different reasons,[11] were quite willing to trust what might be termed judicial subjectivity and competence in the "preferred" area—and especially in that of the First Amendment's protections of religion, speech, press, assembly, and petition[12] —while denying or subordinating it in the economic-proprietarian, the social sphere. In somewhat different language, the governing theme here is, then, that the Court must guard against mistaken self-abnegation, lest the basic freedoms of Americans "be eroded to the point where their restoration becomes impossible."[13]

In justifying the double standard, some specific reasons are commonly advanced, not necessarily in any order of significance. *First*, the Bill of Rights in our Constitution— which has now been *judicially* held to be largely, although not entirely, applicable to the several states via the Fourteenth Amendment's due process of law clause—is assuredly *explicit* in its language. Thus its famed First Article commences with the ringing injunction that "Congress shall make *no law respecting* an establishment of religion, or *prohibiting* the free exercise thereof; or *abridging* the freedom of speech, or of the press; . . . ."[14] In the firm judgment of Justice Black, for one, "no law" means just that:

It is my belief that there *are* "absolutes" in our Bill of Rights, and that they were put there on purpose by men who knew what words meant, and meant their prohibitions to be "absolutes." . . . The phrase "Congress shall make no law" is composed of plain words, easily under-

---

[11] See the superb study of the Holmes-Brandeis tradition and its effect upon American democracy in Samuel J. Konefsky's *The Legacy of Holmes and Brandeis: A Study in the Influence of Ideas* (New York: The Macmillan Co., 1956).

[12] As Stone read Holmes, judges "should not be too rigidly bound to the tenets of judicial self-restraint in cases involving civil liberties." (Asserted by Stone in a letter to Clinton Rossiter, April 12, 1941, and thus quoted by Alpheus T. Mason, *Harlan Fiske Stone: Pillar of the Law*, New York: The Viking Press, 1956, p. 516.)

[13] Loren P. Beth. "The Case for Judicial Protection of Civil Liberties," 17 *The Journal of Politics* 112 (February 1955).

[14] Italics supplied.

stood . . . the language of this Amendment [is not] anything less than absolute.[15]

One need not subscribe to this "absolutist" concept of Justice Black—which rests on somewhat dubious grounds, however generous and attractive the sentiment may be—to
recognize the specificity and explicitness of the language.
That language finds no applicable counterpart, whatsoever,
anywhere in the basic document in purely economic terms,
which must find their salvation in the much more vague,
much more general, language of the "due process of law"
clauses of the Fifth and Fourteenth Amendments and the
latter's "equal protection of the laws" clause. (The generous
Marshallian interpretation of the impairment of the obliga-
tion-of-contracts clause of the Constitution[16] retains little, if
any, effective meaning today.)

   Second, and closely allied to the first point, is the contention that, after all, we are here dealing with the most basic of
all of our freedoms, those upon which all the others rest. For
what purpose are the rights of petition for the redress of
grievances and assembly when the right to vote is gone? Of
what benefit is the right of freedom of speech and press when
prior censorship denudes these of meaning? In short, when
these most basic rights are gone, the rest become irretrievable
as well. It was this reasoning that persuaded Justice Stone to
write a famous footnote to an otherwise unimportant 1938
case, *United States* v. *Carolene Products Co.,*[17] a footnote
that must surely rank as one of the most significant in all
legal history. In it he intimated with conviction that the type
of judicial self-restraint that we normally have a right to

------

[15] Hugo L. Black, "The Bill of Rights," 35 *New York University
Law Review* 867, 874 (April 1960). As he put the matter elsewhere: "I
think that state regulation [of economic affairs] should be viewed quite
differently than where it touches or involves freedom of speech, press,
religion, assembly, or other specific safeguards of the Bill of Rights. It is
the duty of this Court to be alert to see that these *constitutionally
preferred rights* are not abridged." Dissenting opinion, *Morey* v. *Doud,*
354 U.S. 457 (1957), at 471. (Italics added.)
    [16] Art. I, Sec. 10, Cl. 1. See, a.o., his opinions in *Dartmouth College*
v. *Woodward* and *Fletcher* v. *Peck* (cited in fn. 3, *supra*).
    [17] 304 U.S. 144 (1938). See my *Freedom and the Court, op cit.,*
pp. 14 ff.

expect from the judicial branch of the government would be
misapplied in the civil liberties field; that in the case of the
Constitution's specific prohibitions there existed more than
justification, indeed an activist command, for close and even
painful scrutiny. He did not believe this scrutiny to be
justifiable in the economic-proprietarian field, where he, too,
did not find the Constitution specific; that, in fine:

> ... legislation which restricts those political processes
> which can ordinarily be expected to bring about repeal
> of undesirable legislation, is to be subjected to more
> exacting judicial scrutiny under the general prohibitions
> of the Fourteenth Amendment [as applied by the First]
> than are most other types of legislation.[18]

And he confirmed this belief in his solitary, stirring dissenting
opinion in the first *Flag Salute* case[19] two years later, a
dissent that became majority opinion scarcely three years
thereafter:[20]

> The very fact that we have constitutional guarantees of
> civil liberties and the specificity of their command
> where freedom of speech and of religion are concerned
> require some accommodation of the powers which gov-
> ernment normally exercises, when no question of civil
> liberty is involved, to the constitutional demand that
> these liberties be protected against the action of govern-
> ment itself. ... The Constitution expresses more than
> the conviction of the people that democratic processes
> must be preserved at all costs. It is also an expression of
> faith and a command that freedom of mind and spirit
> must be preserved, which government must obey, if it is
> to adhere to that justice and moderation without which
> no free government can exist.[21]

Third, and following logically if one accepts the first and
second contentions, no other agency of our government has

---

[18] Ibid.

[19] *Minersville School District* v. *Gobitis,* 310 U.S. 586 (1940).

[20] *West Virginia State Board of Education* v. *Barnette,* 319 U.S.
624 (1943).

[21] 310 U.S. 586, *loc. cit,* at 606–607.

proved itself willing and/or capable of protecting this vital area of freedom. (Unlike Britain, for one, where the so representative legislative branch continues to exert far-reaching power in demanding that the government preserve and defend civil liberties.) Thus it has fallen to our judiciary to afford that necessary protection, a task and a role that our traditions have always viewed as an intrinsic function of the courts staffed by jurists who are presumably eminently qualified by experience as well as instinct to play the role of guardians of our fundamental rights. It is a role procedurally enhanced by the Supreme Court's all but absolute prerogative of determining the kind of cases that will reach its docket— which thus enables it to concentrate on articulating the libertarian realm.[22]

On the other hand, the judiciary has neither the expertise nor the time, given its heavy docket, to make complex economic judgments. These would appear to belong to the legislative branch of the government, for it is there that the day-to-day process of economic planning and facilitation finds appeal and expression. As Justice Black expressed the matter once: "Whether the legislature takes for its textbook Adam Smith, Herbert Spencer, Lord Keynes or some other is of no concern of ours."[23] Probably no one ever stated the case so well as did Justice Holmes, in typically colorful fashion, to his then 61-year-old colleague, Justice Stone. White mustache bristling, his still-sharp, clear eyes dancing, Holmes intoned:

> Young, man, about 75 years ago I learned that I was not God. And so, when the people [through their elected representatives] want to do something [in that vast realm of economic and social legislation] I can't find anything in the Constitution expressly forbidding them to do, I say, whether I like it or not, "Goddamit, let 'em do it."[24]

---

[22] On that point see Alpheus Thomas Mason, *The Supreme Court from Taft to Warren* (New York: W.W. Norton & Co., Inc., 1964), Ch. 5, "Toward Positive Responsibility."

[23] *Ferguson* v. *Skrupa*, 372 U.S. 726 (1963), at 732.

[24] As quoted by Charles P. Curtis in his *Lions Under the Throne* (Boston: Houghton Mifflin Co., 1947), p. 281.

Or, as that supreme skeptic and philosopher, while chatting about anti-trust legislation, once expressed the matter on another occasion to John W. Davis, the famed corporation and criminal lawyer and unsuccessful 1924 Democratic nominee for the presidency:

> Of course I know, and you know, and every other sensible man knows, that the Sherman [Anti-Trust] Law is damned nonsense, but if my country wants to go to hell, I am here to help it.[25]

Yet in the area of the Bill of Rights, in general, and that of the First Amendment, in particular, he firmly rejected that philosophy, for he was convinced that the Constitution neither provided nor sanctioned such an approach. He, in concert with many other thoughtful jurists, simply did not regard the average American (including his legislative representatives) as being very "enlightened"—to use Justice Jackson's phrase[26] —on the subject of basic civil rights and liberties.

Fourth, it is an axiom of the American political scene that the average economic-proprietarian or social interest or pressure group has more avenues and pathways of *access* to the legislative process, in order to obtain real or fancied redress of public policy grievances, than does the often unpopular minority in the cultural freedoms realm. After all, it is the latter that accounts for the vast bulk of civil liberties litigation, hardly the former! The difficulty is that whatever may be the views of the average American citizen toward the activities of an economic interest, he is more likely than not to regard those of the political minority group or individual as "troublemakers" of one sort or another. Alas, as Justice Frankfurter once observed tellingly, the average civil liberties litigants "are not very nice people."[27] He had particular

---

[25] As told by Francis Biddle, *Justice Holmes, Natural Law, and the Supreme Court* (New York: The Macmillan Co., 1961), p. 9.
[26] See Robert H. Jackson, *The Supreme Court in the American System of Government* (Cambridge: Harvard University Press, 1955), p. 82.
[27] The exact quote, penned in *United States* v. *Rabinowitz*, 339 U.S. 56 (1950), was: "It is a fair summary of history to say that safeguards of liberty have been forged in controversies involving not very nice people."

reference to those accused in the criminal law realm, who have frequently been vehicles for procedural due process decisions by the Court. Often these decisions not only proved favorable to the accused, but became catalysts for liberal interpretations of the constitutional provisions concerned. Thus, there was nothing particularly endearing about one Dollree Mapp, to whom we are "indebted" for the 1961 landmark decision in *Mapp* v. *Ohio*,[28] which held, in Justice Clark's words, "that the right to privacy[29] embodied in the Fourth Amendment is enforceable against the States, and that the right to be secure against rude invasions of privacy by state officers is, therefore, constitutional in origin." Neither do we admire Arthur Culombe, whose Connecticut conviction for two grisly gasoline station murderers was set aside by the Supreme Court on the gounds that his confession was obtained by force and that it lacked the judicial standard of voluntariness.[30] Nor, surely, the convicted rapist and kidnaper, Ernesto Miranda, whose name has become a household word for safeguards—however contentious—in the realms of counsel, confession, and self-incrimination.[31] It is not easy for that type of appellant to obtain his day in court, let alone at the bar of legislature—although it must be recognized that one of the by-products of the rise and sustenance of civil libertarian activism in the early 1950's has been the very marked success of civil rights and liberties interest groups in having their grievances heard and litigated at all levels of the governmental process. There is no question that this represents a significant change from the days of yore.

This development notwithstanding, it remains true that, since the average economic-proprietarian interest group does not normally suffer from the "not-so-nice" label, and more often than not is viewed as both "respectable" *and* influ-

---

[28] 367 U.S. 643. See also p. 68, *infra*.

[29] For some intriguing "privacy" decisions in realms other than that of the Fourth Amendment—concentrating instead on the Ninth—see, a.o.: *Griswold* v. *Connecticut*, 381 U.S. 479 (1965), the "Birth Control Case"; the 1973 "Abortion Cases," *Roe* v. *Wade*, 41 U.S. 213 and *Doe* v. *Bolton*, 410 U.S. 179; and *Planned Parenthood of Missouri* v. *Danforth* (July 1, 1976).

[30] *Culombe* v. *Connecticut*, 367 U.S. 568 (1961).

[31] *Miranda* v. *Arizona*, 384 U.S. 436 (1966). (Miranda was killed in a barroom brawl in 1976—with the police subsequently using a "Miranda card" to read the prime suspect his rights prior to his arrest.)

ential, it has little difficulty in gaining the attention of legislative representatives. There is nothing evil or wrong with this fact of public life. Yet it does point to the relative ease with which the average economic interest group can take steps to redress court-imposed grievances, should the need arise—that there is a superior ability of the average economic interest to gain affirmative access to the governmental process. Of course, there is a significant, often crucial, distinction that should and, indeed, *must* be made between large, powerful firms, such as du Pont de Nemours, for example, and the corner grocer. The *grocer's* influence is hardly on a par with du Pont's. But this does not negate the basic argument of potential access based upon notions of "respectability" and "noncriminality"—which even the lone economic individual possesses, though he may belong to no identifiable interest or pressure group at all.

Recently, the Court modified the traditional "double standard" to give "strict judicial scrutiny" to certain types of equal protection *and* due process cases. Depending on the type of legislative statutory classification, the Court places or views the case before it in different categories or levels, which affects its treatment of the issue at hand accordingly. Thus, for the economic-proprietarian cases discussed earlier in this chapter, the Court still uses the "traditional" equal protec tion test of examining whether the legislature had a "reasonable" or "rational" basis for making its statutory classification. While basic civil rights and liberties issues have for some time now led to a closer case examination by the Court, the demonstration of a classification in a law that affects so-styled "fundamental interests" (e.g., voting rights,[32] the right to interstate travel[33]) *or* touches a "suspect category" (e.g., race,[34] national origin or alienage,[35] and, as of 1968 but apparently no longer after mid-1976, illegitimacy[36]) has resulted *in an even higher level of Court scrutiny.* Once an issue has been placed on that level, the Court, in effect, shifts

---

[32] For example, *Harper* v. *Virginia Board of Elections*, 383 U.S. 663 (1966).
[33] For example, *Shapiro* v. *Thompson*, 394 U.S. 618 (1969).
[34] For example, *Loving* v. *Virginia*, 388 U.S. 1 (1967).
[35] For example, *Graham* v. *Richardson*, 403 U.S. 365 (1971).
[36] For example, *Levy* v. *Louisiana*, 391 U.S. 68 (1968); *Labine* v. *Vincent*, 401 U.S. 532 (1971); *Weber* v. *Aetna Casualty and Insurance*

the burden of proof of its constitutionality *to the government* and requires that *it* demonstrate a *"compelling* state interest" for its legislative classification. Hence, once the "fundamental interest" or *"suspect* category" classification of a case is demonstrated, the "strict judicial scrutiny" which thereby results leads to considerably greater judicial protection of these rights. In essence, then, the Court uses a complicated double-standard-within-a-double-standard to accomplish this contemporary task.[37]

Taken together, as well as separately, the four reasons outlined above represent the case for a justification of a double standard (or standards). It may not be entirely convincing both morally and logically—and it raises very serious, indeed fundamental, questions about the nature of judicial power and judicial process under our system. Yet it is a practical recognition of one of the latter's crucial and realistic facets of government and politics. Within often ill-defined limits, the case of the special judicial protection of civil liberties is strong. But there is an additional consideration related to the concept of a double standard: the vexatious and contentious matter of the "incorporation," "nationalization," or "absorption" of the provisions of the federal Bill of Rights to the several states via the first section of the Fourteenth Amendment, in general, and the due process of law clause, in particular.

"INCORPORATION," DUE PROCESS OF LAW, AND CRIMINAL JUSTICE

Two Types of Due Process of Law

There are two types or kinds of "due process of law," *substantive* and *procedural.* They are not as clearly separable

---

Company, 406 U.S. 164 (1972). But after enjoying a "suspect category" standard for almost a decade, a 6:3 decision by the Court in mid-1976, ruling against a claim by illegitimate children, pronounced the subject matter no longer "suspect," that the sole test to be met by the legislature was the usual one of "reasonableness." (*Norton* v. *Mathews* and *Mathews* v. *Lucas,* 44 LW 5135 1976.)

[37] For two excellent recent treatments of this vexatious and complicated issue, see Gerald Gunther, "The Supreme Court: 1971 Term:

as we might wish, or as some members of the legal profession at times pretend, but it *is* both possible and vital to understand the basic distinction. Simply, *substantive* due process refers to the contents or subject matter of legislation or an executive ordinance; *procedural* due process refers to the manner in which the fruits of the legislative and/or administrative process are carried out by public officials, be they executives, policy-making or subordinate civil servants, or members of the judicial branch. In both substantive and procedural concepts, the test of constitutionality or legality applied by the judiciary is the answer to the question whether in content or in procedure an action by a member of the governmental process has been "capricious," "arbitrary," or "unreasonable," as applied to constitutional powers and guarantees. If the judicial response to its question is affirmative, the law or order presumably falls either on substantive grounds or its execution falls on procedural grounds, and sometimes both violations are present.

Substantive. A recent illustration of violation of *substantive* due process was a Jacksonville, Florida, ordinance that inherited some of its language from the "poor laws" of Elizabethan England. It outlawed as vagrants and "rogues and vagabonds" persons who, among other things, "use juggling or unlawful games," are "common nightwalkers" or "habitual loafers," and who are "able to work but habitually live upon the earnings of their wives or minor children." Plaintiff Papachristou had been convicted under the quaint statute for "prowling by auto." In an opinion for the unanimous Supreme Court, Justice Douglas declared the law unconstitutionally vague, because it did not tell citizens what conduct was forbidden and encouraged arbitrary and erratic arrests and convictions.[38]
Another example from three decades earlier is *Skinner* v.

In Search of Evolving Doctrine on a Changing Court: A Model for a Newer Equal Protection," 86 *Harvard Law Review* 1 (1972), and J. Harvie Wilkinson, III, "The Supreme Court, the Equal Protection Clause, and the Three Faces of Constitutional Equality," 61 *Virginia Law Review* 945 (1975). See also Chapter II, "The Double Standard," of my *Freedom and the Court, op cit.*
[38]*Papachristou* v. *City of Jacksonville*, 405 U.S. 156 (1972).

Oklahoma,[39]   the Oklahoma sterilization law. Oklahoma's
legislature had passed the statute in a burst of moralistic
enthusiasm, confident both of its wisdom and constitutionality. It provided that thrice-convicted criminal offend-
ers, whose crimes amounted to felonies involving "moral
turpitude," could be legally compelled to undergo sterilization.

Arthur Skinner "qualified" under the statute and was
advised that his time as a procreator had run its course. He
appealed the order and ultimately attained the United States
Supreme Court. The highest tribunal, in one of Douglas's
earliest opinions, unanimously declared the law unconstitutional on the grounds that the classification of "criminal"
was "too loose for so serious a business," especially since it
included larceny by fraud (Skinner had stolen three chickens,
which "counted" as one of the three offenses to be punished
by sterilization), but it *excluded* embezzlement. The Court
thus refused to be persuaded that "a man in Skinner's category was more likely to transmit biologically inheritable
traits than one who had embezzled." Although the basic issue
in this case, as presented by Skinner's attorneys, was an
alleged violation of the "equal protection of the laws" clause
of Amendment Fourteen rather than its "due process"
clause, the law fell, in fact, as a violation of substantive due
process because of its arbitrary nature.

A Virginia sterilization law enacted some years earlier, on
the other hand, had already been upheld against substantive
challenges. It provided that inmates of state-supported institutions who have been found to be afflicted with "an *heredi-
tary* form of insanity, idiocy, imbecility, feeble-mindedness,
or epilepsy" might be sterilized by state action. Carrie Buck
was a seventeen-year-old feeble-minded inmate of a state
institution; her feeble-minded mother was also confined
there. Carrie had given birth out of wedlock to an allegedly
mentally deficient baby just prior to her admission to the
institution. Over Carrie's lawyer's argument that the Virginia
statute should fall, among other reasons because it applied
only to the mentally deficient persons confined to state
institutions and not "to the multitude outside," the Supreme

---

[39] 316 U.S. 535 (1942).

Court upheld it on appeal by an 8:1 vote. Speaking through the now 86-year-old Justice Holmes—a Malthusian since his boyhood—the Court ruled that the "principle that sustains compulsory vaccination is broad enough to cover cutting the Fallopian tubes [under the given circumstances] . . . three generations of imbeciles are enough."[40] And Carrie was duly sterilized.

Procedural due process violations are naturally much more common. The concept requires a general standard of fair procedure; in other words, the procedural due process guarantee denies to agents of government what has been called "the power to filch away private rights oy hole-and-corner methods."[41] Obvious examples are coerced confessions, denial of counsel, "stacked juries," and *unreasonable* searches and seizures. A specific illustration of a clear-cut violation of procedural due process is the famous case of *Rochin* v. *California.*[42] Here, Antonio Richard Rochin was surprised in his bedroom by three Los Angeles County deputy sheriffs, who had some information that he was selling narcotics. Without arrest or search warrant, they had broken into the two-story house where Rochin lived with his mother, common-law wife, brother, and sisters. Two morphine capsules that he had allegedly obtained illegally (which happened to be true) lay on the night table by the bed. When the agents spied them and asked, "Whose stuff is this?", Rochin won the ensuing race for the capsules and stuffed them into his mouth. The agents of the law pummeled and kicked him in the unsuccessful hope that he would relinquish the evidence; to the contrary, he swallowed it. They then inflicted on him a rather thorough beating, hoping, again unsuccessfully, that he might vomit the capsules. Ultimately, they tied, gagged, and transported him to a hospital, where they ordered a resident physician to give the immobilized and irate Rochin an emetic through a stomach tube. This inevitably successful procedure resulted in the vomiting of the two capsules, which the heroic police then presented as evidence at his subsequent trial.

---

[40] *Buck* v. *Bell*, 247 U.S. 200 (1927).
[41] Corry and Abraham, *op cit.*, p. 267.
[42] 342 U.S. 165 (1952).

Rochin was convicted on the strength of that evidence against his hardly unreasonable contention that he had been deprived of procedural due process. Yet when he appealed, the entire appellate structure of the California judicial hierarchy rejected his contentions on the ground that although the evidence was the fruit of what would have clearly been an unconstitutional search and seizure on the *federal* level of government, California did not [then] bar the admission at the trial stage of such evidence. This despite the ready acknowledgment by the District Court of Appeal (the state's intermediate appellate tribunal) that Rochin had been treated outrageously and brutally! When the case ultimately reached the United States Supreme Court on certiorari, that body unanimously reversed Rochin's conviction on grounds of rank violation of *procedural* due process of law guaranteed by the Fourteenth Amendment. Speaking through Justice Frankfurter, the Court held that the proceedings constituted "conduct that shocks the conscience"; that this "course of proceedings by agents of government to obtain evidence is bound to offend even hardened sensibilities ... States in their prosecutions [must] respect certain decencies of civilized conduct." And, concluded Frankfurter in words symptomatic of his judicial posture on the entire problem of "incorporation":

> Due process of law, as a historic and generative principle, precludes defining, and thereby confining, these standards of conduct more precisely than to say that convictions cannot be brought about by methods that offend *"a sense of justice."*[43]

Frankfurter took a position diametrically opposed to that of Justice Black. Yet in the firmly held view of Justices Black and Douglas, expressed in separate *concurring* opinions, the case was rightly decided, but for the wrong reasons. In their judgment—and here again we have a preview of the basic clash on the applicability of the Bill of Rights via the Fourteenth Amendment that exists between what we might loosely call the Frankfurter and Black "camps"—the

---

[43] *Ibid.* (Italics supplied.)

constitutional issue was not the Frankfurter-expressed matter of violation of procedural due process of law under Amendment Fourteen at all. Rather, these two staunch champions of basic freedoms held that California's agents had in fact clearly violated individual liberties expressed by, and safeguarded under, *specific* provisions of the Bill of Rights, such as the self-incrimination provisions of the Fifth Amendment.[44] These, in their repeatedly expressed judgment, are ipso facto applicable to the several states as well as the federal government. Here, of course, is the basic dilemma with which we are now concerned.

Some Historical Considerations

In the search for a solution of the incorporation problem, we turn to the past. There is multiple and conclusive historical evidence that the framers of the Bill of Rights intended it to be a barrier against the federal government only. Indeed, it was the then existing states, under the leadership of Madison, which insisted that a Bill of Rights, applicable to the national government, be added to the Constitution. The states had their own bills of rights; they saw to it that the First Congress proposed the series of ten amendments we now know as the Bill of Rights, and they ratified them in 1791. Certainly there can be no doubt about the initial reach of the First Amendment, for example, for its specific language begins with the words, "Congress shall make no law. . . ." The other amendments are couched in more general language, however, and despite the aforementioned incontrovertible evidence, some observers held that they ought to be construed so as to apply to the states as well as to the federal government. The matter came to a head, and was settled (until the passage of the Fourteenth Amendment thirty-five years later) in the famous case of *Barron* v. *Baltimore*,[45] Chief Justice Marshall's last

---

[44] Twelve years later their viewpoint regarding that particular provision triumphed, when in 1964 the Court held 5:4 that "the Fourteenth Amendment secures against invasion by states the same privilege that the Fifth Amendment guarantees against Federal infringement." (*Malloy* v. *Hogan*, 378 U.S. 1.)
[45] Peters 243 (1833).

constitutional law decision, one that has never been overruled per se.

Barron v. *Baltimore.* The case arose as a result of plaintiff Barron's claim at the bar of the Court that the City of Baltimore had deprived him of his property without due process of law. That property, he protested, was protected by the spirit and the letter of that portion of the Fifth Amendment which forbids the taking of private property for public use—also known as the right of "eminent domain"—without just compensation. Barron had owned a fine wharf, but the city's street-paving and stream-diverting operations caused deposits of sand and gravel near it, shallowed the water, and thus prevented the approach of vessels. *Today*, Mr. Barron would seek redress under the *Fourteenth* Amendment, but his only recourse *then* was the *Fifth*. Marshall made short shrift of Barron's argument. Speaking for his unanimous Court, the chief held that the tribunal had "no jurisdiction of the case; and it is dismissed." His opinion stressed the view that "the question . . . presented is . . . of great importance, but not of much difficulty." Thus he ruled that the Bill of Rights, generally, and here the Fifth Amendment, particularly, was "intended solely as a limitation on the exercise of power by the government of the United States, and is not applicable to the legislatures of the States. . . . This court cannot so apply them."[46] He saw no "repugnancy between the several acts of the general assembly of Maryland . . . and the Constitution of the United States." Mr. Barron had no further legal recourse.[47]

The Slaughterhouse Cases. No other litigation of significance arose on the point at issue until after the ratification of the Fourteenth Amendment in 1868. Five years thereafter, however, the Court reconfirmed the *Barron* doctrine by

---

[46] *Ibid.*, pp. 250–251.

[47] Actually, Barron had won his argument at the level of the trial court, which awarded him $4500 in damages, but when the City of Baltimore appealed that decision to the Maryland State Court of Appeals, it won a reversal.

widening the gulf between the Constitution's applicability to the two levels of government in the very first cases involving the new Amendment. It did this by holding that its "privileges and immunities" clause did not, and was not intended to, protect the rights of *state* citizenship, but solely those of *federal* citizenship; that, in the words of Justice Samuel F. Miller's majority opinion for the closely divided (5:4) Court:

> It is quite clear, then, that there is a citizenship of the United States, and a citizenship of a state, which are distinct from each other, and which depend upon different characteristics or circumstances in the individual.[48]

Having made that distinction, Miller was able to draw a sharp line between those "privileges and immunities" which accrued to an individual by virtue of his *state* citizenship, and those which accrued to him by virtue of his citizenship in the *national* government. Only the latter, then, fell under the protective umbrella of the Fourteenth Amendment.

This was bad news for the plaintiffs in the case, the Butchers' Benevolent Association of New Orleans, who had contended that Louisiana "Carpetbag" legislature, unquestionably under corrupt influence, had in 1867 conferred upon one firm what was virtually a monopoly of the slaughterhouse business in New Orleans. It was a monopoly, forbidden under Amendment Fourteen, they insisted, and one that now prevented over 1,000 firms and individuals from continuing in the slaughterhouse business. It was also bad news for the many supporters of the language of the Fourteen Amendment, especially its first section,[49] who had been confident that its adoption would provide certain minimum federal standards below which a state would not be

---

[48] *The Slaughterhouse Cases (The Butchers' Benevolent Association of New Orleans* v. *Crescent City Live Stock Landing and Slaughterhouse Co.),* 16 Wallace 36 (1873), at 74.

[49] ". . . No State shall make or enforce any law which shall abridge the privileges or immunities of citizens of the United States; nor shall any State deprive any person of life, liberty, or property, without due process of law; nor deny to any person within its jurisdiction the equal protection of the laws."

permitted to fall. It was equally bad news to those who held
with the magisterial John W. Burgess that "if history has
taught us anything in political science, it is that liberty is
national in its origin, content and sanction."[50] Yet had the
Slaughterhouse Cases been decided twenty-five years later,
under the substantive due process–oriented Fuller Court, or
even thirteen years later under Chief Justice Morrison R.
Waite, the grievance complained of by the New Orleans
butchers would almost certainly have been adjudged a violation of the (substantive) due process of law clause of the
Amendment. (It was in 1886 that Waite ruled for a unanimous Court that *corporations* were henceforth to be regarded
as "persons" under the Fourteenth Amendment, and were
thus protected by the Constitution against invalid state infringement.[51] This decision gladdened the judicial and
philosophical heart of Justice Stephen J. Field, who had
written the leading dissenting opinion in the *Slaughterhouse
Cases:* to him an absolute right to engage in the trade of
butchering was *the* privilege or·immunity in need of protection there.)[52]

The Fourteenth Amendment Controversy. We now turn to a
far less clear or certain historical question, one still unre-
solved, and one that has presented us through the years with
one of the bitterest of constitutional arguments: When its
framers in the Thirty-Ninth Congress worded Section I of the
Fourteenth Amendment, did they, or did they not, intend to
have it "incorporate" or "nationalize" or "absorb" the provisions of the federal Bill of Rights, and thus make it applicable *in toto* to the several states? Or, put somewhat differently, how far, if at all, does the language of the first
section of that most litigious Amendment of all apply to the
states the twenty-five or so specific rights listed in the Bill of
Rights as a prohibition upon state action?

This grave and perplexing question has not been settled.

---

[50] *Political Science and Comparative Constitutional Law* (Boston:
Ginn and Co., 1890), I, p. 2250.
[51] *Santa Clara County* v. *Southern Pacific Railroad Co.*, 118 U.S.
394 (1886).
[52] 16 Wallace 36 (1873).

But since 1925 it has been resolved on a piecemeal, gradual, pragmatic basis in favor of the contention that many, if not all, of the enumerated rights must be applied to the states, although that enumeration remains incomplete and contentious. Those who would prefer an historical justification, however, have never really been satisfied, despite a torrent of research and comment alleged to provide *the* answer. The question may well be beyond authentic response, for historical evidence is not conclusive. Perhaps the affirmative respondents have a slight edge, based on the duly recorded assertions by the two floor managers of the Amendment, Republican Representative James A. Bingham of Ohio and Republican Senator Jacob Howard of Michigan.[53] But it is simply a matter of fact that it is entirely possible to come up with opposite conclusions based on almost identical primary data—to wit, the records of the congressional debates on the subject. Thus, Justice Black, in what is one of the longest and most elaborately researched dissenting opinions (in *Adamson* v. *California*[54]) insisted that one of the chief objectives the provisions of the Fourteenth Amendment's first section, "separately and as a whole," was designed to accomplish, was to make the *entire* Bill of Rights applicable to the states. He never wavered from this interpretation and advocacy—one supported *ante* by Professor Horace Flack's 1908 book. [55]

Yet, answering Justice Black and basing his response on substantially similar data, Professor Charles Fairman, a well-known expert on constitutional law and history, came to a precisely opposite conclusion and, in the process, accused Black of deliberate distortion in order to prove his point. [56] Another expert in the area, Professor Stanley Morrison of Stanford University, inclines toward the Fairman interpretation, but believes that the latter's categorical negative goes a

---

[53] For a lengthy discussion and analysis, see my *Freedom and the Court*, *op cit.*, pp. 31 ff.

[54] 332 U.S. 46 (1947). The specific *holding* in the case was overruled 18 years later in *Griffin* v. *California*, 380 U.S. 609 (1965).

[55] *The Adoption of the Fourteenth Amendment* (Baltimore: The Johns Hopkins Press, 1908).

[56] "Critique of the Black Dissent in *Adamson* v. *California*," 2 *Stanford Law Review* 5 (December 1949).

bit too far.[57] A fifth protagonist, Professor J. B. James, who like Flack wrote an entire book[58] on the subject, attacks the sweeping Black interpretation of the congressional debates as erroneous, but, with some reservations, shares Black's conclusion that the framers of the Fourteenth Amendment did, indeed, intend to have the Bill of Rights incorporated. Regardless of personal motivations and commitments, these five positions indicate only too well how difficult it is to prove speculative history—and how little authenticity can result from the popular game of psychoanalyzing history! The famed German historian Ranke's outburst that it is essential to determine *"wie es eigentlich gewesen"*[59] is understandable, but at times rather futile, as it assuredly is in this instance. Not futile, however, and indeed crucial to an understanding of the problem, are a discussion and an analysis of the various positions that have been taken by members of the Supreme Court.

To Incorporate or Not, and If So, How?

Pre-Gitlow Developments. This century's preoccupation with the question and problem dates from Justice Edward T. Sanford's historic "assumption" in the 1925 landmark case of *Gitlow* v. *New York.*[60] There, although the appellant lost his free speech and press claims against New York's Criminal Anarchy Act of 1902—the Court dividing 7:2 with Justices Holmes and Brandeis in outraged dissent—Sanford accepted Gitlow's plea for incorporation of First Amendment freedoms by stating that:

> for present purposes we may and do assume that freedom of speech and of the press—which are protected by the First Amendment from abridgement by Congress—

---

[57] "Does the Fourteenth Amendment Incorporate the Bill of Rights—The Judicial Interpretation," 2 *Stanford Law Review* 140 (December 1949).

[58] *The Framing of the Fourteenth Amendment* (Urbana: University of Illinois Press, 1956).

[59] "How it actually was."

[60] 268 U.S. 652.

are among the fundamental personal rights and "liberties" protected by the due process clause of the Fourteenth Amendment from impairment by the states.[61]

This did not help Gitlow, who went to jail (although he was
later pardoned and commenced a lucrative career as a paid
informer for the federal government in internal security cases
in the 1940's and 1950's), yet it proved of momentous
significance within little more than a decade.

But *Gitlow* was not, of course, the first case to raise—or
raise again, given the decision in the *Slaughterhouse
Cases*[62] —the basic problem; it was certainly not unknown to
the judicial profession. Notably Justice John Marshall Harlan
had time and again in dissent proved receptive to petitioners'
claims in behalf of the incorporation theory. Thus his lonely
dissenting opinions in *Hurtado* v. *California* (1884),[63] *Maxwell* v. *Dow* (1900),[64] and *Twining* v. *New Jersey* (1908)[65]
demonstrated his unshakable conviction that the Fourteenth
Amendment was intended to incorporate the *entire* Bill of
Rights, for he regarded *every* right in the Bill as a "fundamental" one. The first of these cases involved a claim under
the grand jury indictment privilege of the Fifth Amendment;
the second involved the same provision of the Fifth *and* trial
by a petit jury under the Sixth Amendment; and the last, the
privilege against self-incrimination under the Fifth. Yet in
each of the cases, Harlan lost to a solid eight-man majority
(although the Court had unanimously applied the Fifth
Amendment's eminent domain concept to the states via
Amendment Fourteen in an 1897 opinion by Harlan[66]).
That majority not only rejected his view of the incorporation
theory, but also denied that petitioners Hurtado, Maxwell,
and Twining had been deprived by California, Utah, or New
Jersey of *any* Fourteenth Amendment "privileges and immunities" or "liberty and/or property" rights. Yet seventeen

---

[61] *Ibid.*, at 666.
[62] 16 Wallace 36 (1873).
[63] 110 U.S. 516.
[64] 176 U.S. 581.
[65] 211 U.S. 78.
[66] *Chicago, Burlington & Quincy RR.* v. *Chicago*, 166 U.S. 226.
Here Harlan spoke for a unanimous--and property-conscious—Court.

years after the *Twining* decision, *Gitlow* appeared on the horizon, destined to provide us with the doorway to the fascinating and controversial constitutional developments to which we now briefly turn.

Enter the "Honor Roll" Approach: Palko v Connecticut.[67]   Within a few years after the 1925 decision in *Gitlow*, the Supreme Court confirmed the freedom of speech aspect of the Sanford "assumption" in a Kansas case,[68] and that of freedom of the press in two important cases decided after Justice Sanford's death in 1930.[69] But the Court was to expand the doctrine: First, in the celebrated *Scottsboro Case*[70] —replete with evidence of the shocking miscarriage of justice in Alabama courts—it broke new ground by incorporating the concept of benefit of counsel in *capital* criminal cases. Second, it extended the First Amendment coverage to free exercise of religion in a California case involving Albert Hamilton, a University of California student who objected to participation in military drill (although the Court held that his religious liberty had not been abridged by compelling him to participate in the exercises as a condition of attending the state institution of higher learning).[71] And third, it included two of the still "left out" guarantees of the First Amendment by incorporating the freedoms of assembly and petition in *De Jonge* v. *Oregon*[72] in 1937, just a few months prior to *Palko.*[73]

Frank Palko had been indicted by Connecticut for *first degree* murder; a jury found him guilty of *second degree* murder, and he was given a life sentence with a recommendation that he never be paroled. Pursuant to a statute of 1886, the state, and with the permission of the presiding judge of the trial court, appealed the conviction on the lesser count by

---

[67] 302 U.S. 319 (1937).

[68] *Fiske* v. *Kansas*, 274 U.S. 380 (1927).

[69] *Near* v. *Minnesota*, 283 U.S. 697 (1931) and *Grosjean* v. *American Press Co.*, 297 U.S. 233 (1936).

[70] *Powell* v. *Alabama*, 287 U.S. 45 (1932).

[71] *Hamilton* v. *Regents of the U. of California*, 293 U.S. 245 (1934).

[72] 299 U.S. 253.

[73] *Palko* v. *Connecticut*, 302 U.S. 319 (1937).

charging legal error. The Connecticut Supreme Court held that there had indeed been "error of law to the prejudice of the state," reversed the judgment below, and ordered a new trial. Over Palko's objections that the second trial would place him twice in jeopardy for the same offense, forbidden by the terms of the Fifth Amendment and, according to his contention, consequently also by those of the due process of law clause of the Fourteenth, he was retried. This time the jury returned a *first* degree verdict, and the trial court imposed the death sentence. Palko appealed to the United States Supreme Court, contending that whatever is forbidden by the language of the Fifth is also forbidden by that of the Fourteenth Amendment. For the important reasons given below, the Court ruled 8:1 against Palko, Mr. Justice Butler dissenting without opinion—and the appellant was subsequently executed. A cynic might say that in view of the importance of the Supreme Court's pronouncements in the case, Palko did not die in vain.

Mr. Justice Cardozo's beautifully written opinion for the eight-man majority is probably the best known of the decisions he penned during his term of six years on the Court. It is a judicial landmark for many reasons, but for our present purposes two closely related aspects are evident: *First*, it recognized justification for the claim that, under certain conditions and in certain areas, the several states *are* bound by the verbiage of the Bill of Rights via that of the Fourteenth Amendment; *second*, it provided a formula by which a modicum of certainty could govern the judicial process in this sphere. In essence, the Cardozo opinion firmly denied the existence of a "general rule" of "incorporation" or "carrying over" via Amendment Fourteen, *but* stated that there are *some* rights in the Bill of Rights that are and must be so "absorbed."

How and where did he draw the line—how did he establish this "honor roll," to which Justice Frankfurter, Cardozo's successor and lifelong admirer, irreverently referred as "the slot machine theory . . . some are in and some are out"? Refusing to regard the due process of law clause of the Fourteenth Amendment as "shorthand" for the Bill of Rights, Cardozo nonetheless established a dichotomy of those fundamental rights that are "of the very essence of a scheme of ordered liberty" and those without which "justice would not perish" because, unlike the former group, he did not regard them as "implicit in the concept of ordered liberty." To expand somewhat on his justification for the "fundamental" group, he wrote movingly of "those fundamental principles of liberty and justice which lie at the base of all our civil and political institutions," and of a "principle of justice so rooted in the traditions and conscience of our people as to be ranked as fundamental." (Note the recurrent theme of the concept *fundamental* versus what might be called the merely *formal*.) Recognizing the difficulty inherent in this dichotomy, and correctly anticipating some of the problems as well as the criticism that would follow, Mr. Justice Cardozo resorted to the "freedom of thought and speech" as his chief illustration, writing: "Of that freedom one may say that it is the matrix, the indispensable condition, of nearly every other form of freedom." And so it is.

As for the "formal" rights, he contended, speaking of the privilege against self-incrimination, that "[J]ustice would not perish if the accused were subject to a duty to respond to orderly inquiry." He insisted that in the realm of these chiefly procedural rights, in general, and the double jeopardy safeguards of the Fifth Amendment, in particular—since it was at issue in *Palko*—the question to be posed by the Court is whether the state action complained of represents "a hardship so acute and shocking that our polity will not endure it? Does it violate those fundamental principles of liberty and justice which lie at the base of our civil and political institutions? . . . The answer surely must be 'no.' " In Cardozo's view, Connecticut had sought no more than parity with the defendant in the right to continue a case "until there shall be a trial free from the corrosion of substantial legal error." A defendant was given the right to appeal errors adverse to him. "A reciprocal privilege . . . has now been granted to the state. . . ." And he concluded: "The edifice of justice stands, its symmetry, to many, greater than before."[74]

---

[74] *Ibid.*, at 328.

Despite the *Palko* double standard between those rights that are and those that are not "implicit in the concept of ordered liberty," Cardozo made it clear that the states would still be subject to the judicial test of whether a properly contested action by a state involved a violation of the due process of law clause of the Fourteenth Amendment per se. In other words, simply because only some of the rights of the federal Bill of Rights are ipso facto applicable to the states via the Fourteenth Amendment, it does not mean that the states are free to violate the constitutional concept of due process of law to which all persons in their jurisdictions are entitled. The judicial test here becomes that contentious one, so ardently and consistently embraced by Justice Frankfurter and his adherents, of whether or not the state conduct complained of "shocks the conscience"—or, in the less delicate language of Justice Holmes, "Does it make you vomit?" Or, to put the matter somewhat differently, it represents a case-by-case approach to each litigation, always turning on the question of whether the action by a state official has transgressed the bounds of constitutionality inherent in the due process of law clause of the Fourteenth Amendment, as tested by the judges. The case of *Rochin* v. *California,* [75] discussed above, illustrates this judicial test, with Justice Frankfurter holding for the Court that the conduct of the Los Angeles sheriff's deputies "shocked the conscience," and hence violated due process of law. The concurring opinions of Justices Black and Douglas, on the other hand, although naturally agreeing with the reversal of Rochin's conviction, stressed their judgment that the reversal should have been based upon a violation of the Fifth Amendment's provision against self-incrimination, which they would have incorporated verbatim then and there, along with *all* the provisions of the Bill of Rights.

This basic disagreement between what will henceforth be referred to as the "Frankfurter" and "Black" positions, was sharpened in a later state self-incrimination, unreasonable search and seizure case: *Breithaupt* v. *Abram*, 1957.

---

[75] 342 U.S. 165 (1952).

Breithaupt v. *Abram*[76] well illustrates the basic problem raised in *Rochin*—and our discussion of the entire incorporation matter. Paul H. Breithaupt, while driving a pickup truck on a New Mexico highway, was involved in a collision with a passenger car. The three occupants of the car were killed and Breithaupt was seriously injured. An almost empty pint bottle of whiskey was found in the glove compartment of Breithaupt's truck. He was taken to a hospital, and while he was lying unconscious in the emergency room, attendants detected a strong odor of liquor on his breath. Upon the request of a state patrolman, an attending physician withdrew 22 cc. of blood from the unconscious man. The sample contained .17 per cent of alcohol, and Breithaupt, who recovered, was ultimately charged with involuntary manslaughter—with the blood test submitted as important and damaging evidence. Breithaupt, largely following the Court's reasoning in *Rochin*, charged violation of due process of law of the Fourteenth Amendment. Speaking for a six-member majority of the Court, Justice Clark, however, pointed out that "the blood test procedure has become routine in our day," and, responding to the petitioner's charge that the procedure involved constituted "conduct that shocks the conscience"—the *Rochin* test—ruled that "a blood test taken by a skilled technician is not such conduct that shocks the conscience," and does not offend a sense of justice.[77] But there were dissenting opinions by Chief Justice Warren and Justice Douglas, both joined by Justice Black. The three jurists contended with feeling that there was no basic distinction between the two cases, since both involved involuntary incrimination; they rejected any "analysis that would make physical resistance by a prisoner a prerequisite to the existence of his constitutional rights"; and held that, in any case, the Fourth and Fifth Amendments of the Bill of Rights, barring unreasonable searches and seizures and self-incrimina-

---

[76] 352 U.S. 432 (1957).

[77] The *Breithaupt* decision was confirmed 5:4 a decade later in *Schmerber* v. *California*, 384 U.S. 757 (1966), Mr. Justice Brennan writing the opinion, with the three *Breithaupt* dissenters joined by Mr. Justice Fortas in the minority.

tion, should be made applicable to the states via the Fourteenth. Again, the basic clash is evident. Yet there are still other positions on "incorporation" worthy of mention, to which we shall turn after an analysis of the division determined by Justice Cardozo in *Palko* and subsequent developments.

The Two Sides of the Palko Line et seq.   Few determinations are as clearly outlined in a case at law as is Justice Cardozo's "honor roll" in *Palko* v. *Connecticut*,[78] and it is quite easy to build a table or draw a chart based upon it. Those rights viewed by the terms of Cardozo's opinion *in 1937* as being "of the very essence of a scheme of ordered liberty," and thus incorporated via Amendment Fourteen, were *then* as follows:

Amendment I: Speech.
                  Press.
                  Free Exercise of Religion.
                  Peaceable Assembly (and Petition).
Amendment V: Eminent Domain.
Amendment VI: Counsel in Capital Criminal Cases.

And, he added, there may be other similar "situations."

But he *expressly exempted* from his incorporation classification those rights among Articles II–VIII of the Bill of Rights which he did not deem to be "of the very essence of a scheme of ordered liberty." His specific 1937 roster of *non*incorporation:

Amendment IV: Evidence Admitted as a Result of an Unreasonable Search and Seizure.
Amendment V: Double Jeopardy.
                  Grand Jury Indictment or Presentment.
                  Self-Incrimination.
Amendment VI: Jury Trial in Criminal Cases.
Amendment VII: Jury Trial in Civil Cases.

Cardozo thus did not specifically treat *every* area of the Bill of Rights—he did not address Amendments II, III, and VIII at

---

[78] 302 U.S. 319 (1937).

all—but he made quite clear that in his judgment the federal principle demanded that the states be permitted to follow their own discretion in much of the area of procedural due process of law, *so long as due process of law was indeed provided in every instance.*

The Cardozo "honor roll" stood the test of time for almost a quarter of a century—save that the First Amendment's separation of state and church clause was specifically incorporated and thus made applicable to the states via Amendment Fourteen in the 1947 *New Jersey Bus Case,*[79] in an opinion by Justice Black, and that the concept of a *public* trial was carried over in 1948.[80] Despite repeated calls by Justices Stone, Black, Douglas, Murphy, and Rutledge for further, if not total, incorporation, it was not until 1961 that an additional one was effected. It came as a result of the 6:3 opinion in *Mapp* v. *Ohio,*[81] written by Justice Clark, which overruled long-standing precedents[82] to hold that "all evidence obtained by searches and seizures in violation of the Constitution is, by that same authority, inadmissible in a state court. . . ." and:

> Since the Fourth Amendment's right of privacy has been declared enforceable against the States through the Due Process Clause of the Fourteenth, it is enforceable against them by the same sanction of exclusion as is used against the Federal Government.[83]

Barely a year passed before another formerly "nonincorporated" segment of the Bill of Rights was carried over:

---

[79] *Everson* v. *Board of Education of Ewing Township,* 330 U.S. 1.
[80] *In Re Oliver,* 333 U.S. 257 (the Michigan "one-man grand jury" case).
[81] 367 U.S. 643.
[82] See especially the famous case of *Wolf* v. *Colorado,* 338 U.S. 25 (1949). In *Wolf*—in many ways a grotesque case—Justice Frankfurter had held for the Court that the safeguards of the Fourth Amendment are "implicit in the concept of ordered liberty," and enforceable against the states via Amendment Fourteen—*but* that it does *not* forbid the admission of illegally obtained evidence in a *state* court! For in the latter the common-law doctrine then still governed (as it does to this day in British courts and most of the other countries of the world), namely: that if the evidence is trustworthy, it is admissible regardless of how it was obtained.
[83] *Mapp* v. *Ohio, loc. cit.,* at 654–655.

the Eighth Amendment's injunction against "cruel and unusual punishment." Cardozo's opinion in *Palko* had not specifically dealt with that clause, and doubt existed as to the limits a state—or the national government, for that matter—could go before its actions in this sphere would constitute a constitutional violation. But as a result of Justice Stewart's opinion in a decision in 1962, involving the validity of a sweeping California criminal statute against narcotics addiction,[84] the prohibition against cruel and unusual punishment is now one of the "nationalized" safeguards. It became the constitutional hook on which the Court, in a welter of nine opinions running to 243 pages, hung its historic 5:4 decision in 1972 that outlawed capital punishment "as it was then imposed under statutes."[85] But in July 1976, in a series of cases reaching it from five states that had carefully redrawn their laws to meet the objections of the 1972 decision, the Court, by a decisive margin of 7:2, upheld the constitutionality of capital punishment, given the presence of precise statutory safeguards and the absence of either impermissible discretionary imposition or a mandatory death sentence.[86]

Of undoubtedly seminal importance is the celebrated 1963 decision in *Gideon* v. *Wainwright*,[87] which incorporated the right to counsel in *all* criminal cases, be they

---

[84] *Robinson* v. *California*, 370 U.S. 660, at 666–667. The Court began to wrestle with the related issue of chronic alcoholics in the 1968 case of *Powell* v. *Texas*, 392 U.S. 514, but for the present refused 5:4 to apply the *Robinson* rationale since, as Justice Thurgood Marshall wrote in the majority opinion, Powell was not "convicted for being a chronic alcoholic, but for being in public while drunk on a particular occasion." (At 532.)

[85] *Furman* v. *Georgia*, 408 U.S. 238.

[86] *Gregg* v. *Georgia* and *Roberts* v. *Louisiana*, 44 LW 5230, 5281 (1976). See the latter's reconfirmation in 1977.

[87] 372 U.S. 335, Chief Justice Warren placed the *Gideon* case third in importance in the cases decided during his sixteen-year career on the bench. (See Ch. I, p. 2, *supra*.) Its liberal extensions in such now famed and controversial decisions as *Escobedo* v. *Illinois*, 378 U.S. 478 (1964), *Miranda* v. *Arizona*, 384 U.S. 436 (1966), and *Orozco* v. *Texas*, 394 U.S. 324 (1969) underscore *Gideon's* significance. A contraction of *Miranda* came in *Harris* v. *New York*, 401 U.S. 222 (1971); another in *Oregon* v. *Haas*, 420 U.S. 714 (1975); another in *Michigan* v. *Mosley*, 44 LW 4015 (1975); and a further one in *United States* v. *Mandujano*, 44 LW 4629 (1976). But the latter year also saw a significant expansion of the embattled *Miranda* decision (*Doyle* v. *Ohio* and *Wood* v. *Ohio* 44 LW 4902). 1977 witnessed a narrowing in *Oregon* v. *Mathiason*.

capital or noncapital. Some observers had assumed that Justice George Sutherland's opinion in the *Scottsboro Case* [88] had made that aspect of the Sixth Amendment applicable to the states in all criminal cases. But the Court subsequently ruled otherwise in a highly contentious case in 1942. Justice Roberts's opinion held 6:3 that the Fourteenth Amendment did *not* require that counsel be furnished to an indigent by a state (here Maryland) in *noncapital* crimes,[89] unless "special or exceptional circumstances" existed—such as "youth," "lack of education," "mental illness." It was this holding which was specifically overruled in *Gideon*, a case that came to the Supreme Court through Clarence Earl Gideon's pencilled *in forma pauperis* petition to the Supreme Court. Lawyerless and penniless, Gideon had been committed to a Florida jail as a result of conviction of a crime (which, with the aid of a court-appointed lawyer following the mandate of *Gideon*, he was later easily able to prove a frame-up). Speaking with evident satisfaction for a unanimous Court, Mr. Justice Black wrote in *Gideon* that it was an "obvious truth" that "in our adversary system of criminal justice any person hauled into court who is too poor to hire a lawyer cannot be assured a fair trial unless counsel is provided for him." [90] Since 1972 the *Gideon* holding extends to *all* imprisonable crimes, even misdemeanors.[91]

The highly significant self-incrimination safeguards of the Fifth Amendment were incorporated in 1964. In a dramatic overruling of its 1908 precedent of *Twining* v. *New Jersey*, [92] the Court broadened the scope of the Constitution's protection for individuals who refuse to testify against themselves in criminal cases. It did this in two rulings of major importance to jurisprudence: first, by holding 5:4 that the Fourteenth Amendment, which assures all citizens due process of law, "secures against states' invasion the same privilege that

---

[88] *Powell* v. *Alabama*, 289 U.S. 45 (1932).
[89] *Betts* v. *Brady*, 316 U.S. 455 (1932).
[90] *Gideon* v. *Wainwright*, 372 U.S. 355. See Anthony Lewis's excellent account of Gideon's trials and tribulations in *Gideon's Trumpet* (New York: Random House, 1964).
[91] *Argersinger* v. *Hamlin*, 407 U.S. 25, which was made retroactive in 1973 (*Berry* v. *Cincinnati*, 414 U.S. 29).
[92] 211 U.S. 78.

the Fifth Amendment guarantees against Federal infringement";[93] and second, by rejecting unanimously "the rule that one jurisdiction within our federal structure may compel a witness to give testimony which could be used to convict him of a crime in another."[94] To emphasize the Court's full intent of its judgment, Justice Goldberg, speaking for the unanimous bench in the second case, made matters crystal clear: "We hold that the Constitutional privilege against self-incrimination protects a state witness against incrimination under Federal as well as state law and a Federal witness against incrimination under state as well as Federal law." Another corner along the road of incorporation had thus been reached and turned.[95]

Still more were to come. In 1965, in a Black opinion, the Court incorporated, 7:2, the Sixth Amendment's right of an accused in a criminal case to confront *adverse* witnesses against him[96] —a right expanded two years later in a dissent-free opinion by Chief Justice Warren to the privilege of having compulsory process also for obtaining *favorable* witnesses.[97] A short while earlier, the Court, in yet another Warren-written opinion, had unanimously incorporated that same Amendment's provision to the right of a *speedy* trial. [98]

---

[93] *Malloy* v. *Hogan*, 378 U.S. 1.

[94] *Murphy* v. *Waterfront Commission*, 378 U.S. 52.

[95] On the merits of the self-incrimination issue itself, on the other hand, see the narrowing of the immunity concept by the Burger Court in two 1975 (5:2) opinions, written by Justice Powell. In them the Court upheld the use of a new type of immunity of witnesses, the 1970 legislatively sanctioned "use" immunity. (*Kastigar* v. *United States*, 406 U.S. 441 and *Zicarelli* v. *New Jersey*, 406 U.S. 472.) The complete immunity from prosecution ("transactional") is thus evidently now replaceable with the more limited type ("use"); the latter allows the prosecution to use evidence in a case about which the witness was compelled to testify under an immunity grant, *provided* it is able to prove that it derived that evidence "wholly independent" of his or her testimony and that it did so "wholly legitimately."

[96] *Pointer* v. *Texas*, 380 U.S. 400.

[97] *Washington* v. *Texas*, 388 U.S. 14 (1967).

[98] *Klopfer* v. *North Carolina*, 386 U.S. 213 (1967). In 1974 Congress, led by the retiring Senator Sam J. Ervin, Jr. (D.-N.C.), passed the Federal Speedy Trial Act. This provided for setting up a schedule to be implemented over a five-year period of time limits, ultimately reaching a low of 100 days, during which criminal charges must either be brought to trial or dropped. (A number of states have adopted similar laws.)

In 1968 it then voted 7:2 to incorporate the right to a trial by jury in all non-petty *criminal* cases.[99] It had already so held as to the basic right to a trial by an "impartial" jury one year earlier.[100] But, the Court ruled by a narrow margin in 1972, that that right does not encompass a constitutional requirement for states to provide either a twelve-member jury[101] or a unanimous jury.[102] Nor does the Seventh Amendment's guarantee of a right to a trial by jury in *civil* cases in suits valued above $20 mandate a twelve-member jury even at the *federal* level (let alone at that of the states).[103] And in 1969, on the last day of Chief Justice Warren's tenure on the highest bench, the Court, in a 6:2 opinion written by Justice Marshall, at last had held the double jeopardy safeguards of the Fifth Amendment to be "a fundamental ideal in our constitutional heritage . . . that . . . should apply to the States through the Fourteenth Amendment."[104] He added that insofar as this new holding was inconsistent with *Palko* v. *Connecticut*,[105] the latter stood overruled.[106]

By late 1976 no other provisions of the Bill of Rights had been incorporated (the concepts of a fair trial and eminent domain safeguards are regarded as having been absorbed long ago). Whether the Bill of Rights will ever be incorporated *in toto* is highly problematical because of the strong implications of federalism in, and the relatively lesser

---

[99] *Duncan* v. *Louisiana*, 391 U.S. 145. But earlier in 1968 it had declined to review the same issue for *civil* cases. (*McBeth* v. *Texas & Pacific Railway Co.*, 390 U.S. 987.) A "petty" case was held (7:1) in 1970 to be one for which incarcerability could not exceed six months. (*Baldwin* v. *New York*, 399 U.S. 66.) In a 5:4 ruling in 1976, however, the Court seemed to narrow *Duncan* by holding that a state may deny a defendant a jury in his initial trial on a criminal charge *if* it allows that defendant, through an appeal, to get a second trial in which there is a jury. *Ludwig* v. *Massachusetts*, 44 LW 5173, (1976).

[100] *Parker* v. *Gladden*, 385 U.S. 363 (1967).

[101] *Williams* v. *Florida*, 399 U.S. 78 (1970).

[102] *Johnson* v. *Louisiana*, 406 U.S. 356 and *Apodaca* v. *Oregon*, 406 U.S. 404.

[103] *Colgrove* v. *Battin*, 413 U.S. 149 (1973).

[104] *Benton* v. *Maryland*, 395 U.S. 784, at 795–796.

[105] 302 U.S. 319 (1937). What was thus overruled was the erstwhile nonapplicability of the double jeopardy provision of the Fifth Amendment to the states, *not*, of course, the Cardozo-authored philosophy of "selective" incorporation as such. The latter remains the law of the land as pronounced by its highest tribunal.

[106] *Benton* v. *Maryland*, loc. cit.

significance to basic human rights of, those very few enumerated rights still remaining "out"—namely, those dealing with grand jury indictment,[107] trial by jury in civil cases, excessive fines and bail, the right to bear arms,[108] and the Article III safeguards against voluntary quartering of troops in private homes. But given the now well-established belief that if there is anything at all "national" in scope and application under the Constitution of the United States of America, it is the matter of civil rights and liberties—total incorporation is no longer of primary importance save as a matter of constitutional theory. With the incorporation of double jeopardy, the last crucial fundamental right then still "out" was nationalized.

Major "Positions" on Incorporation. In summary—and at the risk of oversimplification—there are essentially four major positions held by prominent past and/or present members of the Supreme Court on that key question of incorporation. The *first* position is probably—although arguably[109]—still current Court doctrine, growing out of the Cardozo opinion in *Palko* v. *Connecticut*: the concept of the "honor roll" or "selective incorporation." Consistently rejected by such champions of judicial self-restraint as Justices Frankfurter and the second Harlan, it has commanded a majority approval of the Court since its pronouncement in 1937. It has the virtues of flexibility and compromise and the vices of weighted selectivity and uncertainty.

The *second* major doctrine is that initially advocated by

---

[107] The Supreme Court again denied certiorari on that issue late in 1968 (*Gyuro* v. *Connecticut*, 393 U.S. 937).

[108] If any provision seems to need no judicial protection, this Amendment Two safeguard would seem to be it—so influential have been the anti–gun control forces. In the one case on record that did reach the Supreme Court, the high tribunal (in 1969) denied review for want of a substantial federal question, the tribunal below having held categorically that Amendment Two does not apply to the states—that, indeed, "as the language of the Amendment indicates, it was not framed with individual rights in mind. . . ." (*Burton* v. *Sills*, 394 U.S. 812, appeal dismissed).

[109] For a view that "selective incorporation" is a misnomer, see Jacob W. Landynski, "Due Process and the Concept of Ordered Liberty: 'A Screen of Words Expressing Will in the Service of Desire'?", 2 *Hofstra University Law Review* 1 (Winter 1974).

the first Justice Harlan at the turn of the century: *simply to incorporate the Bill of Rights lock, stock, and barrel.*[110] This doctrine has been consistently espoused through the years by Justice Black and, with reservations—see below—by such justices as Douglas, Murphy, Rutledge, Goldberg—and probably Chief Justices Stone and Warren and Justices Brennan and the second Marshall. It has been the confirmed and warmly embraced conviction of most of these justices that not only does the Fourteenth Amendment mandate the Bill of Rights' incorporation, but that even if history does not provide an entirely adequate guide on this point, both the logic and necessity of democratic society in the last quarter of the twentieth century require such a position. It possesses the virtues of certainty and simplicity and the vices of dogmatism and questionable interpretation of the basic document.

The *third* position is really an extension of the second: namely, that the Bill of Rights in all its majestic guarantees may not suffice to ascertain full "due process of law" and that therefore it may be necessary to embrace a "total incorporation *plus*" approach in order to achieve full justice for the allegedly aggrieved involved. This posture was most prominently expounded by Justices Murphy and Rutledge in their dissenting opinion in the *Adamson* case. In Justice Murphy's words, they agreed that the specific guarantees of the Bill of Rights should be "carried over intact" into the first section of the Fourteenth Amendment, but that "occasions may arise where a proceeding falls so short of conforming to fundamental standards of procedure *as to warrant constitutional condemnation in terms of a lack of due process despite the absence of a specific provision in the Bill of Rights.*"[111] Justices Douglas and Goldberg voiced their adherence to the "incorporation *plus*" doctrine emphatically in the *Connecticut Birth Control Case* in 1965,[112] with

[110] Harlan did not use those words: His emphasis fell on the universally *fundamental* nature of *all* the provisions of the Bill of Rights, thus calling for their absorption via the Fourteenth Amendment.

[111] *Adamson* v. *California,* 332 U.S. 46 (1947), at 124. (Italics supplied.)

[112] *Griswold* v. *Connecticut,* 381 U.S. 479. In that case Chief Justice Warren and Justice Brennan seemed to embrace that doctrine as well.

Douglas remaining its most forceful advocate through the late 1960's and into the early 1970's.

The *fourth* position is that so prominently associated with the name of Justice Frankfurter, for nearly a quarter of a century the occupant of the Holmes-Cardozo "chair" on the Court. He and his supporters—notable among them the first Justice John Marshall Harlan's grandson by the same name and Justice Lewis F. Powell, Jr.—reject total incorporation as not only foolhardy and contrary to the commands of the Constitution, but as clearly violative of the structure and principles of federalism, and, moreover, as a rank example of "judicial legislating." They reject the *Palko* rule of selective incorporation as "natural law," as creating unwarranted, artificial distinctions among basic rights. Instead, the Frankfurter position advocates the so-called "fair trial" or "case-by-case" approach described earlier, under which the Court would examine each case on its own merits, testing it against the requirements of "due process of law." This position, which gives promise of appealing to the four Nixon appointees to the Burger Court,[113] and to Mr. Ford's one,[114] has the virtues of considerable judicial latitude and close individual examination and the vices of unpredictability and uncertainty.

These are some significant considerations that attend the overriding problem of the application to our governmental units of both the substantive and procedural rights that constitute the lifeblood of our constitutional system.

---

[113] Chief Justice Warren E. Burger (1969); Justice Harry A. Blackmun (1970); Justice Lewis F. Powell, Jr. (1972); and Justice William H. Rehnquist (1972).

[114] Justice John Paul Stevens (1975).

III

The Supreme Court
and Fundamental Freedoms
II: Religion, Expression, and Race

It is axiomatic that the Court's role in each of these three fundamental freedoms and attendant collateral constitutional rights is enormously significant. The Supreme Court has been called upon to adjudicate cases arising under them since the end of World War I, and with increasing frequency. Although the Court has strived to establish and/or draw ascertainable lines, some of these remain almost necessarily wavy. No value judgment should be imputed to the order in which they are discussed here—they are presented in the order in which they appear in the Bill of Rights and subsequent amendments: the First and the Civil War Amendments (Thirteen, Fourteen, and Fifteen). We thus begin with the subject matter of the very first sentence of the article in the Bill of Rights, Amendment One.

RELIGION

That First Amendment of the Bill of Rights—which, as we have seen, is now fully applicable to the states via the Fourteenth—declares that "Congress shall make no law respecting an establishment of religion, or prohibiting the free exercise thereof. . . ." To state the guarantees is to state the problem—obviously one of the most complex constitutional ones. Its implied injunction to render unto Caesar what belongs to Caesar recognizes the difficulty, but hardly solves it. Basically, of course, two major concepts are involved in the field of religion as viewed under the terminology of the First Amendment: (1) *Free Exercise of Religion*—to what extent does this clause require deference to action? (2) *Separation of Church and State*—does this vexatious concept prohibit *any* aid to all religion, only *some* aid, or only discriminatory treatment? There is probably no other area in the realm of cultural freedom which is so prone to emotionalism and considerations of privacy for, as Professor Allport put it well, religion encompasses a value that every democrat "must hold: the right of each individual to work out his own philosophy of life, to find his personal niche in creation, as best he can."[1] Happily, America's general record in the religious tolerance realm has been a good, even excellent, one since post-Civil War days, especially in that of the free exercise of religion, which the Court seems consistently to have viewed as a "preferred freedom area."

Free Exercise of Religion

Although it is difficult to separate clearly the two aspects of the religion clause, the Court has been moved to try to distinguish between "prohibiting the free exercise thereof" and the preceding mandate that "Congress shall make no law respecting an establishment of religion." Turning to the former first, we are at once confronted with a basic dilemma, for the phrase embraces two concepts: freedom to believe and freedom to act. As Justice Roberts stated it so succinctly for the Court in the leading case of *Cantwell* v. *Connecticut*,[2] "[T]he first is absolute but in the nature of things, the second cannot be. Conduct remains subject to regulation for the protection of society." Hence, acting upon that philoso-

---

[1] Gordon W. Allport, *The Individual and His Religion* (New York: The Macmillan Co., 1963), p. vii.
[2] 310 U.S. 296 (1940).

phy, both the legislative and judicial branches have from time to time deemed it necessary and appropriate to curb the "action" realm of the free exercise of religion.

Thus, the Supreme Court upheld a federal law forbidding the practice or advocacy of polygamy in the face of the constitutional challenge by Mormons that it violated their freedom of religion;[3] it rejected sundry attacks upon so-called state blue laws, based on the same constitutional objectives;[4] it denied the claim that freedom of religion includes the right to exhibit poisonous snakes in a church;[5] and, while the Supreme Court had not spoken to the issue as of October 1977, most lower courts—but not all[6]— consistently rejected the free exercise claim of a constitutional "right to die" by disconnecting life-prolonging mechanical respirators. On the other hand, a state may not legally require a declaration of belief in God as a qualification for public office,[7] parents may not be compelled to send their children to a *public* school[8] (although they must send them to a properly accredited school[9]), nor may children be forced to go beyond the eighth grade if such compulsory attendance violates established religious beliefs, i.e., those of the Amish;[10] and—since an overruling of a series of precedents in 1946—citizenship may not be denied to otherwise

---

[3] Reynolds v. *United States*, 98 U.S. 145 (1878).

[4] *McGowan* v. *Maryland*, 366 U.S. 420 (1961) and three other cases in the same volume.

[5] *Thompson* v. *Lawson*, 319 U.S. 759 (1943). Reconfirmed in *Pack* v. *Tennessee ex rel Swann*, 44 LW 3501 (1976).

[6] In the "Quinlan Respirator Case," *In the Matter of Karen Quinlan*, New Jersey Superior Court, Judge Robert Muir, Jr., had initially ruled against the Quinlan family's pleas for a court-sanctioned medical termination of the year-long, utterly hopeless, vegetable-life, machine-supported existence of Karen Anne Quinlan (decision of November 10, 1975). But, on appeal, the New Jersey Supreme Court unanimously reversed Judge Muir 7:0 (March 31, 1976), structuring its holding largely on a "right to privacy," based on "religious beliefs" on the part of Karen's father to act in his daughter's best interest. The State of New Jersey declined to appeal the decision.

[7] *Torcaso* v. *Watkins*, 367 U.S. 488 (1961).

[8] *Pierce* v. *Society of Sisters*, 268 U.S. 510 (1925). But states cannot be *compelled* to provide public funds to church-related schools. (*Brusca* v. *State Board of Education of Missouri*, 405 U.S. 1064 1972).

[9] Garber v. *Kansas*, 389 U.S. 51 (1967), certiorari denied.

[10] *Wisconsin* v. *Yoder*, 406 U.S. 205 (1972).

qualified applicants if their religious creed prevents them from bearing arms (so long as they declare a willingness to perform some other type of service).[11] On the other hand, whereas conscientious objection to military service is entitled to every benefit of doubt under the law and the First Amendment,[12] there are limits: e.g., claims to "selective" conscientious objection, which would see the claimant serve in "justifiable" but not "unjustifiable" wars.[13]

The saga of the Jehovah's Witnesses—a militantly evangelical, fundamentalist, minority Protestant religion—perhaps best illustrates the Court's readiness to bend over backwards in behalf of freedom of religion even for those *beliefs* that may well be obnoxious to the vast majority of the body politic. In the four decades following 1937, the Witnesses, guided by the brilliant advocacy of their chief counsel, Hayden C. Covington, won all except twelve of eighty-seven cases they brought to the Supreme Court on appeal![14] Probably the most celebrated among these cases was *West Virginia Board of Education* v. *Barnette*,[15] in which the Court, overruling a decision of less than three years standing,[16] struck down a state requirement that all public school children must salute the flag, over the Witnesses' objection that such a requirement would compel them to "behold a graven image." Speaking for a 6:3 majority, Justice Jackson's memorable words clearly focus the basic issue:

> If there is any fixed star in our constitutional constellation, it is that no official, high or petty, can prescribe what shall be orthodox in politics, nationalism, religion,

---

[11] *Girouard* v. *United States*, 328 U.S. 61.

[12] See *United States* v. *Seeger*, 380 U.S. 163 (1965) and *Welsh* v. *United States*, 398 U.S. 333 (1970).

[13] *Gillette* v. *United States* and *Negre* v. *Larsen*, 401 U.S. 437 (1971), an unanimous holding save for Justice Douglas's dissent on free exercise grounds, emphasizing the "implied First Amendment right" of "conscience."

[14] Stone once said that the Jehovah's Witnesses "ought to have an endowment in view of the aid which they give in solving the legal problems of civil liberties." [As quoted by A. T. Mason, *Harlan Fiske Stone: Pillar of the Law* (New York: Viking Press, 1956), p. 599.]

[15] 319 U.S. 624 (1943) *cf.* the stirring Frankfurter dissent.

[16] *Minersville School District* v. *Gobitis*, 310 U.S. 586 (1940).

or other matters of opinion, or force citizens to confess by word or act their faith therein.[17]

Separation of Church and State

"Free exercise of religion" is relatively uncomplicated compared to the involved and emotion-charged area of separation of church and state, where extreme positions are the rule rather than the exception. Consequently, the Court has found it enormously difficult to draw a line between those who hold that the Constitution forbids *any and all* aid to and/or recognition of religion by government, and those who believe that at least *some* such governmental action is not only constitutional but eminently desirable and a government "duty." Were the verbiage of the First Amendment, and/or were history, a reliable guide, the problem might have been solved; but the verbiage is subject to differing interpretation and analysis, and history—as is true so often—is a guide only in the eyes of those who wish to utilize it for their own evaluation. Thus, both sides óf the controversy cite Madison as proof for either position—yet all that can really be said with conviction about the Madisonian position is that he wanted to make resolutely certain that Congress (and by implication the several states) would never pass a law establishing or respecting a state religion or state church. Hence the Supreme Court has found any attempt to draw a line the proverbial "can of worms." But tried it has, by giving repeated voice to what it has viewed as the Jefferson-Madison "wall of separation" between church and state. In the 1947 *New Jersey Bus Case*[18] —in which the majority ruled that the

---

[17] *West Virginia Board of Education, loc. cit.*, at 642. The holding in the case was reconfirmed in 1973 in *Central School District # 1* v. *Russo*, 411 U.S. 930 (this time on freedom of speech grounds).

[18] *Everson* v. *Board of Education of Ewing Township*, 330 U.S. 1. Yet some fifteen years later, taking the occasion of *Engel* v. *Vitale*, *infra*, Justice Douglas, one of the *Everson* majority of five, announced from the bench on "Opinion Monday," that he *now* believed *Everson* to have been decided wrongly. But it still stands, and will likely continue to stand—indeed, the Court refused to hear an appeal in a New Jersey case later in 1971 on the very same issue. (*West Morris Regional Board of Education* v. *Sills*, 404 U.S. 986.)

wall had *not* been breached by New Jersey's provision of free bus transportation to parochial school children as well as to those attending Ewing township's public schools, *because the grants benefitted the child rather than the church*—Justice Black expressed the doctrine for the 5:4 Supreme Court as follows:

> The "establishment of religion" clause of the First Amendment means at least this: Neither a state nor the Federal Government can set up a church. Neither can pass laws which aid one religion, aid all religions, or prefer one religion over another. Neither can force nor influence a person to go or remain away from church against his will or force him to profess a belief or disbelief in any religion. No person can be punished for entertaining or professing religious beliefs or disbeliefs, for church attendance or nonattendance. No tax in any amount, large or small, can be levied to support any religious activities or institutions, whatever they may be called, or whatever form they may adopt to teach or practice religion. Neither a state nor the Federal Government can, openly or secretly, participate in the affairs of any religious organizations or groups and vice versa. In the words of Jefferson, the clause against establishment of religion by law was intended to erect a "wall of separation between Church and State."[19]

This is a memorable and oft-quoted position, yet whether or not it has been followed by the Court in practice depends upon one's point of view. The *Everson* decision is a case in point.

Moreover, the Court has either upheld, or refused to review, such practices and/or legislation—frequently under the concept of the aforementioned "child benefit" theory—as Louisiana's, New York's, and Pennsylvania's expenditures of public funds to furnish or loan nonsectarian textbooks to children of parochial and other private schools as well as those in public schools[20] (but it has also upheld the precise

---

[19] *Ibid.*, at 15–16.
[20] *Cochran* v. *Louisiana*, 281 U.S. 370 (1930); *Board of Education* v. *Allen*, 392 U.S. 236 (1968); and *Meek* v. *Pittenger*, 421 U.S. 349 (1975). It is interesting to note that in *Allen* Justice Black, the author

contrary);[21] federal grants for lunches in all schools; the use of sectarian chaplains in the armed forces; the practice of public school "released time," when carried on outside public school buildings[22] (the Court did strike down released time practiced in public school buildings[23]); and blanket tax exemption for any and all religious institutions and their property unless they engage in business for profit.[24] Yet the Court has also upheld, by declining to review, state legislation and state court interpretations *banning* free bus transportation to the other than public school children[25] and subventions to parochial school children.[26] Evidently, the Supreme Court has endeavored to follow a doctrine that constitutes a blend between judicial self-restraint or deference to state legislatures and permitting certain so-called "auxiliary" or "indirect" services to religion, reasoning that such marginal aid does not breach the wall. To state that issue is, of course, to invite immediate dispute.

In the early 1960's, however, the Court seemed to embark upon a new path of strictness in interpreting the separation clause—either on its own terminology or by commingling it with the free exercise of religion phrase. Two cases, de-

---

of the *Everson* decision, dissented vigorously, pointing to what he perceived as a crucial difference between the educational function of books and buses. On the other hand, the Court refused to sanction such book loans to *racially segregated* public schools (*Norwood* v. *Harrison*, 413 U.S. 455, 1973). And it declined to review a decision invalidating a Missouri law that had authorized textbook loans to pupils at church-related schools (*Reynolds* v. *Paster*, 419 U.S. 1111, 1975).

[21] *Carlson* v. *Dickman, 371 U.S. 242 (1961) and Dickman v. School District, Oregon City,* 371 U.S. 823 (1962), certiorari denied.

[22] *Zorach* v. *Clauson*, 343 U.S. 306 (1952). Faced with a golden opportunity to reconsider *Zorach* in 1976, the Court pointedly refused to do so. (*Smith* v. *Smith*, 44 LW 3364, certiorari denied.

[23] *McCollum* v. *Board of Education*, 333 U.S. 203 (1948).

[24] See the 1970 *Walz* decision upholding that principle as to tax exemption (*Walz* v. *Tax Commissioners of New York City*, 397 U.S. 664) and the 1972 *Diffenderfer* one as to the taxability of that part of any church property used commercially (*Diffenderfer* v. *Central Baptist Church of Miami*, 404 U.S. 412).

[25] High courts in Wisconsin, Delaware, New York, Iowa, Alaska, Missouri, New Mexico, Oklahoma, and Washington have held parochial student bus benefit laws unconstitutional. See, a.o., *Rhoades* v. *Washington*, 389 U.S. 11 (1967) and *Worell* v. *Matters*, 389 U.S. 846 (1967).

[26] See, for example, the Vermont parochial student fees case of *Anderson* v. *Swart*, 366 U.S. 925 (1961).

cided in 1962 and 1963, respectively, illustrate the new policy, if such it be. Few, if any decisions—and none in the realm of religion—caused such an outcry, whatever the motivation by the critics, as the two 8:1 decisions in the *New York Prayer Case*[27] and the *Abington Township Bible Reading* and *Baltimore City Lord's Prayer Cases.*[28] Since the latter decisions were basically extensions of the former, we shall concentrate upon the New York case.

At issue was a rather general, 22-word nondenominational prayer,[29] drafted by the New York State Board of Regents (an agency composed of state officials). The prayer was recommended, but not required, for reading aloud by the teachers and students of the New York State public schools in each classroom at the start of each school day. A group of Long Island parents, contending the requirement to be a violation of the separation of church and state principle, brought suit against the New Hyde Park Board of Education. In his not very lengthy, not very complex, and not very diplomatically-phrased majority opinion for the Court, Justice Black agreed with the complaining parents. But he did try hard to put into public focus the manifold and probably insoluble problems of personal commitments and majority–minority religion line-drawing that continue to bedevil the religion-constitutional controversy:

> [T]he constitutional prohibition against laws respecting an establishment of religion must at least mean that in this country it is no part of the business of government to compose official prayers for any group of the American people to recite as part of a religious program carried on by government . . . It is neither sacrilegious nor antireligious to say that each separate government in this country should stay out of the business of writing or sanctioning official prayers and leave that purely religious function to the people themselves and to those the people choose to look for religious guidance.[30]

---

[27] *Engel* v. *Vitale,* 370 U.S. 421 (1962).
[28] *Abington Township* v. *Schempp* and *Murray* v. *Curlett,* 374 U.S. 203 (1963).
[29] "Almighty God, we acknowledge our dependence upon Thee, and we beg Thy blessings upon us, our parents, our teachers, and our country."
[30] *Engel* v. *Vitale, loc. cit.,* at 425.

Barely one year later, in another 8:1 decision, this time written by Justice Clark—with considerably less bluntness, and much more of an eye toward soothing the public—the Supreme Court extended the *Engel* doctrine to embrace the state-required daily public school reading of ten verses without comment from the Holy Bible in Pennsylvania,[31] and the long-standing Baltimore, Maryland, practice of daily Bible reading and Lord's Prayer recitation.[32]   Combining the two cases, the Clark opinion—significantly pointing out en route that there is an almost inevitable overlapping between the nonestablishment and free exercise clauses of the First Amendment—concluded on this essential note:

> The place of religion in our society is an exalted one, achieved through a long tradition of reliance on the home, the church and the inviolable citadel of the individual heart and mind. We have come to recognize through bitter experience that it is not within the power of government to invade that citadel, whether its purpose or effect be to aid or oppose, to advance or retard. *In the relationship between man and religion, the State is firmly committed to a position of neutrality.*[33]

Yet far from soothing the uproar caused by the *Engel* decision of one year earlier, the new Supreme Court pronouncement only seemed to increase the threat of retaliatory legislative action. (It did, however, receive some significant church support, particularly among liberal Protestant and Jewish clergy, and featured lengthy concurring opinions by the Roman Catholic (Brennan) and the Jewish (Goldberg) members of the bench.) Deliberate violations of the *Engel* and *Schempp* decisions were not only rampant but were often encouraged by government officials on the state and/or local levels. By 1976 some 215 proposed constitutional

---

[31] *Abington Township* v. *Schempp, loc. cit.*
[32] *Murray* v. *Curlett, loc. cit.*
[33] *Abington Township* v. *Schempp* and *Murray* v. *Curlett, loc. cit.* (Italics supplied.) But in 1974 the Court upheld a lower tribunal's decision sanctioning the inclusion of prayers in a public school commencement program. (*West* v. *Mt. Lebanon School District*, 419 U.S. 967.) On the other hand, the Court upheld another lower court's ban on compulsory chapel services at the national service academies. (*Laird* v. *Anderson*, 409 U.S. 1076, 1972.)

amendments designed to reverse the Court's school prayer and Bible decisions had been introduced in Congress alone, several of these failing but narrowly of passing Congress.

The enactment in 1965 of the Federal Aid to Elementary and Secondary Schools Act was tailor-made for additional Court involvement in the vexatious church-and-state sphere, facilitated by a successful suit by interested federal taxpayers to obtain the heretofore elusive standing to sue on the constitutional question.[34] Tangentially, the basic issue of primary support of parochial schools from public funds came before the Court in a series of highly important cases in 1971.[35] The catalysts were Pennsylvania and Rhode Island laws providing *direct public fund aid* to "purchase secular services" from sectarian schools, including the payment of parochial school teachers for teaching "secular" subjects in the parochial schools. Speaking through Chief Justice Burger, with only Justice White in partial dissent, the Court struck down the statutes as constituting a constitutionally impermissible "excessive entanglement between Government and religion." Endeavoring to explain the basic dimensions of the new "no excessive entanglement" line, Burger concluded:

> The merits and benefits of these schools . . . are not the issue before us in these cases. The sole question is whether state aid to these schools can be squared with the dictates of the Religious Clauses. *Under our system the choice has been made that government is to be entirely excluded from the area of religious instruction and churches excluded from the affairs of government.*[36]

---

[34] *Flast* v. *Cohen*, 392 U.S. 83 (1968), a ruling that amended the long-standing contrary precedent of *Frothingham* v. *Mellon*, 262 U.S. 447 (1923). The winning side's successful counsel at the bar of the Supreme Court was Senator Sam J. Ervin (D.-N.C.), an ardent supporter of strict separation of church and state.

[35] *Lemon* v. *Kurtzman* and *Earley* v. *Dicenso*, 403 U.S. 602 (1971).

[36] *Ibid.*, at 625. (Italics supplied.) A similar fate (8:1), based upon similar reasoning, befell an Ohio law that attempted to provide direct aid payments to parents of children in parochial schools in order to reimburse them for tuition payments. (*Essex* v. *Wolman*, 409 U.S. 808, 1972.) Still, in a rather strangely reasoned 1973 follow-up decision to *Lemon*, the Court, by a vote of 5:3, authorized Pennsylvania to reimburse sectarian schools for such "secular education services" as

It will come as no surprise, however, that the partisans of state aid to parochial schools would by no means be deterred, and they continued to vie with one another for speedy enactments of new legislation, notwithstanding the Supreme Court's apparent firm stance. New cases were bound to reach the highest tribunal readily. When a bevy of them from New York and Pennsylvania did on the Court's last day in 1973, a variety of schemes to provide financial aid to private secondary schools, *including* sundry types of tax relief and tuition reimbursement, were declared unconstitutional by votes ranging from 8:1 to 6:3.[37] Writing for the Court's solid majority, Justice Powell ruled that the *effect* of the various programs was "to advance religion in that [they] subsidized directly the religious activities of sectarian elementary and secondary schools,"[38] thus violating the Constitution's strictures against the commingling of church and state. Throughout the opinion, *the* governing constitutional trifold yardstick for the separation/establishment issue was stressed and re-stressed, namely: that any law in that realm must have, first, a secular legislative purpose; second, its principal or primary effect must neither advance nor inhibit religion; and third, it must not foster an "excessive entanglement" with religion.

Not to be denied, Pennsylvania—undismayed, undaunted, and stubborn—enacted "new" aid to parochial and other private schools measures, comprising such services as counseling, testing, remedial classes in speech and hearing therapy, and funds for instructional equipment like charts, maps, records, films, tape recorders, and projectors, plus an additional textbook loan program. Predictably, when the all but inevitable challenges to the constitutionality of these measures reached the Supreme Court in 1975, all of them, save the textbook loan program, fell 6:3. Justice Stewart again zeroed in on the constitutional *effect* of the multiple legislation upon the mandated separation between church and

---

they had performed prior to the *Lemon* denouement. (*Lemon* v. *Kurtzman,* 411 U.S. 192.)

[37] *Levitt* v. *Committee for Public Education and Religious Liberty,* 413 U.S. 472; *Committee for Public Education and Religious Liberty* v. *Nyquist,* 413 U.S. 756; and *Sloan* v. *Lemon,* 413 U.S. 825.

[38] *Nyquist, loc. cit.,* at 774.

state, and ruled it an "impermissible establishment of religion."[39] Yet there was scant doubt that the Court would again find itself confronted with delicate and difficult decision-making in this emotion-charged issue. Indeed, its 1976 docket contained a number of possible case-candidates for just such judgments, and one of them—to the astonishment of a number of close students of the Court and its posture on the matter—seemed to open a small crack in the "wall" of separation: In a 5:4 decision, featuring a welter of opinions, but *no* majority agreement, the Supreme Court upheld Maryland's program of financial aid for church-related *colleges.* For the first time in history it thus approved a system of state *general purpose* subsidies benefitting church-related educational institutions. Over fervent, often biting dissents by Justices Brennan, Stewart, Marshall, and Stevens—who viewed the subsidies as involving "the disease of entanglement"—five Justices, Blackman, Powell, Burger, White, and Rehnquist, saw no constitutional violation for a variety of reasons. Controlling seemed to be the somewhat less than totally persuasive rationale, that the "character" of the colleges, their "ability to separate their secular and religious functions," and the lower "impressionability" of college students—as contrasted with secondary and primary level students—thus lessened dangers of indoctrination, and thus sufficed to meet the trifold requirements of nonreligious purpose, nonreligious effect, and avoidance of excessive entanglement.[40] It is hardly difficult to foresee considerable additional church-state litigation in the future!

FREEDOM OF EXPRESSION

Justice can hardly be done to this vast and complex topic in a series of volumes, let alone a few pages. Hence we will raise some essential questions in a general way, and then concentrate upon that area of the topic which has proved to be the most contentious and most significant since the 1940's.

---

[39] *Meek* v. *Pittenger,* 421 U.S. 349, at 366.
[40] *Roemer* v. *Maryland Public Works Board,* 44 LW 4939.

Generally

Freedom of expression signifies the freedom to communicate—and, since 1976, specifically including even purely "commercial speech"[41] —in other words, it comprehends the ability to express oneself orally or in writing—in the press, through books, movies, or plays[42] —without *prior* (previous) restraint. Actually, considerably more is meant by freedom of expression than simply speech or press; included within these concepts is a host of other basic liberties, such as the right to picket—which is really a mode of communication as much as speech and press—the right of assembly and petition; now apparently even that of *spending* by and for a candidate for federal elective office, but *not* in the form of unlimited *contributions*;[43] and, as of mid-1976, a constitutional right of below policy-level government workers not to be dismissed for mere patronage reasons![44] For our present purposes, however, the issue is bracketed under the general concept of "freedom of expression," presumably safeguarded under the broad language of the First Amendment and, as we have seen, also fully applicable to the states via the Fourteenth.

No matter how sweeping and unequivocal these guarantees may be, they are not, of course, absolute—despite Justice Black's fervent contentions to the contrary. Under our system of government, the majority is obliged to safeguard and respect the rights of the minority, but it does not have to acquiesce in the "tyranny of the minority." Thus, as various courts have held repeatedly, picketing and sundry street demonstrations, for example, may be an expression of freedom of speech; but, as even Black, under certain conditions, repeatedly made clear, illegal picketing and trespassing and breach of the peace are not; nor is the burning of draft cards; nor the sale to children of sexually suggestive "girlie" and

---

[41] *Virginia Pharmacy Board* v. *Virginia Consumer Council*, 44 LW 4686.

[42] *Southeastern Promotions, Ltd.* v. *Conrad*, 420 U.S. 546 (1975), held, for the first time, that theatrical productions were entitled to the same kind of constitutional protection against advance censorship and prohibitions long enjoyed by newspapers, books, and movies.

[43] *Buckley* v. *Valeo*, 44 LW 4127 (1976).

[44] *Elrod* v. *Burns*, 44 LW 5091 (1976).

similar magazines; nor undressing in public and/or walking about in the nude; nor the featuring in a bar of nude dancers and other "bacchanalian revelries"; nor homosexual acts by consenting adults in private (!); nor the violation of a school board's order, or a police department's, to cut excessively long hair; nor journalists' refusal to tell grand juries the name of confidential sources; nor a prohibition against sex-designated employment advertisement in newspapers.[45] Yet the First Amendment does protect such symbolic and related, basic free expression activities as wearing black armbands to a high school class as an anti–Viet Nam war protest; publicly denouncing the United States flag (see also *Smith* v. *Goguen*, 415 U.S. 566 [1974]); the wearing, in a play, of the uniform of the United States armed forces even if the tenor of the play is unfavorable; the public sporting of a jacket with the words "fuck the draft" emblazoned upon it (see also *Papish* v. *Board of Curators*, 410 U.S. 667 [1973]); showing "stag" movies in private; peaceful assembly-protest on the grounds of the Capitol in Washington, D.C.; newspaper publishing, within a state, of ads for legal out-of-state abortion services; and the right of the press normally to be free from judicial "gag" orders.[46] Yelling "fire" in a crowded theater—to use

---

[45] The several demonstration cases are illustrated by such as *Thornhill* v. *Alabama*, 310 U.S. 88 (1940); *Giboney* v. *Empire Storage & Ice Co.*, 336 U.S. 490 (1949); *Adderley* v. *Florida*, 385 U.S. 39 (1967); *Walker* v. *Birmingham*, 338 U.S. 307 (1967), *Lloyd* v. *Tanner*, 407 U.S. 551 (1972), and *Hudgens* v. *N.L.R.B.*, 44 LW 3499 (1976). The draft card reference is to *United States* v. *O'Brien*, 391 U.S. 367 (1968); that on obscenity to *Ginsberg* v. *New York*, 390 U.S. 629 (1968) (see also *Miller* v. *California*, 413 U.S. 15 [1973], *Paris Adult Theatre* v. *Slaton*, 413 U.S. 49 [1973], and *Jenkins* v. *Georgia*, 418 U.S. 153 [1974]); that on nude dancers to *California* v. *LaRue*, 409 U.S. 109 (1972); that on homosexuals to *Doe* v. *Commonwealth Attorney for the City of Richmond*, 44 LW 3543 (1976); that on sex-designated newspaper ads to *Pittsburgh Press Co.* v. *Pittsburgh Committee on Human Relations*, 413 U.S. 376 (1973); that on undressing in public to *Nelson* v. *Iowa*, 401 U.S. 923 (1971); that on long hair, *Olff* v. *East Side Union High School District*, 404 U.S. 1042 (1972), and *Kelley* v. *Johnson*, 44 LW 4469 (1976); and that regarding an alleged First Amendment right to protect confidential sources against grand jury questioning, *Branzburg* v. *Hayes*, 408 U.S. 655 (1972).
[46] The armband case is *Tinker* v. *Des Moines Independent Community School District*, 393 U.S. 503 (1969); the flag-denouncing one is *Street* v. *New York*, 394 U.S. 576 (1969); the uniform case is *Schacht* v. *United States*, 398 U.S. 58 (1970); the public display of

the famed Holmesian illustration—is an exercise of freedom of speech (as well as a duty of citizenship) if there is a fire; but if the call is false, it represents not freedom of speech but license.[47] *Actual* overt incitement to the overthrow of the United States government by force and violence, accompanied by the language of incitement, is not freedom of expression;[48] the *theoretical* advocacy of such overthrow, on the other hand, is now considered such a freedom.[49] Calling someone "Goddamn racketeer" and "dirty Fascist" is not freedom of speech;[50] calling a convicted thief "thief" or "crook" presumably is—at least until he has paid his debts to society. And a newspaper cannot be *required* to print replies from political candidates attacked in its columns,[51] although it *is* subject to libel laws by ordinary citizens.[52]

In other words, it is plain that the rights protected in this area of freedom of expression are certainly not absolute; hence, common as well as statutory law has imposed a number of limitations over a period of years. In the United States, these limitations, now almost exclusively of a statutory nature, have occurred increasingly on both the national and state levels of government since the days of world War I. To the courts in general, and to the Supreme Court in particular, has fallen the task of drawing a line between the individual's cherished right of freedom of expression and that

---

vulgar language case is *Cohen* v. *California*, 403 U.S. 15 (1971); that on "stag" movies is *Stanley* v. *Georgia*, 394 U.S. 557 (1969); and that on Capitol grounds demonstrations, *Chief of Capitol Police* v. *Jeannette Rankin Brigade*, 409 U.S. 972 (1972). *Tinker* was reaffirmed in 1972 in *Board of Education* v. *James*, 409 U.S. 1042. The case dealing with out-of-state abortion ads is *Bigelow* v. *Virginia*, 421 U.S. 809 (1975); and the sound "freedom from judges' gag" victory for the press is *Nebraska Press Association* v. *Stuart* (decided June 30, 1976).

[47] *Schenck* v. *United States*, 249 U.S. 47 (1919).

[48] *Scales* v. *Unites States*, 367 U.S. 203 (1961).

[49] *Noto* v. *United States*, 367 U.S. 290 (1961).

[50] *Chaplinsky* v. *New Hampshire*, 315 U.S. 568 (1942). But unless statutes like the New Hampshire one involved in that case are *very* carefully and *very* specifically drawn, they will not survive First Amendment claims—as Georgia found out in a 1972 decision (*Gooding* v. *Wilson*, 405 U.S. 518).

[51] *Miami Herald Publication Co.* v. *Tornillo*, 418 U.S. 241 (1974).

[52] E.g., *Gertz* v. *Robert Welch*, 418 U.S. 323 (1974) and *Time, Inc.* v. *Firestone*, 44 LW 4262 (1976). But a different standard obtains vis-à-vis *bona fide* public officials, where the "actual malice" test governs. (See *New York Times* v. *Sullivan*, 376 U.S. 254, 1964.)

of society to safeguard its body politic against excesses. Not only *where* to draw that line, but *how* it shall be drawn, and *who* shall draw it, are problems that call for a Solomon. Amidst both cheers and jeers the Supreme Court has taken on the task.

Line-Drawing: Gamesmanship or Solution? It is well to keep the "double standard" and "preferred freedoms" in mind as we look at some of the several "tests" devised by the Court. It is as impossible as it would be unwise to speak of any one definitive, current, exclusive "test" or "line," but we may outline the two or three major ones to which the Court has resorted from time to time, depending upon personnel and circumstances.

The first such test is the best-known: the famous *"clear and present danger"* test, authored in 1919 by Justices Holmes and Brandeis in *Schenck* v. *United States.*[53] In that case, the Court unanimously upheld the constitutionality of the Espionage Act of 1917 against the charge that its application to Charles T. Schenck's distribution of anti-draft leaflets to potential draftees was a violation of the First Amendment freedoms of expression. In emotion-charged, intemperate language, Schenck had urged the young men involved to resist the draft. Justice Holmes explained his new line or test in the following memorable passage:

> We admit that in many places and in ordinary times the defendants in saying all that was said . . . would have been within their constitutional rights. But the character of every act *depends upon the circumstances* in which it was done. . . . The most stringent protection of free speech would not protect a man in *falsely* shouting fire in a theater and causing a panic. It does not even protect a man from an injunction against uttering words that have all the effects of force. . . . The question in every case is whether the *words used are used in such circumstances and are of such a nature as to create a clear and*

---

[53] 249 U.S. 47, Some students of the field would credit Judge Learned Hand with an important assist, if not the initial idea, in the creation of the doctrine. (See Robert S. Lancaster, "Judge Hand's Free Speech Problem," 10 *Vanderbilt Law Review* 301, February 1957.)

present danger that they will bring about the substantive evils that Congress has a right to prevent. It is a question of proximity and degree.[54]

One week after *Schenck*, with Holmes again speaking for the unanimous Court, two more convictions under the Act were upheld, again based on the clear and present danger doctrine.[55] (Brandeis preferred to categorize it as "a rule of reason." Correctly applied, he believed, it would preserve the right of free speech both from "suppression by tyrannous, well-meaning majorities, and from abuse by irresponsible, fanatical minorities.")

But, as if to demonstrate the difficulty of the line, barely six months later a majority of the Supreme Court, in a 7:2 decision in the case of *Abrams* v. *United States,*[56] allegedly used the clear and present danger test in sustaining the application of the Sedition Act of 1918. After World War I, twenty-nine-year-old Jacob Abrams and five young anarchist-Socialist associates—all Russian aliens, one girl—distributed some English- and Yiddish-language leaflets from rooftops on New York's Lower East Side. The leaflets urged the "workers of the world" to resist the Allied and American military intervention against the Bolsheviks in the Vladivostok and Murmansk areas of Russia. They bitterly denounced President Wilson for his decision to intervene, and called for a general strike to prevent shipment of munitions to the anti-Soviet forces. The English leaflets closed with the following postscript: "It is absurd to call us pro-German. We hate and despise German militarism more than do your hypocritical tyrants. We have more reasons for denouncing German militarism than has the coward in the White House."[57] Visiting

---

[54] *Ibid.,* at 52. (Italics supplied.)

[55] *Frohwerk* v. *United States,* 249 U.S. 204 (1919) and *Debs* v. *United States,* 249 U.S. 211 (1919). Frohwerk had inserted several articles in a Missouri German-language newspaper, challenging the purposes of the war as well as the merits and constitutionality of the draft. Debs was charged with an attempt to cause insubordination in the army and to obstruct recruiting.

[56] 250 U.S. 616 (1919).

[57] As quoted by Zechariah Chafee, Jr. in his classic *Freedom of Speech in the United States,* 6th printing (Cambridge: Harvard University Press, 1967), p. 110. Chapter 3 in this epic work on freedom of

United States District Court Judge Henry DeLamar Clayton of Alabama sentenced three of the defendants to the maximum of twenty, one to fifteen (the girl), and one to three years in a federal penitentiary. (The jury acquitted one.) Their sentences were commuted in 1921 by President Harding on condition that they would all embark at once for Russia at their own expense—which they did. Justices Holmes and Brandeis, the authors of the clear and present danger doctrine, had joined in an impassioned dissenting opinion by the former, based upon the grounds that the "surreptitious publishing of a silly leaflet" by an unknown man (Abrams) did not constitute a "present danger of immediate evil." Wrote Holmes in an oft-quoted statement:

> . . . I think that we should be eternally vigilant against attempts to check the expression of opinions that we loathe and believe to be fraught with death, *unless they so imminently threaten immediate interference with the lawful and pressing purposes of the law that an immediate check is required to save the country.* . . .[58]

Although a clear majority of the Court had thus sidetracked or narrowed the clear and present danger doctrine, the latter sustained its first *official* modification six years later in the famous case of *Gitlow* v. *New York.*[59] Here a 7:2 majority held that Benjamin Gitlow's verbal and written expressions constituted a *"bad tendency"* to "corrupt public morals, incite to crime, and disturb the public peace." In other words, the Court's majority in upholding Gitlow's conviction under New York's Criminal Anarchy statue dodged the clear and present danger doctrine—perhaps "watered it down" would be a more accurate description—by adopting the *"bad tendency"* test: that is, a "bad tendency" to bring about a danger—a "kill-the-serpent-in-the-egg" test that had initially been given its casual terminology in the 1920 case of *Schaefer* v. *United States.*[60] Clearly, the new

---

expression fully describes the circumstances surrounding the *Abrams* case (pp. 108–140).

[58] *Loc. cit.*, at 630. (Italics supplied.)

[59] 268 U.S. 652 (1925).

[60] 251 U.S. 466.

test effectively shifted the balance between the individual and the state in the latter's favor.

Two years after *Gitlow*, in *Whitney* v. *California*,[61] Justice Brandeis, with the stanch support of his colleague Holmes, attempted not only to resurrect the clear and present danger doctrine, but to expand or liberalize it, by joining to it the test of *"imminence"*—i.e., that the danger must not only be "clear and present" but also "imminent" in order to justify suppressive and punitive state action. Both jurists did agree with the decision of their colleagues on the bench in upholding Miss Whitney's conviction under California's 1919 Criminal Syndicalism Act (which was declared unconstitutional in 1968) because of evidence that appeared to point to the existence of a conspiracy to violate the law. However, in their concurring opinion Brandeis and Holmes rejected the majority's interpretation of another section of the Act, which not only made it a crime to advocate or teach or practice "criminal syndicalism," but that was also directed at "association with those who proposed to preach it." Thus, in his restatement of the clear and present danger test, Justice Brandeis gave posterity the following admonition:

> Fear of serious injury cannot alone justify suppression of free speech and assembly . . . there must be reasonable ground to fear that serious evil will result if free speech is practiced. . . . There must be reasonable ground to believe *that the danger apprehended is imminent.* There must be reasonable ground to believe that the evil to be prevented is a serious one. . . . In order to support a finding of clear and present danger *it must be shown either that immediate serious violence was to be expected or was advocated, or that the past conduct furnished reason to believe that advocacy was then contemplated . . . no danger flowing from speech can be deemed clear and present, unless the incidence of the evil apprehended is so imminent that it may befall before there is opportunity for full discussion. . . .*[62]

It was this general philosophy that the Supreme Court practiced at the end of the 1930's and for much of the

---

[61] 274 U.S. 357 (1927).
[62] *Ibid.*, at 376–378. (Italics supplied.)

1940's. During that period its view that there should be "more exacting judicial scrutiny" of First Amendment freedoms was at its apogee. It was then that the Court recognized beyond doubt a constitutionally protected area of "preferred freedom," in line with the famous footnote by Justice Stone in *United States* v. *Carolene Products Co.*,[63] calling for a special niche for "legislation which restricts the political processes."[64] But the picture began to change when Fred M. Vinson assumed the chief justiceship upon the death of Harlan F. Stone in 1946. And when both Justices Murphy and Rutledge died unexpectedly in the summer of 1949, their replacement by Justices Tom C. Clark and Sherman Minton heralded an almost instant departure from the "preferred freedom" doctrine and the "imminence" test. Especially in the delicate and contentious matters of Communist threat and national security, the clear and present danger doctrine began to transform into what some observers viewed as the *"grave and probable"* test; others, perhaps facetiously, as the *"possible and remote"* doctrine. The Vinson Court (1946–1953) began to reserve the clear and present danger test and its imminence appendage for other aspects of freedom of expression—e.g., street corner oratory and press freedom—while fairly consistently applying the bad tendency test to the national security field. However, once Chief Justice Warren had established his leadership in the latter area, too, roughly midway in his sixteen-year term (1953–1969), the Court returned to the "clear and present danger" plus imminence test for the national security realm as well. With the advent of the "Burger Court" in 1969—Warren Earl Burger having replaced Earl Warren in the center chair—a renewed change in direction could not be ruled out. Yet, as of mid-1976, there had been no return to the Vinson approach. The Burger Court had evinced a generous interpretation of the First Amendment's free expression mandates, notwithstanding some possible narrowing in the "obscenity" and press sectors.[65]

---

[63] 304 U.S. 144 (1938).
[64] *Ibid.*
[65] See p. 102, *supra*, for some illustrations. For an extensive up-to-date treatment of freedom of expression, see Chapter V, "The Precious

The Court and National Security

Understandably, there is no area where the Court has trod more carefully, and where it has been more mindful of public opinion or "consensus," than the realm of the Communist cold war threat and national security. Recognizing the threat as well as the problem, the Court has gone out of its way to save congressional statutes and intent, while at the same time insisting that procedures adopted in the execution of the various statutes be fair to individuals concerned. Moreover, it has not been remiss in curbing Congress by *statutory interpretation*, and, in the case of the Warren Court, by occasional declarations of unconstitutionality.[66] It has thus pursued a wavering line, but a relatively predictable one, clearly mindful of its role as a law court as well as a political and governmental institution. Some illustrations will demonstrate the point.

Congressional Investigating Committees. Nothing is dearer to the collective heart of Congress than its power of investigation. That it must have this power in order to legislate intelligently, to inform the public, and to oversee the administrative branch is as obvious as it is historically demonstrable—and the Supreme Court has repeatedly so held. [67] But that this enormous power also readily lends itself to abuses is equally clear, and the Supreme Court has so held as well.[68] Again, the matter has been particularly "sticky" in the multiple instances of investigations of subversive activities—a popular and widely reported activity—particularly in

Freedom of Expression," in my *Freedom and the Court: Civil Rights and Liberties in the United States*, 3rd ed. (New York: Oxford University Press, 1977).
    [66] See pp. 111 ff., *infra*.
    [67] See, a.o., *Anderson* v. *Dunn*, 6 Wheaton 204 (1821); *In re Chapman*, 166 U.S. 661 (1897); *McGrain* v. *Daugherty*, 273 U.S. 135 (1927); *Braden* v. *United States*, 365 U.S. 431 (1961); and *Stamler* v. *Willis*, 393 U.S. 217 (1968), which upheld the constitutionality of the House Committee on Un-American Activities. (It was abolished in 1975, and its functions transferred to the Judiciary Committee.)
    [68] See, a.o., *Kilbourn* v. *Thompson*, 103 U.S. 168 (1880); *Marshall* v. *Gordon*, 243 U.S. 521 (1917); *United States* v. *Rumely*, 345 U.S. 41 (1953); *Watkins* v. *United States*, 354 U.S. 178 (1957); and *De Gregory* v. *Attorney General*, 383 U.S. 825 (1966).

connection with the refusal of witnesses to respond to questions by invoking the *First* rather than the Fifth Amendment. Matters seemed to come to a head in 1957, when the Court was confronted with the case of *Watkins* v. *United States.* [69] In this case the issue was John T. Watkins's refusal, on *First* Amendment freedoms grounds, to answer some questions put to him by the House Committee on Un-American Activities concerning certain of his associates. The Court, 6:1, held specifically that the Committee had failed to "spell out" its jurisdiction and the purpose of its investigation with "sufficient particularity." But the chief justice went further to point out that there *are* limits to the authority of Congress to inquire; that there exists no general authority to expose the private affairs of individuals merely "for the sake of exposure"; that Congress is not a law enforcement or trial agency; and that, in the words of Warren's expansive opinion and *obiter dicta,* "no inquiry is an end in itself; it must be related to and in furtherance of a legitimate task of Congress."[70] These general constitutional limitations were on the very same day also applied to *state* legislative investigations via the Fourteenth Amendment.[71]

Congressional and public reaction was predictably vehement and condemnatory, and various pieces of legislation designed to deprive the federal judiciary of jurisdiction over investigative procedures were introduced in Congress at once. That the legislation, which was tied in with other highly restrictive barriers to the Supreme Court's appellate jurisdiction,[72] failed to be enacted, however, was in no small measure due to what (despite denials and explanations of distinguishing facts) would clearly seem to have been a strategic retreat by the Court in the form of two 5:4 decisions, [73] announced on the same day in 1959, followed by two others

---

[69] 354 U.S. 178.

[70] *Ibid.,* at 187.

[71] *Sweezy* v. *New Hampshire,* 354 U.S. 234 (1957).

[72] See the intriguing struggles surrounding the proposed "Jenner-Butler Bill" well described in Walter F. Murphy, *Congress and the Court* (Chicago: University of Chicago Press, 1962).

[73] *Barenblatt* v. *United States,* 360 U.S. 109 and *Uphaus* v. *Wyman,* 360 U.S. 72.

by the same close vote two years later.[74] The Court majority took pains to distinguish these several decisions from *Watkins* and *Sweezy*, but there was a strong feeling that the majority had read and heeded "the political signs." On the other hand, the Court has continued to reiterate time and again that it would sanction neither patently unconstitutional investigative procedure nor lack of proper authorization to investigate.[75]

Tests of Anti-Communist Legislation. Most controversial of all aspects of the national security field and judicial review has been the delicate task of the Supreme Court in interpreting cases dealing with the major anti-Communist statutes, especially the Smith Act of 1940 and the Internal Security (McCarran) Act of 1950, both designed to curb and prevent activities to further the internal Communist activity. A third statute, the hastily enacted Communist Control Act of 1954 which was more or less ignored by the Justice Department as a basis for prosecution, had not been judicially tested by mid-1976 in any constitutional sense, although it had figured tangentially in two cases.[76]

The first test, appropriately of the Smith Act, came in the celebrated 1951 case of *Dennis* v. *United States*.[77] Here the Supreme Court, in a 6:2 decision, upheld the Act's constitutionality against charges that it infringed on First Amendment rights of freedom of expression and due process of law under the Fifth Amendment. In federal Judge Harold F. Medina's trial court, eleven top leaders of the American Communist Party had been indicted and found guilty of a conspiracy to teach and advocate the overthrow of the United States government by force and violence, and of

---

[74] *Braden* v. *United States*, 365 U.S. 431 (1961) and *Wilkinson* v. *United States*, 365 U.S. 399 (1961).

[75] E.g., *Russell* v. *United States*, 369 U.S. 749 (1962) and *De Gregory* v. *Attorney General of New Hampshire*, 383 U.S. 825 (1966).

[76] *Pennsylvania* v. *Nelson*, 350 U.S. 497 (1956) and *Communist Party* v. *Catherwood*, 367 U.S. 389 (1961). In the latter case the Court ruled 9:0 that the Communist Party could not be barred from state unemployment systems.

[77] 341 U.S. 494.

conspiring to organize the Communist Party to teach and advocate the same. In sustaining the Smith Act, Chief Justice Vinson's majority opinion invoked what he viewed as the "clear and present danger" doctrine in relation to the *conspiratorial nature* of the defendants' activities. But in so doing, he joined to the test that of "probability," adopting the following excerpt from Chief Judge Learned Hand's opinion in upholding the conviction of the defendants when their case had reached his United States Court of Appeals from the trial court below:

> ... [courts] in each case ... must ask whether the gravity of the evil, *discounted by its improbability*, justifies such invasion of free speech as is necessary to avoid the danger.[78]

The chief justice continued that

> [T]he formation by [the convicted persons] of such a highly organized conspiracy, with rigidly disciplined members subject to call when the leaders ... felt that the time had come for action, coupled with the inflammable nature of world conditions, similar uprisings in other countries, and the touch-and-go nature of our relations with countries with whom [the convicted persons] were in the very least ideologically attuned, convince us that their convictions were justified on this score.[79]

Yet there were two passionate dissenting opinions by Justices Black and Douglas. They *denied* the existence of a danger either "clear and present" enough to justify the limitation of freedom of expression; charged that the majority had, in effect, resurrected the bad tendency test of *Gitlow*;[80] and argued for "full and free discussion even of ideas we hate." Justice Douglas belittled the alleged internal strength and threat of the Communist movement, pointing out that in America "they are miserable merchants of unwanted ideas:

---

[78] *Dennis* v. *United States*, 183 F. 2d 201 (1950), at 212.
[79] *Dennis* v. *United States*, 341 U.S. 494 (1951), at 510–511.
[80] *Gitlow* v. *New York*, 268 U.S. 652 (1925).

their wares remain unsold."[81]   Justice Black concluded his dissent with the following observation:

> Public opinion being what it now is [1951], few will protest the conviction of these Communist petitioners. There is hope, however, that in calmer times, when present pressures, passions and fears subside, this or some later Court will restore the First Amendment liberties to the high preferred place where they belong in a free society.[82]

Justice Black's expression of hope seemed to attain at least partial vindication six years later (after the federal government had obtained 145 indictments and eighty-nine convictions under the Smith Act). In June 1957—a month that featured several broadly libertarian decisions by the Supreme Court, including the above-discussed *Watkins*[83] —a six-man majority with but Justice Clark dissenting, handed down a series of significant amendative interpretations of the Smith Act in *Yates* v. *United States,*[84] thus henceforth drastically limiting its application. Writing for the majority, Justice Harlan narrowed the meaning of the term "to organize"—a term that Congress, in retaliation, broadened again in 1962—and attempted to draw an important legal distinction between the *statement of a philosophical belief* and the *advocacy of an illegal action*. The Smith Act still stood, but the federal government would now no longer be able to punish members of the Communist Party for *expressing a mere belief* in the violent overthrow of the government. It would have to prove that individuals on trial for violating the Smith Act actually intended to overthrow the government by force and violence now or in the future, or to persuade others to do so, and the language employed must be "calculated to incite to action . . . to *do* something, now or in

---

[81] *Dennis* v. *United States,* 341 U.S. 494 (1951), at 589.
[82] *Ibid.,* at 581.
[83] *Watkins* v. *United States,* 354 U.S. 178; *Sweezy* v. *New Hampshire,* 354 U.S. 234; *Jencks* v. *United States,* 353 U.S. 657; *Konigsburg* v. *State Bar of California,* 353 U.S. 252; *Schware* v. *Board of Bar Examiners,* 353 U.S. 232.
[84] 354 U.S. 298.

the future, rather than merely believe in something"—thus reintroducing the clarity, if not the imminence, requirement.

Almost as if to rectify the anticipated adverse public reaction to the *Yates* decision, however, the Court four years later upheld 5:4 the so-called membership clause of the Smith Act, ruling through Justice Harlan that a person who was a "knowing, active" member of a subversive group, and who personally had a "specific intent to bring about violence," was convictable under the statute.[85] But in a companion case, with the opinion also authored by Harlan, the Court held unanimously that *here* the government had not validly met the above requirements of a carefully drawn distinction between "knowing" membership and mere "passive" membership in a subversive group, and must thus release the prisoner.[86] On the other hand, as if to demonstrate the vexatious balancing problems anew, the Supreme Court, in its first significant ruling involving the McCarran Act of 1950—in one of the lengthiest opinions in Court history, written by Justice Frankfurter—held 5:4 on the very same day in 1961 that its registration requirements did not violate the First Amendment by their forced disclosure of Communist Party members' names.[87] With characteristic caution, and deference to legislative action, the Court deliberately failed to reach any of the other constitutional questions involved here—especially the difficult matter of compulsory self-incrimination under the Fifth Amendment.

But its hand was forced little more than two years later when in December of 1963 the United States Court of Appeals for the District of Columbia *did* meet the registration issue squarely in *reversing* the federal trial court conviction of the American Communist Party for having failed to register under the McCarran Act. The party's constitutional argument was that since the Smith Act treats it as a criminal conspiracy, compelled registration would be self-incriminating. Accepting this reasoning, the Court of Appeals ruled unanimously that since "mere association with the party

---

[85] *Scales* v. *United States,* 367 U.S. 203 (1961).

[86] *Noto* v. *United States,* 367 U.S. 290 (1961).

[87] *Communist Party* v. *Subversive Activities Control Board,* 367 U.S. 1.

incriminates," statutory registration would force self-incrimination in the face of Fifth Amendment guarantees against it. The United States government appealed this decision to the Supreme Court—which refused to review it, thus letting stand, without comment, the government's defeat on the issue below.[88] But two weeks later, on the last Opinion Monday of its 1963–1964 term, the Court did squarely come to constitutional grips with another section of the McCarran Act that it had purposely ignored in its 1961 decision—that which denied passports to members of the Communist Party and its fronts. In a 6:3 decision delivered by Justice Goldberg—who had replaced Justice Frankfurter in 1962—the Court ruled that Section 6 of Title I "too broadly and indiscriminately restricts the right to travel and thereby [unconstitutionally] restricts the liberty guaranteed by the Fifth Amendment."[89]

Still, there remained the question of whether *individual* members of the Communist Party, rather than the party itself, could be compelled to register under the Act. "No," [90] came the Court's unanimous reply late in 1965! In fact, all that saved the membership provision from a declaration of unconstitutionality on self-incrimination grounds was the Court's somewhat strained judgment that an individual member could conceivably *agree* to incriminate himself. [91] Other aspects of this continuing line-drawing problem in national security have confronted the Court—as when late in 1967 it declared unconstitutional 6:2, on freedom of association grounds, the McCarran Act's provision making it a crime for members of the Communist Party to work in defense plants.[92] (It extended this ruling in 1968, although under a different statute, and on statutory rather than constitutional grounds, to cover the maritime industry.)[93] Reacting angrily, Congress proceeded to alter the jurisdiction of the Subversive Activities Control Board so that *it* might register Communist

---

[88] *United States* v. *Communist Party of the United States,* 377 U.S. 968.
[89] *Aptheker* v. *Secretary of State,* 378 U.S. 500 (1964), at 514.
[90] *Albertson* v. *Subversive Activities Control Board,* 382 U.S. 70.
[91] *Ibid.,* at 81.
[92] *United States* v. *Robel,* 389 U.S. 258.
[93] *Schneider* v. *Smith,* 390 U.S. 17.

individuals and groups itself. But that move was doomed to failure, for in April 1970 the Supreme Court declined to review a decision by the U.S. Court of Appeals for the District of Columbia that had declared the new provision unconstitutional as a violation of the freedom of association guarantees of the First Amendment.[94] Senator James O. Eastland (D.-Miss.) had introduced in 1968, and again in 1970 and 1972, a sweeping, catch-all bill "designed to give new force to the nation's internal security laws." This bill failed to pass, yet President Nixon, on his own, issued an executive order late in 1971, expanding the scope of the SACB, and Congress acted to give that move legislative approval in 1972. However, it slashed the SACB's budget by 50 percent later that year, and the President's budget message for 1973 omitted all funds for it. Moreover, Congress had already voted overwhelmingly in 1971—the House by 356:49, the Senate already on record unanimously—to repeal the 1950 Emergency Detention Act (a part of the Subversive Activities Control Act of that year), which had allowed the government to operate detention camps for suspected spies and saboteurs in times of national emergency. Undoubtedly, future turmoil and legal clashes continue to loom for the troublesome national security sector, which almost necessarily represents such a vexatious public policy puzzle. But it is one that the judiciary has been increasingly willing to adjudicate—within limits.[95] In the final analysis, even in the realm of the precious freedom of expression, it is simply not possible to get entirely away from the concept of "balancing" liberty and authority, freedom and responsibility—a concept scathingly denounced by Justice Black throughout his lengthy and noble career.[96] But when "balancing" is called for, and in the absence of a danger clear, present, and imminent, we must presume the scale to be weighted on the side of the individual.

---

[94] *Subversive Activities Control Board* v. *Boorda*, 397 U.S. 1042.

[95] In addition to the cases discussed specifically on pp. 109 ff. *supra*, see such landmark decisions as *United States* v. *The Washington Post* and *The New York Times* v. *United States*, 403 U.S. 713 (1971) and, of course, *United States* v. *Nixon*, 417 U.S. 683 (1974).

[96] See his *A Constitutional Faith* (New York: Alfred A. Knopf, 1968).

RACIAL AND POLITICAL EQUALITY

The subjects of racial and political equality are, today, so vast and are so inextricably related that, in effect, they cannot be separated. However, for the sake of explication, we shall give a thumbnail consideration of political equality—in isolation, for this purpose—and a more extensive analysis of racial equality.

POLITICAL EQUALITY

Progress along the road to universal adult suffrage in this country (as well as in others) met with many obstacles. After the initial discriminations against Quakers, Catholics, and Jews had subsided, it took a civil war to gain theoretical suffrage for the Negro; until 1920 to gain it for women; and until 1972 for 18-year-olds. The chief struggle, of course, has centered in the blacks' quest for that political equality to which all citizens are entitled under the Constitution. Success first came into view in the 1920's, but it was not actually consummated legally until the Court's famous 1944 decision in *Smith* v. *Allwright*,[97] which by an 8:1 vote declared the "White Primary" to be unconstitutional as a violation of the Fifteenth Amendment. The federal Civil Rights Acts of 1957, 1960, 1964, and 1968 represented important steps in the struggle to make black suffrage a reality—and the outrages perpetrated upon marchers led by Dr. Martin Luther King, Jr., in Selma, Alabama, served as the catalyst for the enactment of the tough and generally successful Voting Rights Act of 1965. Its passage was justly hailed by President Johnson as "a proud moment for this nation." Although total black suffrage may still not be an accomplished fact, the tools for its attainment now demonstrably exist—and so do those for blacks seeking and holding any public office. This is now a fact of political life, especially given the significant expansions of the 1965 statute in 1970 and 1975 and an important

---

[97] 321 U.S. 649.

spring 1972 Supreme Court 6:1 ruling. This holding struck down "durational" registration requirements in state and local elections, suggesting that "thirty days appear to be an ample period of time" for states to register new arrivals to vote.[98] As a result of the 1965 law, its amendments, and favorable judicial decisions, millions of blacks have been added to the voting rolls—reaching a total of beyond 8,500,000 by mid-1976—averaging in excess of 70 percent of those eligible to register even in the deepest South (e.g., Alabama), coming close to 75 percent nationally, and within 10 percent of the white registration. And not only did some 4,000 blacks hold public elective office *prior* to the November 1976 elections in forty-five states and the District of Columbia (including *all* southern and border states), but over 1,500 were in the eleven states of the Confederacy—where only seventy-two blacks held office in 1965; a two-thousand percent increase—with the largest number (194) in the heart of the formerly segregated South, namely Mississippi.[99]

Another related aspect of the matter of political equality is the long, uphill battle of the urban voters to gain their fair share of representation. Any book written before 1962 would have had to note that the longstanding practice of discrimination against urban and suburban voters, created and perpetuated by deliberate legislative malapportionment on the part of rurally dominated state legislatures—sometimes as high or as low as 1,000:1 (Vermont[100]) and 99:1 (Georgia)—would continue indefinitely, for the Supreme Court had consistently refused to accept the matter for adjudication on the grounds that this was a "political ques-

---

[98] *Dunn* v. *Blumstein*, 405 U.S. 330, a Tennessee case. However, a year later the Court upheld 6:3 the 50-day pre-election *registration* requirement for state and local elections in Arizona and Georgia (*Marston* v. *Lewis* and *Burns* v. *Fortson*, 410 U.S. 679). (Ditto, 5:4, a New York State 8- to 11-month *pre-primary* registration requirement).

[99] *The New York Times*, July 28, 1975, p. 9c; *ibid.*, January 20, 1976, p. 1; *The* (Charlottesville, Va.) *Daily Progress*, August 10, 1975, p. A-9; the annual reports by the Voter Education Project (John Lewis, Executive Director); and those of the U.S. Bureau of the Census.

[100] Burlington (pop. 35,531) and Stratton (pop. 36) *each* were given one representative in the Vermont House.

tion."[101] But thanks to persistent litigants and a gradual change in the thinking of a Court majority, the year 1962 wrought a revolutionary change. In the aforementioned, momentous decision in *Baker* v. *Carr*, [102] in which the issue was the sixty-year-long refusal of Tennessee state legislators to redistrict in the face of state constitutional commands to do so regularly, a 6:2 majority of the Supreme Court held that the distribution of seats in state legislatures was subject to the constitutional scrutiny of the federal courts under the equal protection clause of the Fourteenth Amendment. Justice Frankfurter's sixty-eight-page dissenting opinion (his last signed opinion prior to his retirement because of ill health), joined by Justice Harlan, urged the retention of the "political question" status quo, crying out against involvement in the "political thicket" and becoming entangled in a "mathematical quagmire."[103]

That his appeal to "sear the conscience of the people's representatives" was instead now a lost cause, at long last, became rapidly clear with several successive, highly significant extensions of *Baker*. First, one year later, down went the notorious Georgia County Unit system—a blatant practice of discrimination against urban areas such as Atlanta—with Justice Douglas holding for the 8:1 majority that "one person, one vote . . . is the only conception of political equality under historical standards."[104] Less than a year thereafter the Supreme Court addressed itself to the gerrymandering of *congressional* districts. Ruling 6:3 (or 7:2 depending upon one's analysis of Justice Clark's partly concurring and partly dissenting opinion), the Court, speaking through Justice Black, lectured Georgia and the country:

> While it may not be possible to draw Congressional districts with mathematical precision, that is no excuse for ignoring our Constitution's plain objective of making equal representation for equal numbers of people the

---

[101] See *Colegrove* v. *Green*, 328 U.S. 549 (1946) and *South* v. *Peters*, 339 U.S. 276 (1950).
[102] 369 U.S. 186.
[103] *Ibid.*, at 270.
[104] *Gray* v. *Sanders*, 372 U.S. 368 (1963).

fundamental goal for the [national] House of Representatives. That is the high standard of justice and common sense which the founders set for us.[105]

Then, in June 1964, came the most far-reaching follow-up of the *Baker* decision when the Court, in a series of six state cases, held 6:3 in the lead Alabama case of *Reynolds* v. *Sims*[106] that apportionment must be on a "one person, one vote" basis, with *both* state legislative houses reflecting a representation formula of "substantially equal in population." Wrote Chief Justice Warren for his Court: "Legislators represent people, not trees or acres. Legislators are elected by voters, not farms or cities or economic interests. . . . To the extent that a citizen's right to vote is debased, he is that much less a citizen. The weight of a citizen's vote cannot be made to depend on where he lives." A 1967 decision took a direct, although residually still very inconclusive, 8:1 slap against the age-old vice of the gerrymander.[107]   Soon came, 6:2, the extension of the *Reynolds* principle to units of *local* government.[108]   And in 1969 the Court broadened the 1964 congressional districting decision by striking down New York's and Missouri's planned districting that varied from but 14 and 6 percent, respectively, ruling that states must justify *any numerical* variance between districts, *no matter how small,* in order to meet constitutional requirements.[109]   But the "Burger Court" of the early and mid-1970's, gave signs that it would henceforth be inclined to be at least somewhat more flexible, i.e., less strict, with the *states,* although not with Congress, on the general issue—provided the variances and/or deviations did not clearly violate the basic guidelines of the 1960's.[110]

---

[105] *Wesberry* v. *Sanders,* 376 U.S. 1 (1964).
[106] *Reynolds* v. *Sims,* 377 U.S. 533 (1964) and five companion cases (377 U.S. 633–713).
[107] *Rockefeller* v. *Wells,* 389 U.S. 421 (1967).
[108] *Avery* v. *Midland County, Texas,* 390 U.S. 474 (1968).
[109] *Wells* v. *Rockefeller,* 394 U.S. 542 and *Kirkpatrick* v. *Preisler,* 394 U.S. 526.
[110] E.g., *Gordon* v. *Lance,* 403 U.S. 1 (1971)—upholding, 7:2, a Virginia requirement of a 60 percent vote approval to incur bonded indebtedness or increase taxes of political subdivisions; *Whitcomb* v. *Chavis,* 403 U.S. 124 (1971)—validating, 6:3, an Indiana multi-member

The redistricting decisions were heatedly criticized in some quarters and, after *Reynolds*, were sporadically threatened with various forms of congressional counteraction led by Senator Everett McKinley Dirksen (R-Ill.), who came closest in 1967 when a "delayer" bill passed both houses but died in the Senate after its Conference Committee stage. Nevertheless, there is no doubt whatever that, collectively, these landmark decisions (again with the exception of the *Reynolds* case) not only found a more or less friendly reception, but engendered an almost unbelievable flurry of activity toward compliance by the states. Indeed, all of the latter had taken some form of redistricting action by 1972—a far cry from the reaction evoked by the segregation-integration decisions.

RACIAL EQUALITY

The abolition of slavery, the Civil War, and the adoption of the Fourteenth Amendment introduced and/or intensified major interracial problems between black and white in the

election district; and *Abate* v. *Mundt*, 403 U.S. 182 (1971)—sanctioning, 7:2, total voting equalities in five New York towns of 11.9 percent, because the arrangements there were "based on the long tradition of overlapping function and dual personnel in Rockland County government to favor particular political interests or geographic areas." (The *Abate* opinion was written by Justice Marshall, Justices Brennan and Douglas dissenting. Going further, in 1973 the Court sanctioned several deviations in state districting to the tune of 16.4 percent (!) in Virginia; 9.9 percent in Texas; and 7.8 percent in Connecticut. (*City of Virginia Beach* v. *Howell*, 410 U.S. 315; *White* v. *Regester*, 412 U.S. 755 and *Gaffney* v. *Cummings*, 412 U.S. 735, respectively.) It also made allowances for "weighted" voting in special purpose districts, e.g., 6:3, a water storage one. (*Salyer Land Company* v. *Lake Tulare Water Storage District*, 410 U.S. 719.) But it held to its very strict mathematical equality standards on congressional districts, disallowing a 4 percent deviation in the same year of 1973. (*White* v. *Weiser*, 412 U.S. 783.) And, obviously, there are limits on permissible state deviations, as North Dakota found out when in 1975 it attempted to institute multi-member senatorial districts with 20 percent differentials. (*Chapman* v. *Meier*, 420 U.S. 1.) Later that year the Court did allow an eight-member appointive central school board arrangement, based on two members each from four elected town school boards. (*Rosenthal* v. *Board of Education*, 420 U.S. 980.)

United States. Because of the predominant concentration of blacks in southern and border states,[111] particularly in the former, where in certain areas blacks outnumber whites, the core of the attendant difficulties of relationship has been concentrated there. As the northern ghetto riots of the mid- and late 1960's and the emotional busing-of-students issue have demonstrated only too clearly, however, the "racial problem," like the "farm problem," is neither exclusively regional nor is it just *one* nice, easily identifiable, monolithic problem. Whereas in 1900 almost 90 percent of America's blacks lived in the fifteen states below the Mason-Dixon line, by 1975 the figure had "stabilized at about 53 percent," reversing the trend of past decades, with as many blacks moving *to* as *out of* the South.[112]

History and Progress

Representative Types of Discrimination. Discrimination against blacks has long taken place on both the public and private levels, although the increasing sweep of legislative remedies has officially relegated it to the private sphere—one not easy to define. Thus, *public* authorities—chiefly at the state and local level—enacted measures either simply *permitting* or even *requiring* segregation of: buses, streetcars, taxicabs, railroads, waiting rooms, comfort stations, drinking fountains, state and local schools, state colleges and universities, hospitals, sporting events, beaches, bath houses, swimming pools, parks, golf courses, courthouse cafeterias, libraries, jails, housing, theaters, hotels, cemeteries, restaurants, and other similar facilities—be they public, quasi-public, or private in nature—and interracial marriages were simply proscribed. *Private* groups and/or individuals acted to deny blacks access to social clubs, fraternities and sororities, private schools, private colleges and universities, churches,

---

[111] There are eleven southern states: Virginia, North Carolina, South Carolina, Georgia, Florida, Alabama, Louisiana, Mississippi, Texas, Arkansas, and Tennessee. Six are commonly classified as border states: Maryland, Delaware, West Virginia, Kentucky, Oklahoma, and Missouri.

[112] Report of the U.S. Bureau of the Census, quoted in *The New York Times*, July 28, 1975, p. 9c.

cemeteries, hospitals, hotels, housing, restaurants, movies, bowling alleys, swimming pools, bath houses, sporting events, comfort stations, drinking fountains, barber and beauty shops, employment agencies, and employment. Little, if anything, was covert about either public or private discrimination as it was practiced—it was simply a way of life.

The Doctrine of "Separate but Equal." There was little blacks could do initially to combat *private* discrimination, but they commenced to battle the *public* variety in the courts soon after the Reconstruction era had ended with the Hayes Compromise of 1877. They relied principally upon the Fourteenth Amendment's "due process of law" and "equal protection of the laws" clauses; ultimate success coming chiefly as a result of a firm reliance upon the latter. Initially, however, the efforts of the black community seemed doomed to failure, for in 1896 the United States Supreme Court handed down its famous "separate but equal" doctrine in the historic case of *Plessy* v. *Ferguson.* [113] At issue was a Louisiana law commanding segregation of all *intra*state railway carriers, but at the same time requiring these to provide "equal but separate accommodations for the white and colored races." Its 7:1 decision, written for the Court by Justice Henry B. Brown, a Yale graduate from Michigan, upheld the statute as a reasonable exercise of the state's police power against the challenge by Homer Plessy (who, incidentally, was 7/8 white) that it violated the "equal protection of the laws" clause of Amendment Fourteen. Former Kentucky slaveholder Justice John Marshall Harlan's often-quoted lone dissent, at once angry and eloquent, had to wait almost sixty years [114] until it became the opinion of the Court: "Our Constitution is color-blind," he wrote, "and neither knows nor tolerates classes among citizens." But his brothers on the Court all joined in the majority opinion's key contention that "if the civil and political rights of both races be equal, one cannot be inferior to the other civilly or politically." And, continued the generally popular opinion, if the "enforced separation of the two races stamps the colored

[113] 163 U.S. 537.
[114] *Brown* v. *Board of Education of Topeka,* 347 U.S. 483 (1954).

race with the badge of inferiority . . . [it is] solely because the colored race chooses to put that construction upon [the statute].[115]

The "separate but equal" doctrine remained the permissive law of the land until 1954.[116] Segregation continued to be practiced in the public as well as the private sector in more than one-third of the states and the District of Columbia. But, as the years went by, the "separate but equal" doctrine inevitably came under increasing legal attack. Time and again, the Supreme Court struck down certain state practices as not being "equal" in facilities—without, however, going so far as to hold the doctrine itself to be unconstitutional. Yet its days were numbered.

The "Doctrine" Beleaguered. Concentrating at the graduate level of *higher education*, the Court began in the late 1930's to order specific state universities either to admit individually qualified blacks who had been denied such admission and had appealed to the highest tribunal, or else to provide truly "equal facilities"—probably literally impossible. State law schools in Missouri and Oklahoma were the first to be so ordered,[117] followed by the University of Oklahoma Graduate School.[118] But in 1950, in a Texas law school case, the Supreme Court found the so-called "equal" Texas law school for blacks to be "clearly inferior," hence constituting a denial of the equal protection of the Texas law to its black citizens.[119] At the end of the 1950's, the Court had made resolutely clear that state-operated colleges and universities could no longer limit admissions on the basis of race or color,

[115] *Plessy* v. *Ferguson, loc. cit.,* at 559.
[116] *Brown* v. *Board of Education of Topeka, loc. cit.* and *Bolling* v. *Sharpe,* 347 U.S. 497 (1954).
[117] *Missouri* ex rel *Gaines* v. *Canada,* 305 U.S. 337 (1938) and *Sipuel* v. *Board of Regents of the University of Oklahoma,* 332 U.S. 631 (1948). (The first black to be ordered court-admitted actually was Donald Murray in 1936—to the University of Maryland School of Law—by the Maryland Court of Appeals. (*Pearson* v. *Murray,* 169 Md. 478.)
[118] *McLaurin* v. *Oklahoma State Regents for Higher Education,* 339 U.S. 637 (1950). (Oklahoma had admitted McLaurin but compelled him to sit away from the students, eat at a separate table in the cafeteria, and study at a special desk in the library.)
[119] *Sweatt* v. *Painter,* 339 U.S. 629.

and by 1963, blacks, no matter how few, attended one or more graduate or professional institutions of higher learning in *every* state of the heretofore segregated South. To achieve that, however, necessitated the federal troop-enforced, bloodshed-accompanied admission of James Meredith to the University of Mississippi in the fall of 1962; the similarly troop-enforced, but peaceful, entry of three blacks to campuses of the University of Alabama in 1963; and the admission of Harvey Gantt to Clemson University in South Carolina, also in 1963.

During these years the executive and legislative branches of the federal government, as well as its judiciary, had increasingly become involved in segregation battles in other areas. In 1957 Congress passed its first Civil Rights Act since Reconstruction days (later followed by those of 1960, 1964, and 1968). President Truman outlawed segregation in the armed forces by executive order; President Eisenhower established a Commission on Fair Employment Opportunities; the Court in a heavily attacked decision in 1948 had held restrictive housing covenants legal but unenforceable in any court in the land;[120] Presidents Kennedy and Johnson banned discrimination in federally constructed or financially supported housing; and the Supreme Court, in a host of decisions, struck down numerous state laws requiring or permitting segregation in sundry public or quasi-public facilities.[121] Strictly *private* facilities remained unaffected for the time being, in the absence of state or local public "equal accommodations," "equal opportunity," or other anti-discrimination statutes—which did exist in half of the states by the late 1940's (and were adopted by most of the states, although not all, as the years went by). But the judiciary rejected as patently unconstitutional dodges various wide-

---

[120] *Shelley* v. *Kraemer,* 334 U.S. 1 (1948) and *Hurd* v. *Hodge,* 334 U.S. 24 (1948). See also *Barrows* v. *Jackson,* 346 U.S. 249 (1953). In 1968 Congress enacted a federal ban against discrimination in the sale, rental, and advertising of housing.

[121] For example, *Holmes* v. *City of Atlanta,* 350 U.S. 879 (1955); *City of Petersburg* v. *Alsup,* 353 U.S. 922 (1957); *State Athletic Commission* v. *Dorsey,* 359 U.S. 533 (1959); *Burton* v. *Wilmington Parking Authority,* 365 U.S. 715 (1961); *Watson* v. *Memphis,* 373 U.S. 526 (1963); *Moses H. Cone Memorial Hospital* v. *Simkins,* 376 U.S. 938 (1964); *Lee* v. *Washington,* 390 U.S. 333 (1968).

spread attempts to render public facilities "private" by leasing them to private entrepreneurs. [122] Quite obviously, public transportation facilities similarly felt the sting and had to bow to executive and judicial mandates to discontinue compulsory segregation. As early as 1946, Virginia's statute as applied to interstate buses fell; [123] after a series of preliminary and specific "cease and desist" orders, the Interstate Commerce Commission in 1955 issued a blanket order forbidding all racial segregation in interstate buses and trains, including public waiting room facilities; the lower judiciary attacked state segregation laws on public *intra*state carriers; and as of 1960 the Supreme Court began to strike down as violative of the Fourteenth Amendment all statutorily or mandated permitted racial segregation in air, railroad, and bus terminals, together with their waiting rooms and restaurants, be they publicly *or* privately operated. [124] The tough Civil Rights Act of 1964 was designed to strike a death blow at almost all discriminatory aspects and areas of "public accommodations" and "equal employment" opportunities. And, having in 1964 declared unconstitutional a Florida law forbidding cohabitation between whites and blacks while permitting it among whites *or* among blacks, [125] the Court in a unanimous opinion tackled in 1967 the larger issue of the miscegenation problem per se: it threw out Virginia's antiracial intermarriage law on equal protection grounds. [126]

The 1954 Desegregation Decisions. Most, if not all, of the actions just outlined briefly resulted directly, or indirectly, from the most significant judicial decision in the segregation-integration field since *Plessy* v. *Ferguson* [127] in 1896. It came on May 17, 1954, when a unanimous Court—including natives from Alabama (Black), Kentucky (Reed), and Texas

---

[122] For example, *Derrington* v. *Plummer*, 240 F. 2nd 922 (1957); *Griffin* v. *Prince Edward County School Board*, 377 U.S. 218 (1964); *Louisiana* v. *Pointdexter*, 389 U.S. 571 (1968).
[123] *Morgan* v. *Virginia*, 328 U.S. 373.
[124] See *Boynton* v. *Virginia*, 364 U.S. 454 (1960); *Turner* v. *Memphis*, 369 U.S. 350 (1962); and *Bailey* v. *Patterson*, 369 U.S. 31 (1962).
[125] *McLaughlin* v. *Florida*, 379 U.S. 184 (1964).
[126] *Loving* v. *Virginia*, 388 U.S. 1.
[127] 163 U.S. 537.

(Clark)[128] —after deliberating roughly two years, struck down the "separate but equal" doctrine.[129] Speaking for himself and his eight associate justices in a single, brief opinion,[130] Chief Justice Warren called public education "the very foundation of good citizenship" and "a principal instrument in awakening the child." Noting the findings of psychologists and sociologists, the chief justice, in observations heavily criticized later, declared that in segregated, separated facilities "a sense of inferiority affects the motivations of a child to learn." He then turned to the heart of the constitutional issue and pronounced compulsory segregation—contrary to widespread misconceptions he did *not* say anything about "integration" per se—in public schools unconstitutional:

> ... in the field of public education the doctrine of "separate but equal" has no place. Separate educational facilities are inherently unequal ... [Plaintiffs] are, by reason of the segregation complained of, deprived of the equal protection of the laws guaranteed by the Fourteenth Amendment....[131]

Quite aware of the crushing effect this decision would have upon the South and its long-standing traditions, and of the many genuine difficulties involved in compliance, the Court delayed issuing an enforcement order of its decision for one year. But, on May 31, 1955, having invited the views of interested authorities—of whom but a few submitted sug-

---

[128] Chief Justice Warren and Associate Justices Frankfurter, Douglas, Jackson, Burton, and Minton were the other six—non-southern—members of the Court.

[129] *Brown* v. *Board of Education of Topeka*, 347 U.S. 483 and *Bolling* v. *Sharpe*, 347 U.S. 497.

[130] *Brown* v. *Board of Education of Topeka, loc. cit.,* at 494. Warren told a University of Virginia Student Legal Forum meeting that he purposely kept the opinion short "so that any layman interested in the problem could read the entire opinion ... of which I wrote every blessed word.... In drafting it I sought to use low-key, unemotional language." (Charlottesville, Va., April 18, 1973.) He kept its text secret, locked in his safe, until he read it aloud from the bench in full on that historic Monday in 1954. (See Chief Justice Warren's full-length obituary in *The New York Times,* July 11, 1974, p. 35a.)

[131] 347 U.S. 497.

gestions—it ordered the end of compulsory racial segregation in all public schools, charging local authorities with responsibility for compliance under the scrutiny of the appropriate United States District Court. It directed these tribunals to order "a prompt and reasonable start," but willingly kept the door open for consideration of specific local problems. Nevertheless, the Court left no doubt that it expected full and relatively prompt compliance "with all deliberate speed"[132] —a formula evidently suggested by Justice Frankfurter who allegedly found it in a 1911 Holmes opinion dealing with monetary matters between the states. [133] Holmes identified it there as "language of the English Chancery."

Compliance. Although ten years later no state remained completely untouched by public school desegregation as a result of the two *Brown* decisions (Mississippi succumbed in August 1964), compliance in all but the border states was slow or even token. In stark contrast to the ready compliance in the *Redistricting Cases,* [134] every conceivable stratagem was employed to delay and frustrate efforts to comply with the *Brown* decisions. Thus in 1957 federal troops had to be sent to Little Rock, Arkansas, to overcome Governor Orval Faubus's interference with judicial enforcement orders. [135]   In the decade between 1954 and 1964 following the first *Brown* decision, almost 200 state segregation laws were enacted, all designed to frustrate implementation of the hated judgments. Many legal—and perhaps physical—battles would still led ahead. Customs that have stood for generations, no matter what

---

[132] *Ibid.*, 349 U.S. 294 (1955).
[133] *Virginia* v. *West Virginia,* 222 U.S. 17, at 20.
[134] See p. 121, *supra.*
[135] See Cooper *v. Aaron,* 358 U.S. 1 (1958). Five years later, President Kennedy deployed 25,000 federal troops to overcome Mississippi Governor Ross Barnett's obstruction of the Court-ordered admission of a black, James Meredith, to the University of Mississippi at Oxford. And a few months thereafter the President again had to use troops, this time to beat the defiance of a federal court order by Governor George C. Wallace of Alabama to the admission of two black graduate students to the University of Alabama at Tuscaloosa. (Ten years later Wallace "crowned" the first black Homecoming Queen at the same university!)

their moral implications, are not altered readily. Rarely, if
ever, had the Supreme Court found itself under such heavy
and prolonged attack by so large and vocal a segment of the
population with such significant political strength. Yet the
highest tribunal, in a unanimous opinion by Justice Goldberg,
made quite clear again in 1963 that its decision in *Brown*

> ... never contemplated that the concept of "deliberate
> speed" would countenance indefinite delay in elimina-
> tion of racial barriers in schools, let alone other public
> facilities not involving the same physical problems or
> comparable conditions. ... The basic guarantees of our
> Constitution are warrants for the here and now.[136]

The Civil Rights Act of 1964, with its tough provision for
withholding funds from noncomplying school districts, provided tools for acceleration in compliance. And the Court
made increasingly and resolutely clear that it was simply not
going to stand for any more irrelevant delays, emphasizing its
determination with the statement in a unanimous 1968 decision assailing "freedom of choice" plans that "delays are no
longer tolerable."[137] The other shoe fell in October 1969
when the Court, speaking crisply *per curiam*, ended the
"all deliberate speed" guideline once and for all (it had lasted
for fourteen years): it ruled 8:0 that all school districts must
end segregation "at once" and operate "unitary" integrated
schools "now and hereafter."[138]

A Nationwide Problem. As the 1960's had come upon the
scene, what had been fully anticipated became a fact. The
North, which all too frequently had gloated in the face of the
southern predicament, suddenly found that it, too, was
deeply involved in the segregation—integration controversy.
Here it was not a matter of *legal* inequality or *publicly*

---

[136] *Watson* v. *Memphis,* 373 U.S. 526.
    [137] *Green* v. *School Board of New Kent County,* 391 U.S. 430. See
also the three 1967 decisions of: *United States* v. *Wallace,* 389 U.S
215; *Bibb County, Alabama* v. *United States,* 389 U.S. 215; and *Caddo
Parish, Louisiana, School Board* v. *United States,* 389 U.S. 840.
    [138] *Alexander* v. *Holmes County, Mississippi, Board of Education*
396 U.S. 19.

mandated discrimination, for that no longer existed in the North. What did exist, however, was racial discrimination in employment practices, in access to private housing, in private accommodations, and, largely because of the housing and income disparity syndrome so prevalent in the urban areas of the North and West, *de facto* segregation in public schools. Many of these practices had been blunted by the various antidiscrimination statutes present in almost forty states by the early 1960's, and stood to be further reduced by the Civil Rights Acts of 1964 and 1968 (the latter especially in private housing) but much remained to be done—against the backdrop of ever increasingly militant action by restive black communities throughout the land, especially in urban ghettos. This action, which began with boycotts and picketing, "sit-ins," "pray-ins," "stand-ins," "wade-ins," "stall-ins," and a host of similar demonstrations, [139] —often highly effective economically—regrettably turned to sporadic violence, rioting, and bloodshed, beginning in August 1965 in the Watts section of Los Angeles. [140] By the end of 1969 some 260 cities had experienced riots, resulting in more than 280 deaths—forty-three of these in the horrible 1967 riots in Detroit, thirty-four in those of Watts—thousands of injured, tens-of-thousands of arrests, and billions of dollars in property damage!

Enter Busing. The Holmes County, Mississippi, decision ending the "all deliberate speed" guideline to desegregation in late 1969, seemed to be a response, at least in the educational sector. It was during that period that, acting on the

---

[139] This phase of the struggle commenced with the sit-in demonstration staged by four black students from North Carolina Agricultural and Technical College at a Woolworth's lunch counter in Greensboro on February 1, 1960.

[140] The Watts riots lasted six days and resulted in thirty-four deaths, 1,032 injuries, the arrest of 3,952 persons, and $40 million in property damage (more than 600 buildings were damaged, 200 totally destroyed). The Detroit riots of 1967 were even worse. That bloodiest uprising in half a century lasted five days, resulted in forty-three deaths, 347 injuries, 3,800 arrests, 5,000 made homeless, 1,300 buildings reduced to rubble, and $500 million in damages. See my *Freedom and the Court: Civil Rights and Liberties in the United States*, 3rd ed. (New York: Oxford University Press, 1977), pp. 290–292.

first school desegregation suit filed in the *North*, United States District Court Judge Julius J. Hoffman (later of "Chicago Seven" fame) ordered a suburban Chicago school district to desegregate its facilities and student bodies "forthwith."[141] At that point approximately 38 percent of the black students in the South attended desegregated schools, which compared favorably with those in the North, who averaged 35 percent. But how, given some of the verities of geography, could these orders, coming with increasing frequency nationwide, be implemented? The response from courts, some legislatures, and a good many boards of education would become one of the most volatile, most emotion-charged, most politically tinged of contemporary issues: *busing* children to achieve desegregation and/or integration—a device or tool that, according to Chief Justice Warren, the Court never considered in its implementation conference of 1954–55.[142]

The fat was in the fire. A series of cases came up, headed by one for the Charlotte-Mecklenburg, North Carolina, metropolitan school district in which a group of parents contended that the "color-blind" ruling of the Supreme Court in the *Brown* case meant that assignments of students would have to be made on just such a "color-blind" basis, and that, accordingly, busing to achieve integration was patently unconstitutional. In April 1971, speaking for his unanimous Court, Chief Justice Burger—in what must have surprised not only a large segment of the country but, specifically, the land's most highly placed opponent to busing, President Nixon—specifically upheld not only *busing* but also *racial quotas*, pairing or grouping of schools, and gerrymandering of attendance zones as well as other devices designed to "remove all vestiges of state imposed segregation." *...Desegregation plans cannot be limited to the walk-in school*," he declared.[143] The Court stopped short of ordering the elimination of all-black schools or of requiring racial

[141] *United States* v. *School District 151 of Cook County, Ill.*, 301 F. Supp. 201.

[142] Responding to a question of Charlottesville, Va. (see fn. 130, *supra*, April 18, 1973.)

[143] *Swann* v. *Charlotte-Mecklenburg Board of Education*, 402 U.S. 1, at 15, 30.

balance in the schools (and it made clear that the instant decision did *not* apply to northern-style *de facto* segregation, based on neighborhood patterns—or at least not yet[144]). But it said that the existence of all-black schools created a presumption of discrimination and held that federal district judges—to whom it gave enormously broad discretion—may indeed use racial quotas[145] as a guide in fashioning desegregation decrees. On the busing issue, the chief justice, in a nod to that large element of the populace favoring the neighborhood school concept, admitted that "all things being equal, with no history of discrimination, it might well be desirable to assign pupils to schools nearest their homes. But all things are not equal," he continued, "in a system that has been deliberately constructed and maintained to enforce racial segregation."[146] Yet the longstanding Court unanimity of two decades on the segregation issue ended in June 1972, when the four Nixon appointees dissented from what they considered and characterized as an effort to *require racial balance* rather than desegregation—which they charged the majority of five to have approved.[147] Rarely has the Court been unanimous on the issue since.

Both public and private reaction was generally adverse; the president and Congress were clearly displeased; a host of state legislatures endeavored to prohibit busing by statute and even by constitutional amendment; and the candidacy of Governor George C. Wallace of Alabama in both the 1972 and 1976 presidential sweepstakes received a huge boost—not

---

[144] On the other hand, the Court voted 6½:1½ in 1973 that the Denver system, featuring "substantial pockets of demonstrable segregation," was subject—like all other Northern school districts henceforth to "rigorous desegregation standards," even though racial separation—as was eminently true of Denver—was predominantly, although not exclusively, a product of *social patterns* rather than purely formal law. (*Keyes* v. *School District # 1 of Denver*, 413 U.S. 189.)

[145] This notwithstanding the on-its-face prohibition by Sec. 2000e-6 of Title IV of the Civil Rights Act of 1964, which specifically would seem to *forbid* racial quota assignments. But the chief justice brushed that argument aside, invoking the Court's "historic equitable remedial powers" with respect to the full attainment of the equal protection of the laws clause of the Fourteenth Amendment.

[146] *Swann* v. *Charlotte-Mecklenburg Board of Education, loc. cit.,* at 28.

[147] *Wright* v. *Council of the City of Emporia,* 407 U.S. 451.

only in the South, but in the North, and particularly in the urban centers, such as Boston, where anti-busing sentiment reached its zenith in 1975–76. Consistently having defied, or at least but mildly obeyed, U.S. District Court orders to bus its children, the Boston community, led by South Boston (heavily white ethnic, very few blacks), was confronted with a series of drastic ultimata by Judge W. Arthur Garrity, Jr. Rejecting or downplaying these, the Boston School Committee, an elected, popular body, subsequently found itself deprived of many of its powers in December 1975, and some of its schools placed in the hands of a court-appointed receiver. The proverbial fat was in the fire—with the busing issue becoming (along with abortion) the *key* concern of the March 1976 Massachusetts presidential primary races. But the strife-torn public school system continued in effect to be administratively directed by Judge Garrity—whose stern desegregation order was denied review, and thus upheld by the U.S. Supreme Court in mid-1976.[148]

The Boston reaction—and that in similarly affected cities—matched in intensity of feeling that which had greeted collateral federal district court decisions in Richmond, Detroit, and Los Angeles. The latter decisions, however, went further by ordering cross-district busing between the core city (usually heavily black) and the surrounding suburbs (almost always predominantly white). Thus in 1972 Judge Robert R. Merhige, Jr.—in a 325-page opinion(!)—had ordered the merger of the public schools in the City of Richmond, Virginia (then with a black school enrollment of 70 percent) with those of suburban Chesterfield and Henrico counties (almost 91 percent white).[149] The uproar caused by that decision was matched only by a similar one handed down for the Detroit area. One discernible result was a decisive Wallace victory in the March 1972 Florida Democratic presidential primary. Here Wallace had fashioned his campaign almost exclusively upon the busing issue, as he did, more or less, in Massachusetts in 1976. A welter of bills was subsequently introduced in Congress to forbid or delay busing; the president, in a special

---

[148] *White* v. *Morgan*, 44 LW 3717.
[149] *Bradley* v. *School Board of the City of Richmond*, 338 F. Supp. 67.

television broadcast to the nation, asked for legislation to bring about a "moratorium" on busing—which Congress gave him early that June by enacting a delay in the implementation of court desegregation orders that required the busing or transfer of students "for the purposes of achieving a balance among students with respect to race," either until all appeals had been exhausted or until January 1, 1974; several constitutional amendments to prohibit busing were introduced; and Wallace won the Michigan primary, predominantly on the busing issue. In the interim, the orders by the federal district court judges were being appealed, and Judge Merhige's order, for one, was reversed 5:1 by the United States Court of Appeals for the Fourth Circuit in June 1972.[150] "Affirmed by an equally divided Court," was the Supreme Court's response when the case reached it in mid-1973. Virginia's Justice Powell did not participate.[151] One year later, however, Powell joined the majority opinion of the 5:4 Court, written by Chief Justice Burger, absolving Detroit from bowing to a lower court cross-county busing order, absent proof of *deliberate* racial discrimination in drawing school district boundaries. The four dissenting Justices—White, Marshall, Douglas, and Brennan—saw, in Marshall's words, "a giant step backwards."[152] But the vast majority of the country seemed to support the Court majority.

Increasingly becoming an issue in Presidential election politics, "forced busing" grew apace as a major national controversy. A possible defusing or break appeared on the horizon, however, when, just prior to its adjournment in July 1976, the Court ruled 6:2 in a Pasadena, California, case—Justices Brennan and Marshall in dissent—that if the school authorities initially comply with a court-ordered busing plan and thereby achieve a racially neutral student assignment plan, the Court cannot then require the school authorities to read-

---

[150] *School Board of the City of Richmond* v. *Bradley*, 462 F. 2d 1058.

[151] *Bradley* v. *State Board of Education on the Commonwealth of Virginia*, 411 U.S. 913.

[152] *Milliken* v. *Bradley*, 418 U.S. 717 (1974). Detroit commenced a peaceful inner city busing program pursuant to a federal district judge's order on remand of the aforegone case.

just busing zones each subsequent year in an effort to maintain the same initial racial mix in the face of changing population patterns. This rule applies, the Court held in an opinion by Justice Rehnquist, even where the school system is not yet "unitary" in all respects—for instance, where there has not yet been full compliance regarding such things as hiring of teachers.[153] And, concurrently, the Court unanimously declined to review, and thus in effect upheld a lower federal appellate court ruling that school authorities in Chattanooga, Tennessee, need not redraft a desegregation plan to reflect population shifts that had taken place *after* busing and other desegregation measures had been duly and constitutionally adopted.[154]

Meanwhile, on other fronts the pace of governmental pressure to remedy race and sex discrimination had quickened perceptibly. Generous applications and interpretations of the Civil Rights Acts of 1964 and 1968 by the Department of Health, Education and Welfare and the Department of Labor, augmented by executive orders from both the Johnson and Nixon administrations, resulted in still orders to many sectors of American business, labor, and education, Using the threat of withholding federal contracts and/or grants of a host of types of kinds, the federal government insisted on specific "goals" and "guidelines" concerning minority employment, admission, and recognition in personnel practices,[155] generally based on Titles VI, VII, and IX of the Civil Rights Act of 1964, as applied by the executive agencies charged with their interpretative enforcement. Although they would seem to have been expressly forbidden by the same federal statute, quotas, usually referred to as "guidelines," were in effect demanded from such diverse sectors as the construction industry and federally aided colleges and universities. Many states followed suit with their own requirements. Inevitably, these policies raised serious

---

[153] *Pasadena City Board of Education* v. *Spangler*, 44 LW 5114 (1976).

[154] *Mapp* v. *Board of Education of Chattanoogaa*, 75-1231 (1976).

[155] A 6:3 Court majority thus ruled in 1976 that blacks who were denied jobs in violation of the Civil Rights Act of 1964, must be awarded *retroactive seniority* once they succeeded in obtaining those jobs. (*Franks* v. *Bowman*, 44 LW 4356.) But *cf*. the 1977 *Teamster* cases.

questions not only of illegal "quotas" but also of "reverse discrimination," support of "separatism," and "preferential" treatment—the latter also expressly forbidden by the Civil Rights Act of 1964.[156] Here too the Court would ultimately be called upon to draw another set of delicate, difficult lines. However, when it had an opportunity to do so in connection with the preferential admissions policies of the University of Washington in the *DeFunis* case of 1974, it pointedly refused. In a narrowly decided (5:4) unsigned opinion, it declared the issue to be "moot," since Marco DeFunis had been admitted to the law school as a result of an order by a lower court, the reversal of which was stayed by Mr. Justice Douglas in his capacity as Circuit Justice for the Ninth U.S. Circuit. Initially denied admission by the University, DeFunis had filed suit because, as a result of the application of preferential criteria, thirty-seven "minority" applicants had been admitted, of whom thirty-six had predicted first year averages lower than that of DeFunis, a "non-minority" (white Jewish) applicant. Obviously, the Supreme Court was not eager to reach the merits of the case—hence its "mooting." But Justice Douglas, in his lone dissenting opinion on those merits, flayed what he called the "arbitrariness" of admissions policies generally, and warned that the "Equal Protection Clause commands the elimination of racial barriers, not their creation, in order to satisfy our theory as to how society ought to be organized. The purpose of the University of Washington cannot be to produce black lawyers for blacks, Polish lawyers for Poles, Jewish lawyers for Jews, Irish lawyers for the Irish. It should be to produce good lawyers for Americans and not to have First Amendment barriers against anyone."[157]

Indeed, in a possibly far-reaching 7:2 decision two years later, involving a challenge to an examination for applicants to the District of Columbia police force, an examination that blacks failed in higher proportion than whites, the Court now ruled, that not only was it necessary to prove "a racially discriminatory purpose," but that a statute or an official act

---

[156] Title VII, Sec. 703 (j).
[157] *De Funis* v. *Odegaard*, 416 U.S. 312, at 320 ff.

is not unconstitutional just because it places a "substantially disproportionate" burden on one race.[158] This posture may have signalled a qualification of a tough, unanimous 1971 holding, in which the Court had ruled that the 1964 statute bars the administration of examinations that do not "relate" to qualifications to perform work and that the employer bore the burden of proof.[159] Indeed, the Court subsequently unanimously rejected review of an unusual challenge of the Georgia bar exam, which blacks have traditionally failed more than whites.[160] And just prior to the end of its 1975–76 term, it held, now 7:2 and 9:0, in opinions written by its only black member, Justice Marshall, that the Civil Rights Act of 1866 as well as Title VII of that of 1964, prohibit employers from discrimination against whites on the basis of their race in and to the same extent they prohibit racial discrimination against blacks.[161] There was but little doubt that additional litigation on the "reverse discrimination" front would ensue as a consequence of these decisions.

The State Action Problem

Since much of the discrimination claimed falls into categories of *private* discrimination, one of the most vexatious and fascinating problems became the question of where and when and how to draw the line between public or *state* action and *private* action. Briefly, the line is drawn at the point where the *state* becomes involved: when and if it does, its *action* is then subject to the strictures of Section I of the Fourteenth Amendment that:

> No State shall make or enforce any law which shall abridge the privileges or immunities of citizens of the United States; nor shall any State deprive any person of life, liberty, or property, without due process of law; nor deny to any person within its jurisdiction the equal protection of the laws.

---

[158] *Washington* v. *Davis,* 44 LW 4789 (1976).
[159] *Griggs* v. *Duke Power Co.,* 401 U.S. 424.
[160] *Tyler* v. *Vickey,* 44 LW 3714 (1976).
[161] *McDonald* v. *Santa Fe* Transportation Co., 44 LW 5067 (1976).

Since the Supreme Court held long ago in the *Civil Rights* cases of 1883 that only a state, and not a private individual, is forbidden by the Constitution to discriminate,[162] a private individual is thus presumably free to discriminate if he chooses, provided only that he receives no assistance from the state in his discrimination—and, of course, that he does not violate any state laws. This in turn raises the delicate question of *what is and what is not "state action."* It becomes a matter of balancing, and of drawing lines between liberty and equality; between, one might add, the alleged private right to discriminate—so long as no law is violated— and the public right to be constitutionally protected against illegal discrimination.

The Court had held in 1948 and 1953 that—as noted earlier—*private* discriminatory, restrictive housing covenants (in the absence of the steadily spreading legislation on the subject) are *not* state action, but were any court to enforce these, such action *would* be state action.[163] Then in 1967 it declared unconstitutional, 5:4, California's anti–open housing initiative (Proposition 14), which had enabled property owners to "decline to sell, lease, or rent" property "in their absolute discretion," because its majority regarded the action by the voters as proscribed "state action."[164] However, four years later the Court upheld 5:3 the right of local communities in that state to veto proposed public housing projects by special referendum votes.[165] And the Court came full cycle in the *private* housing sector when, following the enactment of the 1968 Civil Rights Act with its limited housing provisions, it ruled 7:2 that under an almost forgotten civil rights law of 1866 (enacted under Amendment

---

[162] 109 U.S. 3.

[163] *Shelley* v. *Kraemer*, 334 U.S. 1 (1948); *Hurd* v. *Hodge*, 334 U.S. 24 (1948); and *Barrows* v. *Jackson*, 346 U.S. 249 (1953).

[164] *Reitman* v. *Mulkey*, 387 U.S. 369. See also *Hunter* v. *Erickson* (1969). But compare *Eastlake* v. *Forest City Enterprises*, 44 LW 4919 (1976).

[165] *James* v. *Valtierra* and *Schaeffer* v. *Valtierra*, 402 U.S. 137. Justice Black, writing the majority opinion, distinguished the earlier ruling from the present by pointing out that the former had related to racial discrimination "and this one does not. . . . Provisions for referendums demonstrate devotion to democracy, not to bias, discrimination, or prejudice."

Thirteen) racial discrimination in the purchase, lease, sale, holding, and conveyance of any real and personal property is expressly forbidden.[166] In effect, the housing sections of the 1968 law were thus rendered moot, save for its enforcement powers! Under the same rediscovered authority, the Court ruled 5:3 in 1969 that a swimming pool and park owned by the residents of a suburban community could *not* exclude a black family that had moved into the neighborhood, because it had obtained a share in both pool and park by leasing one of the community's shareholder's homes.[167]

Nor, as the unanimous Court held in 1973, could a "recreation association" that draws all of its members from *whites* living within three-quarters of a mile of its swimming pool, bar *non*-whites living in that area from using its facilities. (The Court refused to recognize the association as a "private club on any level.")[168]

What of the rights of a private entrepreneur to refuse to provide service? In the event of sit-ins, may he ask the police to eject the intruders? What of the right of peaceable assembly versus that of breach-of-the-peace or trespass? The Court tried on several occasions to find answers to some of these problems. In an important series of 1963 cases, it reversed the conviction of numerous lunch counter sit-ins and other demonstrators in several southern states, because in the cases at issue the state and local authorities involved had *required* segregation either by statute or official policy or announced custom.[169] And barely ten days prior to the enactment of the Civil Rights Act of 1964, the Court, without reaching the fundamental constitutional issue of the presence or absence of "state action" in the trespass conviction of 42 persons

---

[166] *Jones* v. *Alfred H. Mayer Co.*, 392 U.S. 409. In 1976 the Court ruled 8:0 that federal courts can order the creation of low-cost public housing for minorities in a city's white suburbs to relieve racial segregation in housing within the city (here Chicago) *if* the government has been found to contribute to the latter's segregation through its public housing programs. (*Hills* v. *Gautreaux*, 44 LW 4480.)

[167] *Sullivan* v. *Little Hunting Park, Inc.*, 395 U.S. 229.

[168] *Tillman* v. *Wheaton-Haven Recreation Association*, 410 U.S. 431, at 437. The Court again based its rationale on the 1866 statute noted above.

[169] *Peterson* v. *Greenville*, 373 U.S. 244 and *Lombard* v. *Louisiana*, 373 U.S. 267.

who demanded service without racial discrimination at privately owned places of business in three states not having an
official segregation policy, *reversed* their conviction 6:3 on
various statutory and associated grounds.[170] It is an interesting tribute to the herein repeatedly expressed caution against
oversimplifications and snap judgments regarding the judicial
posture and philosophy of the justices, to note that one of
the three dissenters was Justice Black, who, wishing to meet
the constitutional issue, albeit in *dissent*, noted that "this
Court has never said in the school segregation decisions or
any before or since, that the prejudice of individuals could be
laid to the state."[171] From the bench—on the last day of the
Court's 1963–1964 term—this great champion of the individual said sarcastically that the idea that the Fourteenth
Amendment *itself* prohibited segregation in public accommodations made "the last six months' struggle in Congress a
work of supererogation."[172] Like his long-time jurisprudential "adversary," the then retired Justice Frankfurter, Hugo
Black then once again admonished his country and his world
that:

> *The worst citizen no less than the best* is entitled to
> equal protection of the laws of his state and of his
> nation.[173]

Many of the delicate questions of private property rights,
still remained unanswered. And what of such routine services
by the state as licensing, probating of wills, and bona fide
protective services? The answers to some of these lay with
the Civil Rights Act of 1964, which, by becoming law early
in July of 1964, rendered some of the questions moot, e.g.,
denial of service in "public accommodations." Ultimately,
most—such as the question of housing—would lie with the
Supreme Court of the United States.

[170] *Griffin* v. *Maryland*, 378 U.S. 130 (1964); *Robinson* v. *Florida*, 378 U.S. 153 (1964); and *Barr* v. *City of Columbia*, 378 U.S. 146 (1964).
[171] Comment from the bench, June 22, 1964.
[172] As quoted in *The New York Times*, June 23, 1964, p. 16.
[173] *Bell* v. *Maryland*, 378 U.S. 226, at 328, dissenting opinion. (Italics supplied.)

The first test of the 1964 Act was not long in coming, and it did not prove to be a difficult one for the Court to handle. At issue was the just-alluded-to "public accommodations" section of the Act—its very heart—passed by Congress under its power over interstate commerce. It states:

All persons shall be entitled to full and equal enjoyment of goods, services, facilities, privileges, advantages and accommodations of any place of public accommodations as defined in this section, without discrimination or segregation on the ground of race, color, religion or national origin.[174]

The Court's unanimous opinion upholding this crucial segment of the Civil Rights Act of 1964 was delivered by Justice Clark in December of that year. He easily disposed of two challenges to the section, involving a motel and a restaurant, by returning to and reemphasizing the broad construction given to the federal interstate commerce power as far back as the days of Chief Justice Marshall:

How obstruction in commerce may be removed—what means are to be employed—is within the sound and exclusive discretion of the Congress. It is subject to only one caveat—that the means chosen by it must be reasonably adapted to the end permitted by the Constitution. We cannot say that its choice here was not adapted. The Constitution requires no more.[175]

Of Wills and Clubs. As time went by, it became increasingly clear that the Court would continue to regard the probation of wills as a routine "non-state" action,[176] but that that "non-state" status would become constitutionally proscribed "state" action if the subject had a "public character"—such

---

[174] Stat. 437.

[175] *Heart of Atlanta Motel* v. *United States* and *Katzenbach* v. *McClung*, 379 U.S. 241 and 379 U.S. 294, respectively.

[176] *Pennsylvania* v. *Board of Directors of City Trusts of the City of Philadelphia*, 357 U.S. 570 (1958). That principle was reconfirmed in a 1975 case, *Sutt* v. *First National Bank of Kansas City*, 421 U.S. 992, which let stand a bequest to Protestant Christian hospitals in a single county to help care for native-born white patients.

as attempts to bar blacks by will from a public park[177] or the banning of non-whites by will from a private high school that was adjudged to be of a quasi-public nature.[178] On the other hand, the Court did *not* regard as proscribable "state action" the return of the aforementioned public park to the donor's heirs rather than admitting blacks to its use;[179] nor the court substitution of private for public trustees of a private educational institution;[180] nor the closing of *all* of a city's public swimming pools rather than desegregating them.[181]

By 1969 the Court had begun to reach the "private" club syndrome. It held 7:1 that even a lake recreation club in an out-of-the-way Arkansas location was covered by the public accommodations provisions of the Civil Rights Act of 1964 and must therefore admit blacks.[182] The case involved a boating and swimming facility, called Lake Nixon, located in a rural area about twelve miles west of Little Rock. The establishment advertised widely, charged but twenty-five cents for "membership," and had 100,000 "members" in a single year.

The Court found an effect upon interstate commerce, since some of the club's equipment, facilities, and food—e.g., a jukebox and records, canoes, and three or four snack bar items—came from outside the state and could thus be reached by the federal public accommodations legislation. But what of a private club or lodge that discriminates on racial—or, for that matter, on sexual or religious—grounds? Specifically, can the Loyal Order of Moose, for example, limit membership in its 2,000 lodges to white adult Caucasian males who, if married, are married to white Caucasians, and are of "good moral character," "mentally normal," and "express a belief in a supreme being"? If it is truly a private organization, receives no governmental aid, and pays its taxes, the answer would presumably be in the affirmative—for the liberty to

---

[177] *Evans* v. *Newton*, 382 U.S. 296 (1966).
[178] *Brown* v. *Commonwealth of Pennsylvania*, 391 U.S. 321 (1968).
[179] *Evans* v. *Abney*, 396 U.S. 435 (1970).
[180] *Pennsylvania* v. *Board of Directors of City Trusts of the City of Philadelphia*, 353 U.S. 230 (1957).
[181] *Palmer* v. *Thompson*, 403 U.S. 217 (1971). The city voluntarily reopened its pools on a desegregated basis a few years later.
[182] *Daniel* v. *Paul*, 395 U.S. 298 (1969).

associate privately, even on a discriminatory basis, would appear to outweight egalitarian considerations. Yet what if that organization holds a state liquor license? Does that fact qualify it for state action? The Pennsylvania Commonwealth Court had that question before it, involving the black majority leader of the Pennsylvania State House of Representatives, K. Leroy Irvis. As a guest of a member of Lodge #107 of the Loyal Order of Moose, Irvis had been refused food and an alcoholic beverage. The state tribunal held the lodge to be exempt on grounds of privacy and association.[183] But a three-judge federal district court reversed, ruling that the holder of a state liquor license was indeed open to "state action" under the Fourteenth Amendment.[184] The Moose immediately appealed the decision to the United States Supreme Court, which, in June 1972, in a 6:3 opinion written by its most junior member, Justice Rehnquist, ruled that mere liquor regulation does *not* involve the state in the sense of discriminatory state action forbidden by the Fourteenth Amendment.[185] That August, however, the Pennsylvania Supreme Court, while carefully distinguishing its decision from the aforegone one, upheld a ruling by the Pennsylvania Human Rights Commission that Moose Lodge #107 cannot exclude black non-member guests from its dining room and bar as long as it allows nonmember guests to be served—for by opening its facilities to guests, it becomes "a place of public accommodation."[186] The Moose appealed that holding to the Supreme Court, which rejected the appeal for lack of a "substantial federal question," thereby upholding the Pennsylvania ruling.[187] The fascinating elements in-

---

[183] *Commonwealth* v. *Loyal Order of Moose*, 92 Dauph. 234 (1970).

[184] *Irvis* v. *Moose Lodge # 107*, 318 F. Supp. 1246 (1970).

[185] *Moose Lodge #107* v. *Irvis*, 407 U.S. 163. The dissenting justices were Douglas, Brennan, and Marshall. This holding was reconfirmed in 1973 when the Court, 8:1, let stand a decision below that upheld the right of a New Orleans hotel to bar women from its men's grill, under a state ordinance that licenses bars but does not forbid sexual discrimination in places of public accommodation. (*Millenson* v. *New Hotel Monteleone, Inc.*, 414 U.S. 1011.)

[186] *Loyal Order of Moose* v. *Pennsylvania Human Rights Commission* (decided August 1, 1972).

[187] *Ibid.*, 409 U.S. 1052 (1972). On a related matter, the Court in 1976 declined to review, and thereby sustained, a lower court ruling

herent in this new clash between liberty and equality in a free democratic society under a written Constitution, subject to judicial interpretation, engaged lay as well as professional observers.

And so did another fascinating one in 1976: the eagerly awaited Court answer to the question whether *totally private* schools may bar black students solely because of their race. On the basis of the aforementioned Civil Rights Act of 1866, U.S. District Judge Albert V. Bryan, Jr., of Virginia, had rejected the alleged right of two private Virginia secondary schools to do so. Byran was upheld 4:3 by the U.S. Court of Appeals for the Fourth Circuit in 1975, and the highest court in the land took jurisdiction, hearing oral argument in the spring of 1976.[188]

In an historic 7:2 decision,[189] written by Mr. Justice Stewart, who was joined by his colleagues Burger, Brennan, Marshall, Blackman, Powell, and Stevens, the Supreme Court's answer was to uphold the lower courts, ruling that "private, commercially operated, non-sectarian schools" may not deny "admission to prospective students because they are Negroes." Over a strongly worded dissenting opinion by Justice White, who was joined by Justice Rehnquist, the Court majority based its ruling on a section of the Civil Rights Act of 1866—which was passed to enforce the Thirteenth Amendment's ban on slavery—that accords "all persons the same rights to" make and enforce contracts as is enjoyed by white citizens. In response to the challenge that this interpretation and application of the statute violate constitutional guarantees of freedom of association, the right to privacy, and parental rights, the majority found no invasions of any of these safeguards, holding that they "do not provide easy or ready escapes" through which whites "can contravene laws enacted by Congress to enforce the Constitutional right to equality."

But Justice White's dissenting opinion viewed the

---

that health spas are "places of entertainment" within the meaning of the Civil Rights Act of 1964 and thus subject to the Act's prohibitions. (*Shape Spa for Health and Beauty* v. *Rousseve*, 44 LW 3559.)

[188] *Runyon* v. *McCrary*, 44 LW 3279 (1975), *certiorari* granted.
[189] *Ibid.*, 44 LW 5034 (1976.)

legislative history and intent of the section of the 1866 statute at issue utterly differently than that of the majority: It confirms, he wrote, "that the statute means what it says and no more i.e. that it outlaws any legal rule disabling any person from making or enforcing a contract, but does not prohibit *private* racially motivated refusals to contract. . . . What is conferred by [the disputed section of the law] is the right—which was enjoyed by whites—'to make contracts' with other willing parties and to enforce those contracts in court'. . . . The statute by its terms does not *require* any *private* individual or institution to enter into a contract or perform any other act under any circumstances, and it consequently fails to supply a cause of action by respondent students against petitioned schools based on the latter's racially motivated decision not to contract with them." In language and philosophy reminiscent of Justices Harlan II and Frankfurter, he concluded by flaying his seven colleagues for undertaking "the political task of" construing a statute . . . a task appropriate for the legislature, not the judiciary."[190]

Left intriguingly unanswered until a future day and Court by Justice Stewart's majority opinion, were such collateral questions as the right of *sectarian* schools to discriminate on the basis of race and, conceivably, the application of the 1866 to private clubs. What is not difficult to predict is that there will be future litigation involving that fascinatingly vexatious line between liberty and equality!

Rightly or wrongly, it is with the Court that "the buck stops," an observation with which we began this book—a factual observation. For, in the final analysis, it is the Supreme Court that is the defender as well as the interpreter of the basic freedoms of us all. It is the Court that has been, and will unquestionably continue to be, the definer of values and proclaimer of principles. It is an institution at once legal, political, and human. As such, it can escape neither criticism nor controversy, nor should it. For it is the greatest institutional safeguard we possess.

---

[190] *Ibid..*, 44 LW 5044 (1976).

IV

Courts and Public Policy:
*Personnel, Judicial Review,
Activism, and Restraint*

We shall now give our attention to the Court's general role of judicial review, of constitutional and statutory interpretation, and to a view of the men who staff it and the lower courts. To understand the role of the judiciary in policy-making, several aspects of the judicial process must now be analyzed. Some of these may well have already become more or less apparent to the reader as a result of the preceding discussions of the characteristics of our courts, in general, and the United States Supreme Court, in particular, as institutions at once governmental, legal, and political. Nonetheless, they need additional amplification, and our consideration of them will thus naturally commence with a glance at the individuals who comprise the judiciary.

JUDGES AND JUSTICES

Selection and Tenure

The process of staffing the courts is neither mysterious nor particularly Machiavellian—folklore to the contrary. Essentially, there are just two ways of "getting on the bench"—by *election* or *appointment* (although there do exist combinations of the two in some states). *All* federal jurists are appointed; but state jurists may be either elected or appointed, depending upon constitutional and/or statutory provisions.

Election. The several states of the fledgling Union turned to the elective method largely as a result of the post–Constitutional Convention trend to "democratize" government. Election was by the common device of the ballot by the electorate, or the less frequent one of choice by the legislature. Election remains the generally practiced, if hardly universally applauded,[1] approach to court staffing throughout the states for at least *some* members of the judiciary, their terms varying greatly in length from four years to life (Rhode Island).[2] The basic requirement is to obtain one's political party's nomination and then hope for the best in the general election. However, *real* contests are more often the exception than the rule, and active "politicking" by judicial candidates, especially incumbents, is usually—albeit certainly not always—regarded as improper. Moreover, there are some instances in which certain judicial nominees may run on bipartisan (Pennsylvania) or even nonpartisan (Minnesota) tickets for at least some judicial posts; and in several states the "sitting judge" principle is in vogue, whereby both political parties are—at least theoretically—pledged to support the incumbent, no matter what his political affiliation may be.

Appointment. In the states, appointment of at least some jurists for terms of varying length is usually by gubernatorial

---

[1] Chief Justice Roger J. Traynor of the California Supreme Court told a judicial conference in the fall of 1970 that the "greatest single improvement that could be made in the administration of this country would be to get rid of the popular election of judges." (*The New York Times,* October 5, 1970, p. 34.) At that time fully 82 percent of the judges on local and state courts were elected! (*Ibid.*) That figure has dropped only slightly since.
[2] On this point, and court staffing generally, see my *The Judicial Process: An Introductory Analysis of the Courts of the United States, England, and France,* 3rd ed., rev. and enl. (New York: Oxford University Press, 1975), Ch. II. On Supreme Court staffing, see my *Justices*

selection plus senatorial confirmation; but on the federal level *every* prospective judge or justice (a title reserved there to members of the Supreme Court) is nominated by the president and submitted to the Senate for approval by simple majority vote. At levels below the Supreme Court, the initial selection by the chief executive is customarily delegated to the Attorney General and his deputy. However, when it comes to the choice of a new Supreme Court justice, the selection process turns into a much more personal one for the president. Yet, no matter which level of the federal judiciary may be involved, at least three significant facts of political life must be understood and considered in order to obtain a realistic picture of that selection process.

The *first* fact is that it is not practically possible for the chief executive to designate a member of the federal bench, and see him confirmed, without at least the grudging approval of the United States senators from the nominee's home state. Indeed, some powerful senators of the president's political party will insist not only on the right of approval of his choice, but on the right to have particular candidates of their own appointed. As a minimum, this law of politics applies to the judges of the United States District bench and usually to those of the United States Courts of Appeals. But in the case of the Supreme Court nominees, it governs more as a matter of courtesy than necessity, for it is generally agreed that "they" ought to be regarded as the president's personal choices—despite seventeen significant illustrations to the contrary, such as the Senate's rejection of Cleveland's nominations of William B. Hornblower and Wheeler H. Peckham; Grant's choices of Ebenezer R. Hoar and George R. Williams; the 1930 rejection by 39:41 of Hoover's selection of U.S. Court of Appeals Judge John J. Parker; the 1968 filibuster against Johnson's attempted promotion of Abe Fortas to chief justice;[3] the Senate's 45:55 rejection of the Nixon nomination of Clement F. Haynsworth, Jr. and that of G. Harrold Carswell, 45:51, in 1969

---

and Presidents: A Political History of Appointments to the Supreme Court (New York: Oxford University Press, 1974 and Viking Press, 1975).

[3] When an attempt to invoke closure failed that fall (45:43), Fortas asked the president to withdraw his nomination. (In 1969 he resigned from the bench.)

and 1970, respectively. The reasons for these rejections varied, but they comprised political opposition to the appointing president; the candidate's personal involvement with a delicate political problem; "senatorial courtesy";[4] the questionable ability of the nominee; his political "unreliability";[5] his ethics; or "getting" at the Court itself—e.g., the 1968 anti-Fortas filibuster, which was really directed against the Warren Court's judicial posture.

The *second* important factor in the selection process is the increasingly significant role played by the twelve-member[6] Committee on the Federal Judiciary of the American Bar Association, whose functions began to receive maximum attention and presidential cooperation during the Truman administration. Although some observers question the wisdom of delegating to a private group—which is not without certain specific professional and perhaps personal interests and biases—the right to evaluate all federal judicial personnel prior to the nomination stage, the Committee has developed into a respected and powerful element of the nominating process. Its procedure is to investigate all prospective nominees, below Supreme Court level,[7] over a six- to eight-week period and then to "rate" them for the attention

---

[4] The term signifies a firmly accepted custom whereby the president is expected, as a matter of political patronage practice and courtesy, to consult with the nominee's home state senator(s) prior to his designation—provided the senator is a member of the president's political party. Failing to respect this custom, the president will usually see the invocation of "senatorial courtesy" under which the aggrieved senator's colleagues will, on his call for the nominee's defeat, support him as a matter of fraternal courtesy. The magic words, uttered by the president's senatorial adversary, are that the nominee is "personally obnoxious" to him!

[5] See the detailed article by Henry J. Abraham and Edward M. Goldberg, "A Note on the Appointment of Justices of the Supreme Court of the United States," 46 *American Bar Association Journal* 147 (February 1960).

[6] One member from each of the 11 federal judicial circuits plus one chairman, 13 as of 1976 with the special addition of the first black.

[7] Since a late 1971 confrontation between the Committee and President Nixon and his Attorney General, John N. Mitchell, the latter submitted his recommendation for the Nixon Administration's last two Supreme Court nominations directly to the president, thus bypassing the A.B.A. Committee until the nominee's name had become public— but the Committee issued its evaluations anyway. President Ford restored the *status quo ante* as soon as the first opportunity (the John Paul Stevens nomination in 1975) arose.

of the Attorney General in one of four categories: "EWQ" (Exceptionally Well Qualified); "WQ" (Well Qualified); "Q" (Qualified); or "NQ" (Not Qualified). It should be noted here, however, that the lowest ranking is not necessarily a reflection on the nominee's character or ability. For instance, as a matter of policy the A.B.A.'s Committee will not normally approve anyone who has reached the age of sixty-four, no one above sixty unless ratable at least "WQ"; it is loath to recommend lawyers without trial experience; and it generally insists on fifteen years of experience in "the rough and tumble of legal practice."[8] To cite one year of the Committee's activities, in 1962 President Kennedy nominated and saw appointed 100 federal judges. Of these, the Committee had rated sixteen "EWQ," forty-five "WQ," thirty-one "Q," and eight "NQ." That the names of eight "NQ" judges were nevertheless forwarded to and approved by the Senate is proof of the political pressures that prey upon the chief executive—especially at the start of a new administration that represents a change in party. Still, a number of other "NQ" ratees were never nominated by President Kennedy, a testimonial to the important role of the A.B.A.'s influential Committee.

The *third* factor is a rather subtle but increasingly demonstrable one:[9] the role, difficult to assess but clearly present, that incumbent and retired members of the tribunal—especially at the highest level in the person of the Chief Justice of the United States—play in suggesting nominees to the president. We know, for example, that Chief Justice Taft was not at all reluctant in expressing his thoughts to Presidents Harding, Coolidge, and Hoover—"bombarding" the chief executives with suggestions is a more apt description; that his successor, Hughes, followed a similar course of action with Hoover and F.D.R.; that Associate Justice Stone went so far as to write to President Hoover that he would be willing to resign and relinquish his seat if it would take that sacrifice to propel the president into nominating Justice

---

[8] Committee member Robert L. Trescher to author, December 9, 1971.

[9] See Henry J. Abraham and Bruce Allen Murphy, "The Influence of Sitting and Retired Justices on Presidential Supreme Court Nominations," 3 *Hastings Constitutional Law Review* 1 (Winter 1976).

Cardozo to the Supreme Court; that President Kennedy apparently consulted with Chief Justice Warren and Justice Frankfurter in 1962 regarding Arthur J. Goldberg, Frankfurter's successor to the bench; and that President Johnson consulted Warren concerning his successor as chief justice.

"Mixed" Appointment and Election. In order to combat the chief criticism of the elective and appointive methods, yet still retain the virtues of these methods, different versions of a compromise plan have evolved in a third of the states,[10] with California and Missouri as the pioneers.

The *California Plan,* adopted by referendum vote in 1934, extends to some,[11] but not all, of California's judges. Under it, the governor nominates one prospective jurist to a Commission of Qualifications, composed of the chief justice of the State Supreme Court, the presiding judge of the pertinent District Court of Appeals, and the attorney general. If the Commission accepts the governor's nominee, he is declared appointed for *one year,* after which he must offer himself to the electorate for the full twelve-year term of office. He runs unopposed on a ballot which simply asks the question "Shall [name] be elected to the office for the term prescribed by law?"

The *Missouri Plan* uses a somewhat different method. Here, nonpartisan nominating boards, known as Appellate Commissions and operating on different court levels,[12] select *three* candidates for every vacant judgeship, from whom the governor appoints *one* for a one-year probationary term of office. Thereafter, as in California, the incumbent offers himself to the electorate for a full twelve-year term, running unopposed on a nonpartisan ballot containing the question "Shall Judge [name] of the [name] Court be retained in office?"[13]   Members of the non-salaried Appellate Commis-

---

[10] Variants existed in 1977 in Alaska, Colorado, Florida, Georgia, Idaho, Indiana, Maryland, Montana, New York, Ohio, Pennsylvania, Vermont, Wyoming, Iowa, Kansas, Nebraska, Oklahoma, and Utah.

[11] Those of the Supreme Court and the District Courts of Appeals.

[12] Supreme Court; District Courts of Appeals; Circuit Courts; other lower courts.

[13] Not surprisingly, the response is almost inevitably affirmative. Thus, during the first three decades of its life—from 1940 through 1970—of 179 judicial contests conducted, the Missouri electorate re-

sions are designated for staggered six-year terms of office; they may hold neither public nor political party office. A typical Commission, that for the Missouri Supreme Court and the lower appellate courts, consists of the chief justice of the former as chairman; three lawyers selected by the state Bar (one from each of the three Courts of Appeals); and three citizen laymen, appointed by the governor from the three appellate districts.

On the whole, these mixed systems have proved to be both popular and successful in the jurisdictions where they have been tried, for they combine the democratic notion of accountability to the electorate with an appealing method of selecting prospective judicial personnel that is based upon a type of separation of powers. Still, a question arises as to how much effort will be engendered by a sitting judge to establish a "popular" record for the benefit of the electorate. Perhaps there is really no effective substitute for the responsibility and accountability that are found, at least in theory, in the appointive method, provided it is backed by long tenure. As it stands, "on balance our judicial system still represents primarily a compromise between representativeness and neutral competence."[14]

Tenure of Office and Emoluments. On the state level tenure is either of substantial length or for "good behavior"—i.e., life. On the federal level, "good behavior" tenure is constitutionally mandated for all constitutional court judges; legislative court jurists may be given term appointments, and often are, but there has been an increasing tendency for Congress to accord them life tenure as well. Retirement provisions are different for the state and federal governments. Under the federal plan, adopted in 1937, federal judges may retire on full pay at seventy if they have served ten years on the federal bench, at sixty-five after fifteen years of such

---

jected *but one* candidate—and he received 46.4 percent affirmative votes. (He happened to be a circuit court judge prominently identified with the then discredited Pendergast political machine. See Richard A. Watson, "Judging the Judges," 53 *Judicature* 289, February 1970.)

[14] Herbert Kaufman, *Politics and Policies in State and Local Government* (Englewood Cliffs, N.J.: Prentice-Hall, Inc., 1963), p. 60.

service.[15] In early 1977, salaries of state judges *averaged* $25,000 (but with New York and Illinois paying double); that of the federal jurists, from $44,500 for judges of the Customs Court to $75,000 for the Chief Justice of the Supreme Court (tied as of 1975—1976 to the cost-of-living index, with an upper annual increment limit of 5 percent).

Removal of state judges is normally possible only by impeachment and conviction; but in some states they are removable by joint gubernatorial-legislative action (New Hampshire); in some by legislative resolution (Utah); in some by recall by popular vote (Arizona); and in others by special tribunals such as the Court on the Judiciary in New York.[16] On the federal level, however, judges are involuntarily removable only via impeachment by a simple majority vote of the House of Representatives and conviction therefor by the Senate by a two-thirds vote of the members present and voting, there being a quorum on the floor. Of the thirteen impeachment proceedings formally initiated by the House to date, ten were directed against federal judges;[17] nine other judges resigned before formal charges could be lodged against them. Of the nine impeachment *trials* involving federal judges that have actually taken place, five resulted in acquittals,[18] four in removals.[19] Among the former was the sole one involving a justice of the Supreme Court—Associate Justice Samuel Chase, who was acquitted by a four-vote margin in

---

[15] These requirements are waived in the presence of physical disability, where retirement pay is computed on the basis of length of service. Widows and dependents receive an annual sum equivalent to 37.5 percent of the judge's average salary.

[16] In 1963, it ousted two state judges for "unethical judicial conduct"; also one each in 1970, 1971, and 1973. The Louisiana Supreme Court by a 6:1 vote ordered a state court judge ousted in 1970 for his involvement and arrest in a vice raid at a motel stag party.

[17] The other three were against Senator William Blount of Tennessee in 1789; President Andrew Johnson in 1868; and Secretary of War William Belknap in 1876. Only nine of the ten impeachments of federal judges went to trial; the one directed against Judge Mark H. Delahay became academic when he resigned before the trial could commence. (He had been impeached by voice vote.)

[18] Samuel Chase (1805); James H. Peck (1830); Charles Swayne (1905); George W. English (1926); and Harold Louderback (1933).

[19] John Pickering (19:7 in 1804); West W. Humphreys (38:0 in 1862); Robert W. Archbald (*viva voce* in 1913); and Halsted L. Ritter (56:28 in 1936).

1805, with Vice President Aaron Burr presiding over the Senate proceedings and with Chief Justice Marshall as an important defense witness.

Qualifications and Nominations

On the whole, the only *statutory* requirement for judicial nomination present in the *states* for most courts is a law degree; for others not even an LLB. is required (e.g., certain magistrates). No statutory requirement *whatsoever* exists on the *federal* level, but the need for a law degree there is unquestionably an unwritten law: no nonlawyer stands even the slightest chance of nomination, no matter how learned he may be otherwise (although Justice Black often suggested that at least one nonlawyer serve on the Supreme Court of the United States).

The matter of *judicial experience* is in a different category: considerable lip service is paid to it, and some chief executives have insisted upon it for certain levels (e.g., President Eisenhower for his nominees to the Supreme Court after Earl Warren); but its absence has by no means been a block to nomination even to the United States Supreme Court. Of the 101 men who had served on that tribunal between 1789 and late 1977, only twenty-two had had ten years or more on any lower court levels at the times of their appointments. The last one with that much experience prior to Chief Justice Burger's appointment in 1969 had been Justice Cardozo, who had served for eighteen years on New York benches when President Hoover nominated him to succeed Justice Holmes in 1932. Forty-three had had none at all—yet among these are some of the most revered and illustrious names in America's judicial annals: six of the fifteen chief justices—Marshall, Taney, S. P. Chase, Waite, Fuller, and Warren; and such associate justices as Story, Miller, Bradley, Brandeis, Sutherland, Roberts, Frankfurter, and Robert Jackson. In the oft-quoted words of Justice Frankfurter, neither judicial experience nor geographic considerations nor political affiliation should play the slightest role in the considerations leading to appointment to even the highest bench in the land—such selection should be "wholly on the basis of functional fitness." To him, the essential qualities of a Supreme Court justice were but three: those of the philosopher, historian, and prophet (to which, as we have already noted, Justice Brennan added a fourth: "inordinate patience"). To further seal his basic contention, Frankfurter told an attentive audience of lawyers and law students:

> One is entitled to say without qualification that the correlation between prior judicial experience and fitness for the Supreme Court is zero. The significance of the greatest among the Justices who had such experience, Holmes and Cardozo, derived not from that judicial experience but from the fact that they were Holmes and Cardozo. They were thinkers, and more particularly, legal philosophers.[20]

Nonetheless, the issue of judicial experience is never quite dormant, and there is no doubt that at least some consideration is given to it, depending upon the stance of the nominating authority. Individual members of Congress call sporadically for some statutory requirement—usually providing for upwards of five years of service on a lower court benches[21] — but no such legislation has ever been passed. And it is not likely to be, given continued opposition by the Bar, the executive, and the judiciary itself.

Presidential Nominating Motivations. A favorite indoor sport of the practitioners of the law and politics, as well as the public at large, is to speculate upon the reasons why an individual is nominated by the chief executive—federal or state—to serve on a tribunal. This becomes a particularly intriguing guessing game at the level of the Supreme Court of the United States, whose appointees obviously receive more public prominence than those at lower levels.

Presidential motivations in selecting a future justice of the Supreme Court are both complex and multiple, and vary with each president. There is, however, a fairly reliable quin-

---

[20] "The Supreme Court in the Mirror of Justices," 105 *University of Pennsylvania Law Review* 781 (1957).
[21] In 1968–1969, for example, thirteen such measures were introduced in Congress.

tet of factors that is present in most presidential choices to the august tribunal. In no particular order, they are the nominee's:

1. objective merit (including judicial experience);
2. political "availability";
3. ideological "appropriateness";
4. personal "attractiveness" to the president;
5. geographical, religious, racial, sexual, and other sociopolitical background.

Not all of these considerations necessarily play a role in each selection, but a majority of them unquestionably does; one of them is usually uppermost in significance; and probably all are given at least some thought by the president and his advisers.

Thus, the *merit* factor proved to be decisive in President Hoover's reluctant designation of Justice Cardozo, but the other four factors also played key roles, affirmatively or negatively. Hoover did not really wish to nominate Cardozo, although he recognized clearly the judicial greatness and personal integrity of this dedicated, experienced, principled, and brilliant New York jurist—a bachelor, a Democrat, and a Sephardic Jew. Public and private demands for Cardozo's nomination to succeed to the Holmes seat on the Court were clear and persistent, and were spearheaded by such important figures as Idaho's influential and powerful Republican Senator William E. Borah—not commonly known for his love of easterners—and by Justice Stone, who offered to relinquish his seat in favor of Cardozo when Hoover raised the argument that the Court already had two New Yorkers on the bench (Stone and Chief Justice Hughes). When Hoover suggested possible "religious and sectarian" repercussions—Justice Brandeis also was Jewish—Borah told the president that "anyone who raises the question of race [sic] is unfit to advise you concerning so important a matter."[22] Amidst universal public applause, Hoover then surrendered, and the Senate

---

[22] Claudius O. Johnson, *Borah of Idaho* (New York: Longman's Green and Co., 1936), p. 452.

unanimously confirmed Cardozo within moments after his nomination reached the floor.

Political "availability" includes both the official party allegiance of the designee and his acceptability—or at least his "nonobnoxiousness"—to his home state senators, provided these are of the president's own political party. By and large, an old political maxim governs here; namely, that "there are just as many good *Republican* [or *Democratic,* as the case may be] lawyers—so why appoint someone from the enemy camp?"[23] There have been deviations from this concept, and there are always a few "sops" thrown to the opposition, but there is no mistaking the pattern. To illustrate: President Wilson appointed 73 Democrats and 1 Republican as federal jurists; Harding, Coolidge, and Hoover a total of 198 Republicans and 20 Democrats; F.D.R. 194 Democrats and 8 Republicans; Truman 128 Democrats and 13 Republicans; Eisenhower 178 Republicans and 11 Democrats; Kennedy 105 Democrats, 10 Republicans, 1 Independent, and 1 member of the New York Liberal Party; Johnson 155 Democrats and 12 Republicans; and Nixon 205 Republicans, 16 Democrats, and 2 Independents. Thus the pattern is clear. It is true that thirteen Supreme Court justices of opposite party allegiance were appointed,[24] yet ready explanations governed each instance.[25] The overall percentage of same-as-president's-party appointments has ranged from a low of 82.2 (Taft) to 98.6 (Wilson).

Ideological "appropriateness" played a role in most of the above thirteen cases. This concept is also known as a nominee's "real politics"—i.e., what is surmised to be, on the

---

[23] "Think Republican," Chairman C. B. Rogers Morton of the Republican National Committee urged President Nixon in his consideration of possible successors to Mr. Chief Justice Warren and Mr. Justice Fortas. (*The New York Times,* May 17, 1969, p. 1.)

[24] Nelson-D. (Tyler-W.); Field-D. (Lincoln-R.); H. E. Jackson-D. (B. Harrison-R.); Lurton-D., promotion of E. D. White-D., and J. R. Lamar-D. (Taft-R.); Butler-D. (Harding-R.); Brandeis-R. (Wilson-D.); Cardozo-D. (Hoover-R.); promotion of Stone-R. (F.D.R.-D.); Burton-R. (Truman-D.); Brennan-D. (Eisenhower-R.); and Powell-D. (Nixon-R.). Some would add the Frankfurter appointment (Ind.) by F.D.R.

[25] See my *The Judicial Process,* op cit., pp. 65—72, and my *Justices and Presidents,* op. cit., Ch. III, especially pp. 58—60.

basis of an educated guess, the candidates's actual personal philosophy, regardless of formal party adherence—a philosophy that the appointing authority presumes, with fingers crossed, to express itself on the bench. As President Theodore Roosevelt put it succinctly in a well-known statement to Senator Henry Cabot Lodge (R.-Mass.) concerning the "appropriateness" of Horace H. Lurton, ". . . the *nominal* politics of the man has nothing to do with his actions on the bench. His *real* politics are all important. . . ." And he then proceeded to outline how "right" he was on sundry public questions.[26]   But more than once a chief executive's hopes and advance analysis have proved to be erroneous. The case of Madison's appointment of Joseph Story, Theodore Roosevelt's of Holmes, Wilson's of James C. McReynolds, and Eisenhower's of Earl Warren and William J. Brennan, Jr. are obvious illustrations of the point. Consequently, it is not easy to "pack" the Court—although many have tried. Perhaps most famous was President Franklin D. Roosevelt's effort, in 1937, and first was President Washington, who insisted on a set of five criteria[27] for his nominees. "You shoot an arrow into a far-distant future when you appoint a Justice," aptly commented Alexander M. Bickel, "and not the man himself can tell you what he will think about some of the problems that he will face."[28]   In characteristic language and with candor, President Truman observed that "packing the Supreme Court can't be done, because I've tried it and it won't work. . . . Whenever you put a man on the Supreme Court he ceases to be your friend. I am sure of that."[29]

A nominee's *personal "attractiveness" to the president* may play a decisive role in a president's decision to select an individual, regardless of the other factors at issue. Close personal friendship thus unquestionably accounted in large measure for the Supreme Court nomination of Messrs. Vin-

---

[26] Henry Cabot Lodge, *Selections from the Correspondence of Theodore Roosevelt and Henry Cabot Lodge, 1884–1918* (New York: Charles Scribner's Sons, 1925), Vol. II, p. 228.

[27] (1) advocacy of federalism; (2) a "fighting participant" in the Revolution; (3) "fitness"; (4) judicial experience; (5) "proper" geography.

[28] *The New York Times*, May 23, 1969, p. 24.

[29] As reported in *The Philadelphia Bulletin*, April 29, 1959.

son, Clark, and Minton by President Truman, that of Byron R. White by President Kennedy, and that of Abe Fortas by President Johnson.

The last among the five outstanding factors embraces the American melting-pot considerations of *religion*, *geography*, and now *race* and *sex*. They are usually present—either negatively or positively. The case of Justice Cardozo illustrates the first: neither the presence of two other New Yorkers nor that of his co-religionist Brandeis was permitted to stand in the way, although President Hoover saw them as genuine and overriding barriers. In the "positive" sense, President Eisenhower's designations of Charles Evan Whittaker of Illinois and Potter Stewart of Ohio reflected his concern with the absence of the Midwest on the Court. And the fact that thirty-one states had sent justices to the Supreme Court as of its 1975–1976 term would appear to bear out the regional factor consideration. The same is true for religion: that William J. Brennan was from New Jersey (key state) and a Roman Catholic (a religion then not "represented" on the Court) was surely not lost on President Eisenhower and his advisers when Brennan was nominated to the Supreme Court during the presidential election year of 1956. Although President Truman ignored the "religious" factor when he appointed Tom C. Clark to succeed Justice Murphy in 1949, and President Nixon did likewise with his appointment of Harry A. Blackmun to replace Justice Fortas, it has become an accepted axiom of American politics that there should be a Jew and a Roman Catholic on the highest bench at all times. As of the 1975–1976 term, six Roman Catholics [30] and five Jews[31] had served on the Court; the other ninety had been Protestants.[32] The pressure to establish a niche for another minority group, the blacks, culminated in President Johnson's appointment of Thurgood Marshall in June 1967. And a "woman's seat" is all but certain sooner or later.

---

[30] Taney, E. D. White, McKenna, Butler, Murphy, Brennan.

[31] Brandeis, Cardozo, Frankfurter, Goldberg, Fortas.

[32] Episcopalian, 26; Presbyterian, 17; Unitarian, 6; Baptist, 5; Congregationalist, 3; Methodist, 4; Disciples of Christ, 2; Quaker, 1; Unspecified Protestant, 25.

The Typical Justice of the Supreme Court of the United States. A composite of the typical jurist on the highest bench of the land, reflecting the various aspects and factors of the selection process as well as statistical facts of the past, would look as follows at the time of accession to the Court:

A 50–55 year-old male; white (the first black came to the Court in 1967); generally Protestant; of Anglo-Saxon stock (all except six to date); high social status; reared in an urban environment; well-educated; member of an economically comfortable, civic-minded, politically active family; with B.A. and LLB. or J.D. degrees; experienced in some public or civic office.[33]

We shall now examine the jurist's role in the Court's ultimate power—judicial review.

JUDICIAL REVIEW

Genesis

The power of judicial review is the most awesome and potentially the most effective weapon in the hands of the judiciary of the United States, in general, and the Supreme Court, in particular. Peculiar to countries that, like the United States, operate under a federal system, it is a power at once controversial and misunderstood, maligned and applauded. Any definition would have to state at least the following:

Judicial review is the ultimate power of any court to declare unconstitutional and hence unenforceable: (1) any law; (2) any official action based upon a law; and (3) any other action by a public official that it deems to be in conflict with the Constitution.

---

[33] For an interesting study in this connection, see John R. Schmidhauser, *The Supreme Court: Its Politics, Personalities and Procedures* (New York: Holt, Rinehart and Winston, Inc., 1960), Ch. 3, *passim.* See also my *Justices and Presidents, op cit.,* Ch. III, "Why They Get to the Supreme Court: Qualifications and Rationalizations," *passim.*

What a court does accordingly (obviously, a court also practices judicial review when it upholds a law or action) is to
apply the *superior* of two laws, here the United States Constitution, against a statute, some action or activity by a public
official, or even a segment of the constitution of a constitu-
ent unit of government. But it does not do this lightly or
frequently: it does so only after careful, minute analysis,
reflection, and weighing of alternatives, in line with the
canons of the taught tradition of the law—against a backdrop
of judicial self-restraint. Every court of record in the United
States, no matter how high or low, possesses this fascinating
power, this "principled" process of enunciating and applying
enduring values of our society."[34] Our concern here is with
the exercise of this power by the federal Supreme Court.

It is a power not lightly or frequently exercised—and
whenever the Court can find its way clear to do so, it avoids
the drastic remedy of meeting the constitutional issue—for
meeting it may well mean the exercise of the ultimate "no-
saying" weapon. The Court would much rather handle a
delicate problem by statutory interpretation (as we have
noted in Chapter III) than by going to the constitutional
jugular, especially since it is often possible thus to achieve
similar results. Such Supreme Court decisions as those dealing
with the loyalty-security field[35] and the range and extent of
the Smith Act of 1940[36] are obvious cases in point. Others
are legion. Conscious of its conservative role as the weakest
of the triumvirate of governmental branches, and aware of
public sensitivity in the fields at issue, the Court chose a
course of action in all those instances that comes close to
having the proverbial cake (judicial judgment) and eating it
too (acting as a restraining and explanatory agency, yet
avoiding nullification).

---

[34] Alexander M. Bickel, *The Least Dangerous Branch* (Indianapolis:
Bobbs-Merrill Co., 1962), p. 58).
[35] For example, *Cole* v. *Young*, 351 U.S. 536 (1956) and *Schneider*
v. *Smith*, 390 U.S. 17 (1968).
[36] For example, *Yates et al* v. *United States*, 354 U.S. 298 (1957);
Scales v. *United States*, 367 U.S. 203 (1961); and *Noto* v. *United
States*, 367 U.S. 290 (1961).

Some Examples. The Court does, from time to time, exercise judicial review in its ultimate sense. As of October of 1977, it had done so some 950 times in the instance of *state* legislation and state constitutional provisions (over 850 of these came after 1870), and 122 times in the case of *federal* enactments.[37] An example of the exercise vis-à-vis state legislation is the declaration of unconstitutionality of an Arizona statute that made it unlawful to operate within the state a railroad train consisting of more than fourteen passenger or seventy freight cars, because the law was held to place an undue burden on interstate commerce.[38] One dealing with a section of a state constitution is the voiding of a provision of the Maryland Constitution that compelled all officeholders to declare their belief in God as a condition of employment, because such a requirement was held to constitute a "religious test for public office," thus invading the individual's right of freedom of religion.[39] On the federal level, involving an *Act of Congress*, a section of the Food and Drug Act concerned with the procedure of factory inspection was struck down as unconstitutionally vague under the due process of law clause of the Fifth Amendment.[40] A famous example of judicial review over an *ultra vires action of an official of the United States* was the Supreme Court's ringing "No" to President Truman when he seized the steel mills in 1951. The "No" was based on the chief executive's alleged usurpation of legislative power.[41] And a more recent one, of course, was the Court's unanimous order to President Nixon in July 1974 to surrender the notorious "Watergate Tapes."[42]

The most contentious of these various modes of judicial review has always been the striking down by the Court of an Act of Congress or a portion thereof. (Under the principle of "separability," the Court will always try to save as much of a

---

[37] For a table of these through March 1976, see my *The Judicial Process, op. cit.*, pp. 288–293.

[38] *Southern Pacific Co.* v. *Arizona*, 325 U.S. 761 (1945).

[39] *Torcaso* v. *Watkins*, 367 U.S. 488 (1961).

[40] *United States* v. *Cardiff*, 344 U.S. 174 (1952).

[41] *Youngstown Sheet and Tube Co.* v. *Sawyer*, 343 U.S. 579 (1952).

[42] *United States* v. *Nixon*, 417 U.S. 683.

law's framework as is constitutionally feasible in a given case).[43] It is here that the issue of majoritarian rule would appear to be most clearly and perceptibly joined—for it is here that the highest echelon of the judicial branch, in the ultimate authority of nine *appointed* individuals, says to a majority of the highest echelon of *elected* and, presumably, *representative* legislative branch, that it has violated the basic law of the land. In other words, it is here that one branch of government becomes *the* authoritative interpreter of the Constitution, the protestations of another "equal" branch of the government to the contrary notwithstanding.

The Arbiter. Yet an arbiter there must obviously be! Theoretically it is both plausible and attractive—to some, but certainly not to all, citizens of the Republic—to contend that in a bona fide democracy what the majority wants the majority should get, giving due regard to the rights of the minority—as spelled out in the basic document that governs the body politic. Certainly, or so the argument goes, majoritarian government becomes a hollow shell indeed, if a duly elected, legally constituted body of the people's representatives is denied the right and the ability to respond to people's majoritarian wishes, as expressed by their representatives assembled in Congress. Why should an undemocratically constituted body of nine elitists, who are not responsible to the people via the ballot box, be accorded the overriding power to strike down what the people want? Is not Congress, and is not the executive branch of government equally capable of judging and interpreting the constitutionality of a proposed measure or course of action? Are they not equally devoted to the principle of government under law? It may be quite all right, so the argument continues, for the judiciary to "interpret" and to "adjudicate," but *not* to strike down as unconstitutional anything that a majority has enacted within the confines of the law and the Constitution. This, in sub-

---

[43] The series of decisions declaring portions of the Uniform Code of Military Justice Act of 1950 unconstitutional are cases in point: e.g., *United States* ex rel. *Toth* v. *Quarles*, 350 U.S. 11 (1955); *Reid* v. *Covert*, 354 U.S. 1 (1957); *Kinsella* v. *Singleton*, 361 U.S. 234 (1960); and *Grisham* v. *Hagan*, 361 U.S. 278 (1960).

stance, was Thomas Jefferson's argument once he had turned
against judicial review. (He had been a supporter of that
power until the judiciary began to sanction the hated Alien
and Sedition Acts of 1789 rather than declare them unconstitutional.)

The answer to this argument is obvious *and* complicated.
It is obvious because our Founding Fathers never intended
our governmental organization and base to be a *pure* democracy. They were afraid of the excesses of democracy, as they
saw it and thought it, and constituted the basic document
with safeguards against any potential "tyranny of the majority." This was done not only vis-à-vis the relationship
between the individual and the government, but also vis-à-vis
the relationship of the various governmental branches. Thus
was born a *federal* system of government, with not only a
division of powers between it and the states, but a central
government in which the three main branches were separated
yet still checked and balanced one another. And the new
format was spelled out in a written document—the Constitution of the United States of America. Far from wanting to
see a governmental form like the pure democracy of
Athenian days, or even a fusion of powers like that of our
British cousins, the Founding Fathers thus determined that
majorities must be checked and observed at almost every
turn. Who would be more qualified than the judiciary to be
both legitimator and arbiter, to render a final judgment
regarding infractions of the basic law? Hence the Founding
Fathers widely recognized the idea of judicial review as the
surest tool for the arbiter, and although they failed to spell
out the power, it is clear that they agreed with the Father of
the Constitution, James Madison, who wrote that the

> [J]udiciary is truly the only defensive armor of the
> Federal Government, or rather for the Constitution and
> laws of the United States. Strip it of that armor and the
> door is wide open for nullification, anarchy, and convul-
> sion.[44]

---

[44] As quoted by Charles Warren in *The Supreme Court in the
United States History* (Boston: Little, Brown, 1937), Vol. I, p. 740.

As the years went by, however, and despite the Marshallian stroke of judicial statesmanship and statecraft in *Marbury* v. *Madison*[45] (see below), doubts about the extent of
the role of the legitimator and arbiter have never completely
been laid to rest—even in the minds of some of the most
famous jurists. Thus both Justice Holmes and Judge Learned
Hand—two towering figures in American jurisprudence—although recognizing the need for a federal legitimator and
arbiter, consistently wondered whether it would be absolutely essential at the level of the operation of the national
government. They were convinced that a legitimator and,
assuredly, an arbiter were indeed needed to have the last
word in disputes involving the mechanism of the federal
system, i.e., disputes between the central government and the
states, for they recognized that the Union could not survive
otherwise in the image of its creation. *But* they did not
believe that the "Republic would come to an end" if the
courts were deprived of the power of judicial review regarding legislation passed by Congress.

This position, however laudable in terms of judicial self-
restraint, ignores that role of the judiciary, in general, and of
the Supreme Court, in particular, which casts it as the
guardian of our individual liberties—a role which has occupied it increasingly during the course of this turbulent
century. As such it has become the greatest institutional
safeguard for the individual and the small group. Here, in
saying "No" to government—both national and state—it has
become the last bulwark against majoritarian excesses. In
being willing to stand up and be counted, in refusing to be
cowed by criticism and opprobrium, it has acted as a "moral
goad" to the other two branches. Unlike the legislative and
executive wings, the judiciary does not count constituents; is
neither engaged nor interested in a popularity contest; and is
far from that arena which so frequently has seen the other
two, and notably the legislature, close to what Judge Learned
Hand himself viewed as "the pressure of public hysteria,
public panic, and public greed." And even if a transfer of the

---

[45] Cranch 137 (1803).

judicial guardianship to other institutions of government were theoretically desirable, which few thoughtful citizens believe, it would be politically impossible. What sane citizen would wish to have the ultimate exercise of his individual liberties, including the provisions of the Bill of Rights, be at the mercy of partisan political bodies?

Historical Justification? The other prong of the basic argument is far more complicated, for even if we accept the Court's necessary role as arbiter and legitimator—as most Americans do, depending somewhat upon whose ox is being gored—what of the historical justification of the practice? This query has been a constant one ever since *Marbury* v. *Madison*—for that matter, even prior to that historic decision—because the Founding Fathers *did not* spell out the power of judicial review in so many words, and its presence today results from a combination of historical experience, judicial interpretation, and rather obvious necessity.

Little would be gained by a lengthy rehashing of the historical argument and evidence. It is a fact that the Constitution makes no *specific* reference to judicial review. It is also a fact that the Founding Fathers clearly envisaged it; that it was debated at length in the Constitutional Convention in Philadelphia in 1787; that the most authoritative historical research available on the point—that by Charles Beard[46]—indicates that between twenty-five and thirty-two of the forty delegates to the Constitutional Convention generally favored judicial review; that such significant framers as Madison, Hamilton, and Gouverneur Morris went publicly on record as so holding; and that, indeed, the supremacy clause of Article VI of the Constitution and Article III, Section 2, of the basic document strongly imply the power at issue. It is fair to conclude that the debate over the *legitimacy* of judicial review has been settled by history.

Marbury v. *Madison.* We cannot pass on to consider some of its ramifications in the judicial and governmental process

---

[46] *The Supreme Court and the Constitution*, rev. ed. (Englewood Cliffs, N.J.: Prentice-Hall, Inc., 1962).

without pausing to glance at its judicial "birth," as it were—
with Chief Justice Marshall in the role of midwife—in the
hallowed case of *Marbury* v. *Madison.*[47] It is a case that has
been aptly called "the rib of the Constitution,"[48] and which
Justice Frankfurter characterized as "indispensable" to the
"character of a written constitution."[49] Marshall, who had
been a delegate to the Ratifying Convention of Virginia, a
one-term congressman from that state, John Adams's Secretary of State, and a brilliant lawyer, understood the Constitution and the needs of his land. He was determined to mold
them as he deemed wise and appropriate. His chance came in
what, with the possible exception of his decision in *McCulloch* v. *Maryland*[50] some sixteen years later, is the most
significant decision on constitutional law ever rendered by
the Court. That he should have disqualified himself from
sitting the case; that it could readily have been disposed of
without meeting the constitutional issue; and that the construction itself was unnecessarily tortuous—none of these
considerations now matters in the face of Marshall's momentous holding that "an act repugnant to the Constitution is
void" and that it lies with the courts to determine the
question of validity.

The background of *Marbury* v. *Madison* is sufficiently
well known to obviate any lengthy discussion.[51] Briefly,
John Adams, second president of the United States, had been
defeated for re-election in 1800 by his arch political rival,
Thomas Jefferson. In order to salvage at least something for
his thoroughly trounced Federalist Party, Adams, in 1801,
with the aid of an obliging lame-duck Federalist Congress,

---

[47] 1 Cranch 137 (1803).
[48] Glendon A. Schubert, *Constitutional Politics* (New York: Holt,
Rinehart and Winston, Inc., 1960), p. 178.
[49] "John Marshall and the Judicial Function" in *Government Under
Law* (Cambridge: Harvard University Press, 1956), p. 8.
[50] 4 Wheaton 316 (1819).
[51] For a full and penetrating treatment, see Supreme Court Justice
Harold H. Burton's article, "The Cornerstone of Constitutional Law:
The Extraordinary Case of Marbury v. Madison," 36 *American Bar
Association Journal* 805 (October 1950). For a more historical piece,
see John A. Garraty, "The Case of the Missing Commissions," in
Quarrels That Have Shaped the Constitution (New York: Harper &
Row, 1964).

caused to have two statutes adopted—the Circuit Court and the District of Columbia Acts—that enabled him to nominate, and have his Senate confirm, fifty-nine federal judges—including his own Secretary of State, John Marshall—and thus "pack" the judicial branch with "safe and loyal" Federalists. Presumably these would see to it that any excesses of the incoming Republican "radicals" and "Jacobins" would be held to a minimum. Prophetically, it became Marshall's job, as the outgoing Secretary of State, to deliver the commissions of these last-minute appointees, often called the Adams "Midnight Judges." But because of the pressure of time and last-minute preparations for the inauguration—when he would have to swear in his cordially disliked distant cousin as chief executive of the United States—Marshall failed to deliver seventeen of the judicial commissions, literally leaving them on the desk of his successor, James Madison. When Jefferson and Madison found these undelivered commissions, the new president exclaimed: "The nominations crowded in by Mr. Adams after he knew he was not appointing for himself I treat as mere nullities."[52] And, according to one account, the commissions were "disposed of with the other waste paper and rubbish of the office."[53]

Among the disappointed appointees were William Marbury and three colleagues,[54] who had been duly nominated and confirmed as justices of the peace for the District of Columbia. They hired Adams's Attorney General, Charles Lee, to take their case to court. Lee saw his best chance in Section 13 of the Judiciary Act of 1789, the basic statute that had organized the federal judiciary. This gave to the Supreme Court the authority to issue *writs of mandamus* (Latin for "we command"), writs commanding a public officer to perform his official, ministerial, nondiscretionary duty. In 1803, the case of *Marbury* v. *Madison* thus reached the original docket jurisdiction of the highest court of the land, with Chief Justice John Marshall presiding. Marshall promptly issued an order to Madison to show cause why the

[52] Charles Warren, *The Supreme Court in United States History*, rev. ed. (Boston: Little, Brown, 1937), Vol. I, p. 201.

[53] Charles S. Hyneman, *The Supreme Court on Trial* (New York: Atherton Press, 1963), p. 75.

[54] Denis Ramsey, William Harper, and Robert Townshend Hooe.

requested writ should not be issued against him—an order that was ignored by the Secretary of State. The stage was now set for the momentous opinion and decision.

Marshall, shrewd and wise, recognized that he was confronted with a Hobson's choice: if he were to *grant* the writ of mandamus in the face of almost certain disobedience by Madison (acting upon Jefferson's instructions), the fledgling Supreme Court would be powerless to do anything about enforcing its order; yet if he were to *refuse* to grant the writ, Jefferson would triumph. Facing that unenviable choice squarely, Marshall ingeniously managed to have his cake and eat it too. In what his biographer, Senator Albert J. Beveridge of Indiana, described as "a coup as bold in design and daring as that by which the Constitution had been framed," [55] Marshall—conscious of and delighting in what was indubitably an emotion-charged, fascinating political situation— *declared Section 13 of the Judiciary Act unconstitutional.* It was unconstitutional, he wrote for his unanimous Court, [56] because Congress had given to the Supreme Court a power which it could not legally receive: for that power represented a *statutory* addition to the Court's *original* jurisdiction—a jurisdiction that could be altered *only by constitutional amendment* (as indeed it had been by the Eleventh Amendment in 1798, following the case of *Chisholm* v. *Georgia*[57] of 1793). "An act repugnant to the Constitution is void," crowed the chief justice, explaining that it is

emphatically *the province and duty of the judicial department to say what the law is.* Those who apply the rule to particular cases, must of necessity expound and interpret that rule . . . A law repugnant to the Constitution is void; . . . courts as well as other departments are bound by that instrument.[58]

True, said Marshall, Marbury and his friends were clearly entitled to their commissions, and he denounced Jefferson

[55] *The Life of John Marshall* (Boston: Houghton Mifflin Co., 1919), Vols. I and III, pp. 323 and 142, respectively.
[56] Associate Justices Paterson, S. Chase, and Washington (Moore and Cushing not sitting in the case).
[57] 2 Dallas 419.
[58] *Marbury* v. *Madison*, 1 Cranch (1803). (Italics supplied.)

and Madison from the bench in scathing terms. Proceeding with *dicta* that consumed twenty of the twenty-seven pages of the case, he announced that not only did the legal right to the commission exist, but that Lee had been correct in assuming that the laws of the country afforded a remedy. Unfortunately, that remedy was unconstitutional.

And thus judicial review was born formally as the potent weapon we know today—although it had actually already been applied in five minor instances prior to *Marbury*, in effect as early as 1792 and 1794.[59] But Marshall had now given it the dignity of both full dress and full explanation. And he delighted in the knowledge that by his *coup de main*, blending apparent rather than real judicial self-abnegation with very real judicial assumption of power, he had not only established the judicial branch's claim to equi-powerful part- nership in the tripartite governmental system, but had at- tained a major goal of the democracy-distrusting Federalists. Nonetheless, although Marshall evidently strained the judicial process by making *Marbury* v. *Madison* the catalyst for the pronunciamento of the judical veto, there is not the slightest doubt that judicial review is crucial to the federal character of the governmental process in the United States, the prin- ciples of separation of powers, and those of limited govern- ment. Whatever his motives were—and they were at once noble and crafty—the great chief justice rendered a monu- mental service to the Republic in expounding the doctrine. Far from being a usurpation, judicial review, a product of our common Western history and the "logical result of centuries of European thought and Colonial experiences,"[60] has con- clusively powerful claims to authenticity—buttressed by a strong line of precedents and convincing contemporary litera- ture. That its exercise has inevitably become a "can of

---

[59] See *Hayburn's Case*, 2 Dallas 409 (1792); *United States* v. *Yale Todd*, decided in 1794, but not cited until it became a footnote 57 years later in *United States* v. *Ferreira*, 13 Howard 40 (1851); *Ware* v. *Hylton*, 3 Dallas 199 (1796); *Clerke* v. *Harwood*, 3 Dallas 342 (1797); and *Hylton* v. *United States*, 3 Dallas 171 (1796). In *Yale Todd* the Court had declared a federal pension claim law *unconstitutional*, but in all the other precedents here cited, it had *upheld* legislation that was challenged on constitutional grounds.

[60] Mauro Cappelletti, *Judicial Review in the Contemporary World* (Indianapolis: Bobbs-Merrill Co., 1971), p. 25.

worms" is both understandable and fascinating—and very much a matter of line-drawing.

LINE-DRAWING AND JUDICIAL POLICY

Judging and Legislating

Even those who are philosophically opposed to the principle of judicial review grant that courts must possess the authority to interpret and to adjudicate, but that they must not "legislate." In that view they do not differ significantly from those who favor the principle of judicial review. The difficult problem—and it is one that is crucial to an understanding of the continuing controversy that has embroiled the judiciary, in general, and the Supreme Court, in particular—is where to draw the line between *"judging"* and *"legislating,"* especially since there is no agreement on these definitions! In a sense all judging is "legislating" and all legislating is "judging." What the basic indictment of the Court refers to, of course, is its alleged making of policy, its "law-making," even given its ultimate power of judicial review—for these are presumably matters reserved to the legislature. In fact, there is little or no disagreement with this basic premise. The difficulties arise in what one views as proper adjudication and how one regards judicial decisions. What appears to be a bona fide exercise of judicial power to some will appear as an unjustifiable judicial assumption of legislative authority to others. Thus, to revert to some of the key themes of Chapter III, when the Supreme Court held the use of the twenty-two-word New York State-mandated nondenominational prayer in the public schools to be a violation of the principle of separation of church and state, and hence an unconstitutional infringement of the First Amendment,[61] those who favored the decision regarded it as not only a proper but a necessary exercise of the judicial function. Those who opposed it, on the other hand, castigated the decision as unwarranted judicial legislation that denied the legislative majority the right to set public policy.

---

[61] *Engel* v. *Vitale*, 370 U.S. 421 (1962).

When after long years of refusing to hear the question of legislative districting on grounds that it was of a "political nature" and thus beyond its jurisdiction, the Court finally reversed itself in 1962 in *Baker* v. *Carr*[62] and declared the issue justiciable in line with the requirements of the Fourteenth Amendment (and later Article I of the main body of the Constitution),[63] there were those who agreed wholeheartedly, and those—including Justice Felix Frankfurter, who wrote a sixty-eight-page dissenting opinion in the case— who thought the Court had ventured into the sphere of legislating. And it goes without saying that similarly opposing views extended to the Court's dramatic right-to-counsel cases of the 1960's;[64] greeted what is probably the most far-reaching social policy decision of the century—the unanimous desegregation case of *Brown* v. *Board of Education*;[65] and engulfed the Court's contentious holdings in the emotion-charged *Abortion Cases* of 1973 and 1976.[66]

Ox-Goring? The *Brown* case, however, raises the intriguing— if rather obvious—point that much of the criticism of the Court in the judging-legislating dichotomy is a direct reaction to the goring of personal oxen. The emotion-charged problems of racial desegregation and integration are tailor-made for such a charge. Thus, the earlier counterparts of those most vehement in their attack on the Court for "outrageous judicial usurpation of legislative power" in 1954 had lauded the Court a century before when it decided the famous case of *Dred Scott* v. *Sanford*[67] "their" way! And the partisans of the 1954 *Brown* decision had been conversely denunciatory

---

[62] 369 U.S. 186 (1962).
[63] *Wesberry* v. *Sanders*, 376 U.S. 1 (1964).
[64] E.g., *Gideon* v. *Wainwright*, 372 U.S. 335 (1963); *Escobedo* v. *Illinois*, 378 U.S. 478 (1964); and, especially, *Miranda* v. *Arizona* 384 U.S. 436 (1966).
[65] 347 U.S. 483 (1954).
[66] *Roe* v. *Wade*, 410 U.S. 113 and *Doe* v. *Bolton*, 410 U.S. 179 (1973) and *Planned Parenthood of Missouri* v. *Danforth*, 44 LW 5197 (1976). Cf. *Beal* v. *Doe* and *Poelker* v. *Doe* (June 20, 1977).
[67] 19 Howard 393 (1857). The case featured nine opinions, Mr. Chief Justice Taney delivering the principal one, Justices Curtis and McLean dissenting. Taney's opinion for the Court held, a.o., that no Negro could be a citizen; that the Negro was a person of "an inferior order"; that he was a slave and thus his master's permanent property,

of *Dred Scott* in 1857. A myriad of similar illustrations quickly come to mind to lend substance to the basic charge that much of the criticism of the Court is sheer sophistry and ax-grinding. For another well-known area, one need only look to the avalanche of declarations of unconstitutionality of New Deal legislation by the pre-1937 Court on sundry constitutional grounds (thirteen of these coming between 1934 and 1936) when the majority of the justices, backed by the foes of the New Deal, insisted that all they did was "to lay the article of the Constitution which is invoked beside the statute which is challenged" and then decided "whether the latter squares with the former." In the thirteen cases just alluded to, the New Deal laws never seemed to "square" in the eyes of Justice Van Devanter, Sutherland, McReynolds, and Butler, and frequently not in those of Chief Justice Hughes and Justice Roberts. Yet they almost always did seem to "square" in the eyes of Justices Brandeis, Stone, and Cardozo. Now who had the better "eyes" and what does the verb "to square" mean? Considerable subjectivity attends the problem, primarily on the part of those whose own ox is being gored, but also on the part of the justices themselves. Still, any interpretation that dismissed the basic argument as one of a purely personal-interest nature is guilty of considerable oversimplification of a highly vexatious and significant issue.

Judicial "Monks or Scientists"?   One thing is clear: judges are judges, but they are also men, not "disembodied spirits." In the words of Justice Frankfurter, a principal apostle of judicial self-restraint, "as men, they respond to human situations. They do not reside in a vacuum." Justice McReynolds insisted characteristically that a jurist cannot and should not be "an amorphous dummy, unspotted by human emotions." As Chief Justice Warren wrote, "our judges are not monks or scientists, but participants in the living stream of our national life, steering the law between the dangers of rigidity on the one hand and formlessness on the other."[68] He thus echoed

---

no matter whether the latter took him to free or slave territory; and that the Missouri Compromise was unconstitutional.

[68] "The Law and the Future," 52 *Fortune* 106 (November 1955).

the realistic appraisal four decades earlier by Thomas Reed Powell, who had observed that "[j]udges have preferences for social policies as you and I. They form their judgments after the varying fashions in which you and I form ours. They have hands, organs, dimensions, senses, affections, passions. They are warmed by the same winter and summer and by the same ideas as a layman is."[69] In interpreting our basic document, judges do, of course, "legislate," a fact of judicial life recognized "without hesitation" by Justice Holmes when he wrote that, indeed, jurists "do and must legislate." He, like his successors, Cardozo and Frankfurter, fully believed in judicial self-abnegation. But, he added—and it is a "but" crucial to the issue under discussion—they can legislate "only interstitially; they are confined from molar to molecular motions."[70] These motions are rigidly circumscribed by walls that are unseen by the layman, walls built of the heritage of the taught tradition of the law. No one expressed this at once more pungently and beautifully than Justice Cardozo who, after acknowledging that "the great tides and currents which engulf the rest of men, do not turn aside in their course, and pass the judges idly by,"[71] wisely explained that a jurist

is not to innovate at pleasure. He is not a knight-errant, roaming at will in pursuit of his own ideal of beauty or of goodness. He is to draw his inspiration from consecrated principles. He is not to yield to spasmodic sentiment, to vague and unregulated benevolence. He is to exercise a discretion informed by tradition, methodized by analogy, disciplined by system, and subordinated to "the primordial necessity of order in the social life."[72]

Guidelines of the Taught Tradition of the Law. The "consecrated principles" of which Justice Cardozo spoke are part and parcel of the taught tradition of the law, which guides

---

[69]"The Logic and Rhetoric of Constitutional Law," 15 *Journal of Philosophy, Psychology, and Scientific Method* 656 (1918).

[70]*Southern Pacific Co.* v. *Jensen*, 244 U.S. 205 (1916), at 221.

[71]*The Nature of the Judicial Process* (New Haven: Yale University Press, 1921), p. 168.

[72]*Ibid.*, p. 141.

and motivates the judges in their decisions. Many facets combine to bring this tradition and these principles of life, and although they are almost inevitably interpreted along somewhat divergent lines by different judges (of whom Justices Black and Frankfurter are excellent illustrations), they *are* ascertainable. There is that abiding sense of judicial integrity that comes with the robe; a consciousness of precedent; rules of procedure; recognition of the Court's threefold role as a governmental, political, and legal institution; the presumption of constitutionality of legislation; an awareness of membership in the body politic, of the responsibility of not being too far out of step with consensus—certainly not in the *long* run; the concept of equality before the law and at the bar of the Supreme Court. A few words of explanation for some of these guidelines, particularly those of a policy-procedure nature are in order:

1. *Adherence to Precedent.* As a principle of judicial policy, adherence to precedent—the doctrine of *stare decisis et quieta non movere* ("let the decision stand and do not disturb the calm")—is obviously both necessary and desirable. It is normally accepted as a rule of thumb unless there is clear reason for change. This, of course, requires a careful weighing of alternatives available, for it often comes down to a choice of precedents. Precedents abound, and not all precedents are of equal rank. Lord Coke lauded ". . . the known certaintie of the law [which] is the saftie of all. . . ." but he was neither adverse to overturning precedent nor to manufacturing one. Indeed, we must not expect what Chief Justice Hughes called "the icy stratosphere of certainty." According to Justice Brandeis, *stare decisis*

> is usually the wise policy because in most matters it is more important that the applicable rule of law be settled than that it be settled right. . . . This is commonly true even where the error is a matter of serious concern, provided correction can be had by legislation. *But in cases involving the Federal Constitution, where correction through legislation is practically impossible, this Court has often overruled its earlier decisions.* The Court bows to the lessons of experience and the force of better reasoning, recognizing that the process of trial

and error, so fruitful in the physical sciences is appropriate also in the judicial function.[73]

And, in so doing, the Court both "judges" and "legislates." In the wistful words of Justice Stewart, endeavoring to explain his change of mind vis-à-vis precedent in an important labor case: "Wisdom too often never comes, and so one ought not to reject it merely because it comes late."[74]

2. *Procedural Guidelines.* Organized, predictable procedure is of the essence to any judicial body, and particularly to the highest tribunal, for the vast majority of its work, and certainly its *raison d'être*, is appellate. Hence: (a) A definite *"case"* or *"controversy"* at law or in equity between bona fide adversaries under the Constitution, involving the protection or enforcement of valuable legal rights, or the punishment, prevention, or redress of wrongs directly concerning the party or parties bringing suit, must exist before the Court will entertain its consideration. (b) The party or parties bringing suit must have *standing.* This requires proof that he who brings suit is personally and substantially injured by a statute or governmental action or is in substantial danger of such injury, and/or that he is a member of the class or group to whom the action or statute applies. (c) As was already explained in Chapter I, the federal constitutional judiciary may not render *advisory opinions.* This matter was settled as early as 1793, when Chief Justice Jay told President Washington that he would not answer certain questions put to him by the chief executive because the Court could not tender legal advice since its role was confined to decisions of cases that arose in the course of bona fide legislation. (d) The Court will not entertain generalities, which means that a petitioner must not only invoke a specific clause of the Constitution but that the matter to be litigated must comprise a specific *live* constitutional issue. (e) The Court will not pass on the constitutionality of a statute or official action at the behest

---

[73] *Burnett* v. *Coronado Oil and Gas Co.*, 285 U.S. 293 (1932). (Italics supplied.)

[74] *Boys Market* v. *Retail Clerks' Union*, 398 U.S. 235 (1970), at 255. In fact, he quoted Justice Frankfurter—one of the staunchest adherents to precedent—in *Henslee* v. *Union Planters Bank*, 335 U.S. 595 (1949), at 600.

of one who has *availed himself of its benefits,* but subsequently decided to challenge its legality. (f) Prior to making
applications for review, *all remedies below must have been
exhausted* in prescribed lower court procedure, scrupulously
followed. (g) The federal question raised at the bar of the
Court must be *substantial* rather than trivial, must be the
pivotal point of the case, and must be a part of the plaintiff's
case rather than a part of his opponent's defense. (h) Although it is axiomatic that "matters of law grow downward
into roots of fact, and matters of fact reach upward, without
a break, into matters of law,"[75] it is true as a matter of
policy-procedure that the Supreme Court, as an appellate
tribunal, will not normally accept matters of *fact* rather than
those of *law* for bases of review.

3. *Presumption of Constitutionality of Legislation.*
Even if the challenge to a legislative enactment is entirely
valid and proper, the Court—true to its role as a judicial
rather than a law-making body—*will presume its constitutionality.* If it must meet the constitutional issue per se—
something it will try hard to avoid in line with its dedication
to uphold rather than destroy the will of the law-making
majority—it will, as Chief Justice Hughes put it so cogently in
1937, at a critical moment in the Court's history, endeavor to

> save and not to destroy. We have repeatedly held that as
> between two possible interpretations of a statute, by
> one of which it would be unconstitutional and the other
> valid, our plain duty is to adopt that which will save the
> act. Even to avoid a serious doubt the rule is the
> same.[76]

It follows logically, then, that if a case or controversy can
conceivably be decided upon *any other than on constitutional grounds*—such as by statutory construction, which
constitutes the greatest single area of the Court's work, or if
it can rest on an independent state ground—the Court will
normally be more than eager to decide it thus. "The most

---

[75] John Dickinson, *Administrative Justice and the Supremacy of
Law* (Cambridge: Harvard University Press, 1927), p. 55.
[76] *National Labor Relations Board* v. *Jones and Laughlin Steel
Corporation,* 301 U.S. 1.

important thing we do is *not* doing," said Justice Brandeis once in this connection, and the Court has thus saved itself many a battle with Congress. In fact, it is here that the Court, to an important degree, can have its cake and eat it too, for statutory construction may well mean that the teeth of a law are being pulled even while the appearance *cum* illusion of its existence remains. For example, when the Court ruled in *Yates* v. *United States*[77] that the theoretical advocacy of the overthow of the government by force and violence was not a violation of the Smith Act of 1940, it went to great lengths to point out that it had *not* overruled its landmark decision of six years earlier upholding that statute in *Dennis* v. *United States*,[78] but that it merely construed and interpreted its meaning. Thus the Act per se still stood against First and Fifth Amendment challenges, but in construing the essential difference between "theoretical advocacy" and "advocacy in the realm of action," the Court had in effect amended the Smith Act and rendered convictions under it by the government far more difficult. Its author, veteran Congressman Howard Smith (D.-Va.), protested on the floor of the House that the Court had misconstrued congressional intent; yet with the exception of a relatively minor amendment involving the meaning and extent of the verb "organize," Congress failed to do anything to alter the Court's ruling. Any search for congressional "intent or purpose" inevitably becomes somewhat of an exercise in psychoanalysis and, as Justice Cardozo once observed acidly, "a great principle of constitutional law is not susceptible of comprehensive statement in an adjective."[79]

Be that as it may, the Court will not ordinarily impute illegal motives to the lawmakers. But it is inevitable that different interpretations will be put upon the Court's policy of deference to the legislature, especially when, as illustrated above, statutory construction all but accomplishes the decimation of law while holding aloft its shell. It is hence not surprising that even on the Court itself, those in the minority

---

[77] 354 U.S. 298 (1957).
[78] 341 U.S. 494 (1951).
[79] *Carter* v. *Carter Coal Co.*, 298 U.S. 238 (1936), at 327, dissenting opinion.

will frequently accuse the majority of ignoring the will of Congress by indulging in judicial legislating. A contemporary example is the dissenting opinion of Justice Clark in a 5:4 decision, in which the majority held that a resident Swiss alien, one George E. M. Fleuti, who had left the country "briefly and casually," did not, on his return, make an "entry" of the kind that under the congressional statute at issue in the case could subject him to deportation for "pre-entry misbehavior." With dripping sarcasm, Clark began his dissenting opinion as follows:

I dissent from the Court's judgment and opinion be-cause "statutory construction" means to me that the Court can *construe* but not that it can *construct* them. The latter function is reserved to the Congress.[80]

The words "construe" and "construct" were pointedly un-derlined. Naturally, the majority's interpretation or construc-tion was and is always subject to change by Congress, which can, in effect, pass a law saying "We did not mean what you said we did; *here* is what we *really* meant." But although this is done from time to time it is the exception rather than the rule; for, temperamentally, Congress is normally quick to criticize but slow to act—which indubitably lends itself to the interpretation that the Court may well have been right in its judgment in the first place.

It is of the highest importance to recognize that, as a matter of fundamental policy, the Court brings a genuine sense of deference to the legislative will; but there are limits, and in some areas these limits are now reached earlier than in others. *Prior* to 1937—to use the most obvious illustration of the point—that limit was reached by a majority of the Court rather quickly in the realm of substantive due process as applied to economic-proprietarian and social legislation grow-ing out of the experimental programs of the New National-ism, the New Freedom, and the New Deal. Yet infinite restraint was shown regarding governmental enactments or practices concerning the cultural freedoms in the Bill of

---

[80] *Rosenberg* v. *Fleuti*, 374 U.S. 449 (1963). Justice Clark was joined in this dissent by Justices Harlan, Stewart, and White.

Rights. Conversely, the *post-1937* Court majority turned the tables on the limit-line dramatically and drastically: since that time it has been almost impossible for government, state as well as federal, to do "wrong" in the realm of economic-proprietarian and social legislation—yet it is constantly in hot water with the Court regarding the Bill of Rights and the due process and equal protection of the laws clauses of the Fourteenth Amendment. Having made this essential point of judicial metamorphosis, it remains true that, by and large, the Supreme Court of the United States insists that it is not designed either to serve as a check against inept, unwise, emotional, narrowminded legislators—or against unwise, unfair, silly, poor, injudicious, stupid, even undemocratic legislation or executive-administrative action. The cardinal question for the Court is always, and must always remain: "Is it legal? Is it constitutional? Can it stand?" It is not easy to stand aloof in the face of legislation and actions that offend the mind and heart—but with that, in the words of the judicial philosopher *par excellence* of our age, Justice Holmes, "we have no [official judicial] concern."[81] No one made the point more eloquently than Justice Frankfurter, when, writing in dissent, he warned:

> It is not easy to stand aloof and allow want of wisdom to prevail, to disregard one's own strongly held view of what is wise in the conduct of affairs. But it is not the business of this Court to pronounce policy. It must observe a fastidious regard for limitations on its own power, and this precludes the Court's giving effect to its own notions of what is wise or politic. That self-restraint is of the essence in the observation of the judicial oath, for the Constitution has not authorized the justices to sit in judgment on the wisdom of what Congress and the executive branch do. . . .[82]

This, of course, is another way of reiterating the point made by Chief Justice Waite more than eighty years earlier in the landmark case of *Munn* v. *Illinois*,[83] where he wrote that for

---

[81] *Noble State Bank* v. *Haskell*, 219 U.S. 575 (1910).
[82] *Trop* v. *Dulles*, 356 U.S. 86 (1958).
[83] 94 U.S. 113 (1876).

"protection against abuses by legislatures the people must resort to the polls not the courts." Or, to turn to the more contemporary statement by Justice Harlan, writing in his now famous dissent in *Reynolds* v. *Sims* in 1964: "The Constitution is not a panacea for every blot upon the public welfare; nor should this Court, ordained as a judicial body, be thought of as a general haven for reform movements."[84]

JUDICIAL ACTIVISM AND JUDICIAL RESTRAINT: MORE ON "LINES"

It is easy and appropriate to agree with the basic philosophy of judicial self-restraint, but it cannot settle the concurrent interpretative problem of finding that line when the "Constitution expressly forbids." It cannot settle it by any ready and easy formula, for no formula, other than the basic commitment to judicial self-restraint, is either discernible or devisable—and not even the many and energetic modern apostles of the scientific method and behavioralism can help us draw such a line. In essence, the matter comes back to individual interpretation by the jurists concerned. In the final analysis, it is the Supreme Court that must decide the ultimate constitutional question—and, as we have seen again and again, it does so often only because the other two branches, and notably the legislature, have failed or refused to perform their jobs and have passed the proverbial "buck" to the Court. Now the Court can, of course, continue that game, but there comes a time when it will refuse to play and, rising to its responsibility as it conceives of it, will tackle the issue, no matter how delicate, or how violent the public response. Obvious examples are the controversies involving desegregation, criminal justice, and legislative redistricting. In accepting the challenge and in deciding the emotion-charged, difficult public issues and policies involved, the Court indeed did judge *and* legislate. Perhaps it did so because, as ex-Attorney General Francis Biddle often suggested, these com-

---

[84] 377 U.S. 533, at 624.

prise the areas of the "can't helps." But, above all, it did so because it *is* the guardian and interpreter of the Constitution; a Constitution, in Chief Justice Marshall's words, "intended to endure for ages to come and, consequently, to be adapted to the various crises of human affairs,"[85] a Constitution that, as Justice Holmes stated, must ever be alive to "the felt necessities of the time."

Dichotomies. Not surprisingly, against this background various justices approach their tasks of judging and interpreting in such a way as to indicate radically different judicial philosophies. Vast oversimplification—and sometimes deliberate crass misinterpretation—has attended these manifestations of differences. Often lay and professional commentators on this basic problem have simply tried to explain it by classifying two "kinds" of justices on the bench: those they deem to be "liberals" and those they deem "conservative." Two less helpful, less accurate, and more confusing classifications can hardly be imagined! For just *who* is being so classified, and *why*? Broadly speaking, the tag "liberal" has been given to those justices on the post-1930 Court who have been willing to give a generous interpretation to the Bill of Rights and the Civil War Amendments, on the one hand, and have consistently upheld governmental legislation in the socioeconomic realm, on the other (e.g., Justices Holmes, Brandeis, Stone, Cardozo, Black, Douglas, Murphy, Rutledge, Warren, Brennan, Goldberg, Marshall). The label "conservative" has been awarded to those who have variously given less generous interpretations *either* in one *or* in both of these areas (e.g., Justices Van Devanter, McReynolds, Butler, Sutherland, Hughes, Roberts, Frankfurter, Reed, Jackson, Burton, Byrnes, Vinson, Minton, Clark, Whittaker, Harlan, Jr., Stewart, White, Burger, Blackmun, Powell, Rehnquist). A more facile oversimplification is hardly imaginable!

True, the "quads" (Van Devanter, Sutherland, McReynolds, and Butler) did predictably and consistently vote together to strike down almost every piece of socioeconomic experimentation that came before them—and they were

---

[85] *McCulloch v. Maryland,* 4 Wheaton 316 (1819).

often, but not always, joined by Hughes and Roberts. But it was Hughes and Roberts who exercised the 1937 "switch-in-time-that-saved-nine"—whatever their contentious motivations may have been in fact. Moreover, Van Devanter and Sutherland had a much more "liberal" outlook on the exercise of executive power, especially in foreign affairs, than did McReynolds and Butler, *and* the former two would often vote to support First and Fourteenth Amendment claims, whereas McReynolds and Butler rarely did. True also that Justices Frankfurter, Reed, Jackson, and Burton practiced considerably more judicial self-restraint in constitutional questions concerning the Bill of Rights than their brothers Black, Douglas, Murphy, and Rutledge, to use obvious examples. *But,* they were equally as "liberal" as the latter four when it came to the upholding of governmental legislation and regulation in the socioeconomic sphere. To indicate further the folly of tags "liberal" and "conservative," Justice Jackson's Bill of Rights record *before* he went to Nürnberg as Chief Prosecutor for the United States in the War Crimes Trials was decidedly more "liberal" in the First Amendment area than *after* his return. Justice Clark was generally regarded as a "conservative" on civil liberty questions by the critics, but he had a "liberal" record in the majority of First Amendment cases—other than those in the area of "national security." Clearly, the "liberal" versus "conservative" dichotomy is as unhelpful as it is inaccurate and confusing.

Judicial "Activism" versus "Restraint."   More helpful classifications, if we must have them, are those jurists who are regarded as adhering to a judicial philosophy of "self-restraint"[86] versus those who are styled "activists." The former's juris-

---

[86] Professor Philip Kurland makes six basic assumptions for the doctrine of judicial self-restraint:

"One is history and the obligation that constitutionalism imposes to adhere to the essential meaning put in the document by its framers. A second is the intrinsically undemocratic nature of the Supreme Court. A third is a corollary to the second, an abiding respect for the judgments of those branches of the government that are elected representatives of their constituents. A fourth is the recognition that judicial error at this level is more difficult of correction than other forms of judicial action. A fifth is respect for the judgments of earlier courts. But [sixth], the essential feature of judicial restraint that has gained prudence adheres to a "legal positivist" approach, the latter's to that of a "legal realist." In short, the "self-restrainters" will bend over backwards to permit the political branches of the government to act or not to act or to have the upper hand, even in areas of marginal constitutionality, provided that the action (or legislation) is not *really* a violation of the Constitution *as they see it*. The "activists" on the other hand believe in a more affirmative, some would say aggressive judicial policy, and are more ready to say "No" to governmental enactments and actions because they would normally more quickly see a constitutional violation by the political branches. Moreover, unlike the "self-restrainters," the "activists" would be inclined to "legislate," to "make policy." This was the case, or so the charge goes, in the highly significant 1962 case of *Baker* v. *Carr*,[87] for example, when the Supreme Court held the question of state apportionment and redistricting to be justiciable at the bar of the courts. In that 6:2 decision, the opinion was written by Justice Brennan ("moderate activist"), joined by the chief justice ("activist"), Justice Black ("qualified activist"), and Justice Stewart ("moderate self-restrainter"); it was concurred in by separate opinions by Justice Douglas ("advanced activist") and Justice Clark ("moderate self-restrainter"); and lengthy dissenting opinions were filed by Justices Frankfurter and Harlan (both "self-restrainters"). The position of the latter two is symptomatic of the basic cleavage in judicial philosophies: Frankfurter and Harlan insisted that the majority had usurped legislative functions; had entered the "political thicket"; had accepted a "political question" for review; and would thus find itself involved in a "mathematical quagmire."

Yet if the "line-up" in *Baker* v. *Carr* illustrates that Court's division on the question of involvement (Justice Whittaker did not participate in the case), it also illustrates the difficulty of labels—even here—for what labels do we now

---

most attention and aroused the greatest doubts probably because few men are themselves big enough to abide by its command—is the notion of rejection of personal preference." (Philip B. Kurland, *Mr. Justice Frankfurter and the Supreme Court* [Chicago: University of Chicago Press, 1971], p. 5.)

[87] 369 U.S. 186.

give Justices Clark and Stewart? Moreover, *each* and every one of the above justices—and certainly not exempting Justice Douglas, the chief villain-example in the eyes of those who abhor "activism"—would deserve the label "self-restrainter" regarding governmental action in the socioeconomic sphere!

Categorizations. What it comes down to basically, then, is the position of the justices on the question of *when* the Court should enter the field to say "No." There is no question that Justices Black and Douglas, for example, generally said "No" long before Justices Frankfurter and Harlan did in the realm of most, but by no means all, provisions of the Bill of Rights. In that sense, we are thus confronted by two jurisprudential poles—Black and Douglas being characterizable as "activists" (although they often split, Douglas the avowedly far more advanced, except in the realms of speech and press[88]), Frankfurter and Harlan philosophical devotees of British majority rule and legislative supremacy, "self-restrainters." Ironically, this gives the Black-Douglas group the same label as the Sutherland-Van Devanter-Butler-McReynolds group of the 1930's, since the latter practiced obvious "activism" in the economic realm. Yet in varying degree they, especially McReynolds and Butler, were "self-restrainters" in civil liberties! It must be made crystal clear, however, that Black, for one, vehemently and eloquently rejected any and all "labelling" until the day he died in 1971, after more than thirty-four years of distinguished service on the Supreme Court,[89] and that, moreover, his libertarian creed was operative only if he found *literal* (specifically expressed) warrant for it in the Constitution's verbiage.

---

[88] Yet even here Black was willing to proscribe *conduct,* as distinct from *expression,* whereas Douglas rarely, if ever, did. See for example, the demonstration and/or "sit-in" cases of *Brown* v. *Louisiana,* 383 U.S. 131 (1966) and *Adderley* v. *Florida,* 385 U.S. 39 (1966). Two other dramatic splits between the two, with Douglas siding with the individual, were the "black armband" and "fuck the draft" cases of *Tinker* v. *Des Moines Independent Community School District,* 393 U.S. 503 (1969) and *Cohen* v. *California,* 403 U.S. 15 (1971), respectively. Harlan sided with Black in the former but with Douglas in the latter! Lines *are* elusive.

[89] See his *A Constitutional Faith* (New York: Alfred A. Knopf, 1968), pp. 15–22.

Although it *is* possible to find these two broadly divergent philosophies of law on the bench, and although it *is* evident that the two poles are identifiable *in certain areas*—that they do exist, and that they are even predictable to an extent—any explanation that would label the Black-Douglas group as judging with its "heart" and the Frankfurter-Harlan group with its "head" is a gross oversimplification. In the final analysis it comes down to a basic difference of reading constitutional commands in the light of the judicial function (and there are remarkable differences *within* each group[90]). To conclude with the classic illustration of the First Amendment, Justice Black read as an *absolute* injunction against governmental action the words: "Congress shall make no law . . . abridging the freedom of speech, or of the press; . . ." To him and his followers this is indeed an absolute—"No to me means no," as he said so often. Yet in the eyes of Justice Frankfurter—whom Yale Law Professor Fred Rodell called "the Emily Post of the Supreme Court"—and his followers, no matter how unwise a law in the area may be, it must stand in line with the canons of judicial self-restraint. As he put the matter in his concurring opinion in *Dennis* v. *United States*, upholding the Smith Act of 1940 against First and Fifth Amendment challenges:

> . . . The demands of free speech in a democratic society as well as the interest in national security are better served by candid and informed weighing of the competing interests, within the confines of the judicial process, than by announcing dogmas too inflexible for the non-Euclidian problems to be solved. . . . [But] full responsibility for the choice cannot be given to the courts. Courts are not representative bodies. They are not designed to be a good reflex of a democratic society. Their judgment is best informed, and therefore most dependable, within narrow limits. Their essential quality is detachment, founded on independence.[91]

Black agreed with much of the five last sentences and he wholeheartedly concurred insofar as the philosophy, stated

---

[90] See fn. 88, supra.
[91] 341 U.S. 494 (1951).

so cogently by Frankfurter, applied to the socioeconomic realm. But he dissented vigorously from the "balancing" theme of the opening passages. To Black and his followers, freedom of expression—provided it is that and not proscribable "conduct"—(a) is not balanceable, for it is an absolute; and (b) its constitutionality is peculiarly the province of the judicial branch whose responsibility it is to safeguard that matrix of all freedoms.

The Court and Public Policy

In spite of the above considerations, several important facts of judicial life point to a cardinal lesson of the Court's role in the legal, political, and governmental process: *The Court may have the last say, but potentially it has the last say only for a time.* The Supreme Court's only genuine power is the power to persuade—purse and sword are in other hands. The Court may be reversed in a variety of ways, and this has frequently been done. Thus, it may be reversed, totally or partly, *by legislative action*—as it was, for example, when Congress granted E. I. du Pont de Nemours and Co., Inc., legislative relief[92] after the firm had lost twice at the bar of the Supreme Court in an involved and expensive stock acquisition and holding matter.[93] It may *reverse itself by overruling* an earlier decision—as it did when it unanimously upheld the wage-and-hour provisions of the Fair Labor Standards Act of 1938 in *United States* v. *Darby*[94] in 1941, specifically overruling its earlier decision which struck down 5:4 a similar congressional enactment in 1918 in *Hammer* v. *Dagenhart.*[95] It may alter an earlier decision by *distinguishing or modifying it,* thus in effect reversing itself, as it did so exasperatingly in the five *Covert-Krueger* cases[96] between 1955 and 1960—

[92] Public Law 87–403, signed by President Kennedy on February 2, 1962, known as the Williams-Bennett bill.
[93] *United States* v. *E. I. du Pont de Nemours and Co.,* 353 U.S. 586 (1957) and 366 U.S. 316 (1961).
[94] 312 U.S. 100.
[95] 247 U.S. 251.
[96] *Kinsella* v. *Krueger,* 371 U.S. 470 and *Reid* v. *Covert,* U.S. 487 (June 11, 1956); ditto, 352 U.S. 901 (November 5, 1956); ditto, 354 U.S. 1 (June 10, 1957); *Kinsella* v. *Singleton,* 361 U.S. 234 and *Grisham* v. *Hagan,* 361 U.S. 278 (January 18, 1960).

here by no means solely, or even predominantly, due to changes in membership on the Court, as has been true in many instances. And, finally, the Court's judgment may be effectively reversed by the *passage of a constitutional amendment*, which was accomplished with the enactment of Amendments Eleven, Thirteen, Fourteen, Fifteen, Sixteen, Nineteen, Twenty-four, and Twenty-six.[97] If not without some toil and trouble, the Supreme Court may thus be overruled by other forces of government, headed by Congress, or it may overrule itself. Most of its decisions do "stick," but quite a few are rendered moot.

In Step. There is no doubt that, generally speaking, the policy of the Court—whose members, after all, are "children of their times"—never departs drastically from the policy of the law-making majority *in the long run.* Notable exceptions are decisions involving the Bill of Rights, especially Amendments One and Five, and the egalitarian and due process facets of the Fourteenth—exceptions clearly demonstrated during 1940–1949, 1954–1957, and again markedly since 1962, although less so in the criminal justice sector with the advent of the Burger Court of the early 1970's. *In the short run*, the Court has often been out of step with that law-making majority, but there it either succeeded in its short-run educational mission or it "came around" in the long run; and, in the appropriate words of Edward S. Corwin, "the run must not be too long a run, either!" The justices, in the timeless observation of Alexis de Tocqueville of over a century ago, do indeed possess enormous power, "but it is the power of public opinion"—although the Court must be a leader of it, not merely its register. The Supreme Court is quite conscious of the overall exhortation, well expressed by Francis Biddle, that "we must not get away too far from life, and should continually touch the earth for renewed vitality."[98]   If the

---

[97]The Eleventh concerned the original jurisdiction of the Court; Thirteen, Fourteen, and Fifteen were the Civil War Amendments; Sixteen, the Income Tax; Nineteen, Women Suffrage; Twenty-four, the Poll Tax, and Twenty-six, the 18-year-old vote in state and local as well as federal elections.
[98]Biddle, *op. cit.*, p. 73.

Court is to thrive, it must, in line with Professor Wallace Mendelson's admonition, "respect the social forces that determine elections and other major political settlements. No court can long withstand the morals of its era."[99] The Court is much better at saying what the government *may* or *may not* do than at prescribing what it *must* do and *how* it must go about doing it. Indeed, the Court should resolutely shun prescriptive policy-making.

The Custodian. Nonetheless, the Supreme Court of the United States must play its role as educator and legitimator-arbiter—it must remain true to its function as teacher in an eternal national constitutional seminar. No other branch can fill that role. It acts, in the words of one commentator, "as the instrument of national moral values that have not been able to find other governmental expressions" [100] —always assuming, of course, that it functions within its authorized sphere of constitutional and statutory application and interpretation. Thus, it defines values and proclaims principles and—as our "sober second thought" [101] —is the natural forum in our society for the individual and for the small group. "The Court's essential function," wrote Chief Justice Warren tellingly in 1968, "is to act as the final arbiter of minority rights." [102] It is simply the greatest institutional safeguard we possess. Despite the storms that have buffeted and whipped it, it has remained our national conscience as well as our institutional common sense. And, as Justice Robert H. Jackson told his countrymen in *The Supreme Court in the American System of Government*, [103] the small but superb book that became his epitaph:

---

[99] *Justices Black and Frankfurter: Conflict in the Court* (Chicago: University of Chicago Press, 1961), pp. 75–76. See also Robert A. Dahl, "The Supreme Court and Majority Control," in his *Pluralist Democracy in the United States: Conflict and Consent* (Chicago: Rand McNally & Co., 1967), pp. 154–170.

[100] Anthony Lewis, *The New York Times Magazine*, June 17, 1962, p. 38.

[101] Charles L. Black, Jr., *The People and the Court: Judicial Review in a Democracy* (New York: The Macmillan Co., 1960), p. 12.

[102] As quoted in *The Philadelphia Inquirer*, October 4, 1968, p. 2.

[103] Cambridge: Harvard University Press, 1965.

The people have seemed to feel that the Supreme Court, whatever its defects, is still the most detached, dispassionate, and trustworthy custodian that our system affords for the translation of abstract into concrete constitutional commands.[104]

As such, it continues to fulfill the fascinating, crucial, however, delicate, role of heeding the "felt necessities of the time," while holding aloft the proud banner of constitutional fundamentals.

---

[104] *Ibid.*, p. 23.

For Further Reading

There is a wealth of background reading available to the student of constitutional law, the judicial process, and civil rights and liberties. Space permits the listing of but a very few of the many important ones among these. (* denotes availability in paperback.)

*Abraham, Henry J., *Freedom and the Court: Civil Rights and Liberties in the United States*, 3rd ed. (New York: Oxford University Press, 1977). Expository-analytical treatment of the problem of freedom and the role of the Supreme Court.

*Beard, Charles A., *The Supreme Court and the Constitution* (Englewood Cliffs, N.J.: Prentice-Hall, Inc., 1938). Still the most persuasive explanation in print for the authenticity of judicial review.

Beveridge, Albert J., *The Life of John Marshall* (Boston: Houghton Mifflin Co., 1916). The most significant biographical study of a Supreme Court member to date; provides keen insights in a historical framework.

Black, Hugo L., *A Constitutional Faith* (New York: Alfred A. Knopf, 1968). Written as a valedictory work, it shines with first principles and the touching faith of one of America's greatest constitutionalists.

*Cardozo, Benjamin N., *The Nature of the Judicial Process* (New Haven: Yale University Press, 1921). Probably the

most important single work ever written on the subject.
A "must."

*Chafee, Zechariah, Jr., *Free Speech in the United States* (Cambridge: Harvard University Press, 1941). Still *the* classic in the field. (Reprinted in 1967.)

Clark, Ramsey, *Crime in America: Observations on its Nature, Causes, Prevention and Control* (New York: Simon & Schuster, 1970). A recent Attorney-General of the United States reports, evaluates, summarizes.

*Corwin, Edward S., *The Higher Law Background of American Constitutional Law* (Ithaca: Cornell University Press, 1929). Superb analysis of the historical-theoretical foundations of the topic.

Cox, Archibald, *The Role of the Supreme Court in American Government* (New York: Oxford University Press, 1976). Excellent summary by Harvard's authority on constitutional law (and the first "Watergate" Special Prosecutor).

Harris, Robert J., *The Quest for Equality* (Baton Rouge: Louisiana State University Press, 1960). One of the few trenchant and analytical studies of the meaning and range of the equal protection clause—an "action" call.

*Jackson, Robert H., *The Supreme Court in the American System of Government* (Cambridge: Harvard University Press, 1955). A brief, but superb analysis of the Court as a legal, political, and governmental institution.

Kelly, A. H., and W. A. Harbison, *The American Constitution—Its Origin and Development*, 5th ed. (New York: W. W. Norton and Co., 1976). The best historical-analytical study of constitutional development extant.

Lusky, Louis, *By What Right?: A Commentary on the Supreme Court's Right to Revise the Constitution* (Charlottesville, Va.: The Michie Co., 1975). A trenchant critical analysis and evaluation of the Court's policy-making role by a leading, veteran observer.

*McCloskey, Robert G., *The Modern Supreme Court*, (Cambridge: Harvard University Press, 1972). The best brief history of the Court from the Stone Court through 1971. (Ed. by Martin Shapiro.)

Mason, Alpheus T., *The Supreme Court: Palladium of Freedom* (Ann Arbor: University of Michigan Press, 1962). A keen evaluation.

*Myrdahl, Gunnar, *An American Dilemma: The Negro Prob-

lem and Modern Democracy, rev. ed. (New York: Harper
& Row, 1962). Unquestionably still the most significant
study of the problem on record.

Stokes, Anson Phelps, *Church and State in the United
States*, condensed and edited by Leo Pfeffer (New York:
Harper & Row, 1964). The key work on the separation of
church and state, both historically and analytically—
albeit from a very controversial point of view.

Warren, Charles P., *The Supreme Court in United States
History*, rev. ed. (Boston: Little, Brown, 1937). Until the
promised new mammoth history of the Court is finished
(some volumes are now available), Warren's remains the
most authoritative.

APPENDIX

The Constitution
of the United States of America

We the people of the United States, in order to form a more perfect Union, establish Justice, insure domestic Tranquility, provide for the common defence, promote the general Welfare, and secure the Blessing of Liberty to ourselves and our Posterity, do ordain and establish this CONSTITUTION for the United States of America.

ARTICLE I

Section 1. All legislative Powers herein granted shall be vested in a Congress of the United States, which shall consist of a Senate and House of Representatives.

Section 2. The House of Representatives shall be composed of Members chosen every second Year by the People of the several States, and the Electors in each State shall have the Qualifications requisite for Electors of the most numerous Branch of the State Legislature.

No Person shall be a Representative who shall not have attained the Age of twenty-five Years, and been seven Years a Citizen of the United States, and who shall not, when elected, be an Inhabitant of that State in which he shall be chosen.

[Representatives and direct Taxes shall be apportioned among the several States which may be included within this Union, according to their respective Numbers, which shall be determined by adding to the whole Number of free Persons, including those bound to Service for a Term of Years, and excluding Indians not taxed, three-fifths of all other persons.][1] The actual Enumeration shall be made within three Years after the first Meeting of the Congress of the United States, and within every subsequent Term of ten Years, in such Manner as they shall by Law direct. The Number of Representatives shall not exceed one for every thirty thousand, but each State shall have at Least one Representative; and until such enumeration shall be made, the State of New Hampshire shall be entitled to chuse three, Massachusetts eight, Rhode Island and Providence Plantations one, Connecticut five, New York six, New Jersey four, Pennsylvania eight, Delaware one, Maryland six, Virginia ten, North Carolina five, South Carolina five, and Georgia three.

When vacancies happen in the Representation from any State, the Executive Authority thereof shall issue Writs of Election to fill such Vacancies.

The House of Representatives shall chuse their Speaker and other Officers; and shall have the sole Power of Impeachment.

Section 3. The Senate of the United States shall be composed of two Senators from each State, chosen by the Legislature thereof,[2] for six Years; and each Senator shall have one Vote.

Immediately after they shall be assembled in Consequence of the first Election, they shall be divided as equally as may be into three Classes. The Seats of the Senators of the first Class shall be vacated at the Expiration of the second Year, of the Second Class at the Expiration of the fourth

---

[1] This provision was modified by the Sixteenth Amendment. The three-fifths reference to slaves was rendered obsolete by the Thirteenth and Fourteenth Amendments.

[2] See the Seventeenth Amendment.

Year, and the third Class at the Expiration of the sixth Year, so that one-third may be chosen every second Year; and if Vacancies happen by Resignation, or otherwise, during the Recess of the Legislature of any State, the Executive thereof may make temporary Appointments until the next Meeting of the Legislature, which shall then fill such Vacancies.

No Person shall be a Senator who shall not have attained to the Age of thirty Years, and been nine Years a Citizen of the United States, and who shall not, when elected, be an Inhabitant of that State for which he shall be chosen.

The Vice President of the United States shall be President of the Senate, but shall have no Vote, unless they be equally divided.

The Senate shall chuse their other Officers, and also a President pro tempore, in the absence of the Vice President, or when he shall exercise the Office of President of the United States.

The Senate shall have the sole Power to try all Impeachments. When sitting for that Purpose, they shall be on Oath or Affirmation. When the President of the United States is tried, the Chief Justice shall preside; And no Person shall be convicted without the Concurrence of two-thirds of the Members present.

Judgment in Cases of Impeachment shall not extend further than to removal from Office, and disqualification to hold and enjoy any Office of honor, Trust or Profit under the United States; but the Party convicted shall nevertheless be liable and subject to Indictment, Trial, Judgment and Punishment, according to Law.

Section 4. The Times, Places and Manner of holding Elections for Senators and Representatives, shall be prescribed in each State by the Legislature thereof; but the Congress may at any time by Law make or alter such Regulations, except as to the Places of chusing Senators.

The Congress shall assemble at least once in every Year, and such Meeting shall be on the first Monday in December, unless they shall by Law appoint a different Day.[3]

Section 5. Each House shall be the Judge of the Elec-

---

[3] See the Twentieth Amendment.

tions, Returns and Qualifications of its own Members, and a Majority of each shall constitute a Quorum to do Business; but a smaller Number may adjourn from day to day, and may be authorized to compel the Attendance of absent Members, in such Manner, and under such Penalties as each House may provide.

Each House may determine the Rules of its Proceedings, punish its Members for disorderly Behavior, and, with the Concurrence of two-thirds, expel a Member.

Each House shall keep a Journal of its Proceedings and from time to time publish the same, excepting such Parts as may in their Judgment require Secrecy; and the Yeas and Nays of the Members of either House on any question shall, at the Desire of one-fifth of those Present, be entered on the Journal.

Neither House, during the Session of Congress, shall without the Consent of the other, adjourn for more than three days, nor to any other Place than that in which the two Houses shall be sitting.

Section 6. The Senators and Representatives shall receive a Compensation for their Services, to be ascertained by Law, and paid out of the Treasury of the United States. They shall in all Cases, except Treason, Felony, and Breach of the peace, be privileged from Arrest during their Attendance at the Session of their respective Houses, and in going to and returning from the same; and for any Speech or Debate in either House, they shall not be questioned in any other Place.

No Senator or Representative shall, during the Time for which he was elected, be appointed to any civil Office under the Authority of the United States, which shall have been created, or the Emoluments whereof shall have been encreased during such time; and no Person holding any Office under the United States, shall be a Member of either House during his Continuance in Office.

Section 7. All Bills for raising Revenue shall originate in the House of Representatives; but the Senate may propose or concur with Amendments as on other Bills.

Every Bill which shall have passed the House of Representatives and the Senate, shall, before it become a Law, be presented to the President of the United States; If he approve he shall sign it, but if not he shall return it, with his Objections to that House in which it shall have originated, who shall enter the at large on their Journal, and proceed to reconsider it. If after such Reconsideration two-thirds of that House shall agree to pass the Bill it shall be sent, together with the Objections, to the other House, by which it shall likewise be reconsidered, and if approved by two-thirds of that House, it shall become a Law. But in all such Cases the Votes of both Houses shall be determined by Yeas and Nays, and the Names of the Persons voting to and against the Bill shall be entered on the Journal of each House respectively. If any Bill shall not be returned by the President within ten Days (Sundays excepted) after it shall have been presented to him, the Same shall be a Law, in like Manner as if he had signed it, unless the Congress by their Adjournment prevent its Return, in which Case it shall not be a Law.

Every Order, Resolution, or Vote to which the Concurrence of the Senate and House of Representatives may be necessary (except on a question of Adjournment) shall be presented to the President of the United States: and before the Same shall take Effect, shall be approved by him, or being disapproved by him, shall be repassed by two-thirds of the Senate and House of Representatives, according to the Rules and Limitations prescribed in the Case of a Bill.

Section 8. The Congress shall have Power To lay and collect Taxes, Duties, Imposts and Excises, to pay the Debts and provide for the common Defence and general Welfare of the United States; but all Duties, Imposts and Excises shall be uniform throughout the United States;

To borrow money on the Credit of the United States;

To regulate Commerce with foreign Nations, and among the several States, and with the Indian Tribes;

To establish an uniform Rule of Naturalization, and uniform Laws on the subject of Bankruptcies throughout the United States.

To coin Money, regulate the Value thereof, and of foreign Coin, and fix the Standard of Weights and Measures;

To provide for the Punishment of counterfeiting the Securities and current Coin of the United States;

To establish Post Offices and post Roads;

To promote the Progress of Science and useful arts, by securing for limited Times to Authors and Inventors the exclusive Right to their respective Writings and Discoveries;

To constitute Tribunals inferior to the supreme Court;

To define and punish Piracies and Felonies committed on the high Seas, and Offenses against the Law of Nations;

To declare War, grant Letters of Marque and Reprisal, and make Rules concerning Captures on Land and Water;

To raise and support Armies, but no Appropriation of Money to that Use shall be for a longer Term than two Years;

To provide and maintain a Navy;

To make Rules for the Government and Regulation of the land and naval Forces;

To provide for calling forth the Militia to execute the Laws of the Union, suppress Insurrections and repel Invasions;

To provide for organizing, arming, and disciplining the Militia, and for governing such Part of them as may be employed in the Service of the United States, reserving to the States respectively, the Appointment of the Officers, and the Authority of training the Militia according to the discipline prescribed by Congress;

To exercise exclusive Legislation in all Cases whatsoever, over such District (not exceeding ten Miles square) as may, by Cession of particular States, and the acceptance of Congress, become the Seat of the Government of the United States, and to exercise like Authority over all Places purchased by the Consent of the Legislature of the State in which the Same shall be, for the Erection of Forts, Magazines, Arsenals, dock-Yards, and other needful Buildings;—And

To make all Laws which shall be necessary and proper for carrying into Execution the foregoing Powers, and all other Powers vested by this Constitution in the Government of the United States, or in any Department or Officer thereof.

Section 9.   The Migration or Importation of such Persons as any of the States now existing shall think proper to admit, shall not be prohibited by the Congress prior to the Year one thousand eight hundred and eight, but a tax or duty may be imposed on such importation, not exceeding ten dollars for each Person.

suspended, unless when in Cases of Rebellion or Invasion the public Safety may require it.

No Bill of Attainder or ex post facto Law shall be passed.

No capitation, or other direct Tax shall be laid, unless in Proportion to the Census or Enumeration herein before directed to be taken.[4]

No Tax or Duty shall be laid on Articles exported from any State.

No Preference shall be given by any Regulation of Commerce or Revenue to the Ports of one State over those of another; nor shall Vessels bound to, or from one State, be obliged to enter, clear, or pay Duties in another.

No Money shall be drawn from the Treasury, but in Consequence of Appropriations made by Law; and a regular Statement and Account of the Receipts and Expenditures of all public Money shall be published from time to time.

No Title of Nobility shall be granted by the United States: And no Person holding any Office of Profit or Trust under them, shall, without the Consent of the Congress, accept of any present, Emolument, Office, or Title, of any kind whatever, from any King, Prince, or foreign State.

Section 10.   No State shall enter into any Treaty, Alliance, or Confederation; grant Letters of Marque and Reprisal; coin Money; emit Bills of Credit; make any Thing but gold and silver Coin a Tender in Payment of Debts; pass any Bill of Attainder, ex post facto Law, or Law impairing the Obligation of Contracts, or grant any Title of Nobility.

No State shall, without the Consent of the Congress, lay any Imposts or Duties on Imports or Exports, except what may be absolutely necessary for executing its inspection Laws: and the net Product of all Duties and Imposts, laid by any State on Imports or Exports, shall be for the Use of the Treasury of the United States and all such Laws shall be subject to the Revision and Controul of the Congress.

No State shall, without the Consent of Congress, lay any duty of Tonnage, keep Troops, or Ships of War in time of Peace, enter into any Agreement or Compact with another State, or with a foreign Power, or engage in War, unless

---

[4] See the Sixteenth Amendment.

The privilege of the Writ of Habeas Corpus shall not be actually invaded, or in such imminent Danger as will not admit of delay.

ARTICLE II

Section 1. The executive Power shall be vested in a President of the United States of America. He shall hold his Office during the Term of four Years, and, together with the Vice President, chosen for the same Term, be elected, as follows

Each State shall appoint, in such Manner as the Legislature thereof may direct, a Number of Electors, equal to the whole number of Senators and Representatives to which the State may be entitled in the Congress; but no Senator or Representative, or Person holding an Office of Trust or Profit under the United States, shall be appointed an Elector.

The Electors shall meet in their respective States, and vote by Ballot for two persons, of whom one at least shall not be an Inhabitant of the same State with themselves. And they shall make a List of all Persons voted for, and of the Number of Votes for each; which List they shall sign and certify, and transmit sealed to the Seat of the Government of the United States, directed to the President of the Senate. The President of the Senate shall, in the Presence of the Senate and House of Representatives, open all the Certificates, and the Votes shall then be counted. The Person having the greatest Number of Votes shall be the President, if such Number be a Majority of the whole Number of Electors appointed; and if there be more than one who have such Majority, and have an Equal Number of Votes, then the House of Representatives shall immediately chuse by Ballot one of them for President; and if no Person have a Majority, then from the five highest on the List the said House shall in like Manner chuse the President, but in chusing the President, the Votes shall be taken by States, the Representation from each State having one Vote; A quorum for this Purpose shall consist of a Member or Members from two-thirds of the States, and a Majority of all the States shall be necessary to a

Choice. In every Case, after the Choice of the President, the Person having the greatest Number of Votes of the Electors shall be the Vice-President. But if there should remain two or more who have equal Votes, the Senate shall chuse from them by Ballot the Vice President.[5]

The Congress may determine the Time of chusing the Electors, and the Day on which they shall give their Vote; which Day shall be the same throughout the United States.

No person except a natural born Citizen, or a Citizen of the United States, at the time of the Adoption of this Constitution, shall be eligible to the Office of President; neither shall any Person be eligible to that Office who shall not have attained the Age of thirty-five Years, and been fourteen Years a Resident within the United States.

In Case of the Removal of the President from Office, or of his Death, Resignation, or Inability to discharge the Powers and Duties of the said office, the same shall devolve on the Vice President, and the Congress may by Law provide for the Case of Removal, Death, Resignation or Inability, both the President and Vice President, declaring what Officer shall then act as President, and such Officer shall act accordingly, until the Disability be removed, or a President shall be elected.

The President shall, at stated Times, receive for his Services, a Compensation, which shall neither be encreased nor diminished during the Period for which he shall have been elected, and he shall not receive within that Period any other Emolument from the United States, or any of them.

Before he enters on the Execution of his Office, he shall take the following Oath or Affirmation:—"I do solemnly swear (or affirm) that I will faithfully execute the Office of President of the United States, and will to the best of my Ability, preserve, protect and defend the Constitution of the United States."

Section 2. The President shall be Commander in Chief of the Army and Navy of the United States, and of the Militia of the several States, when called into the actual Service of the United States; he may require the Opinion in writing, of the principal officer in each of the executive

---

[5] This paragraph was superseded by the Twelfth Amendment.

Departments, upon any subject relating to the Duties of their respective Offices, and he shall have Power to Grant Reprieves and Pardons for Offenses against the United States, except in Cases of Impeachment.

He shall have Power, by and with the Advice and Consent of the Senate, to make Treaties, provided two-thirds of the Senators present concur; and he shall nominate, and by and with the Advice and Consent of the Senate, shall appoint Ambassadors, other public Ministers and Consuls, Judges of the supreme Court, and all other Officers of the United States, whose Appointments are not herein otherwise provided for, and which shall be established by Law: but the Congress may by Law vest the Appointment of such inferior Offices, as they think proper, in the President alone, in the Courts of Law, or in the Heads of Departments.

The President shall have Power to fill up all Vacancies that may happen during the Recess of the Senate by granting Commissions which shall expire at the End of their next Session.

Section 3. He shall from time to time give to the Congress Information of the State of the Union, and recommend to their Consideration such Measures as he shall judge necessary and expedient; he may, on extraordinary Occasions, convene both Houses, or either of them, and in Cases of Disagreement between them, with Respect to the Time of Adjournment, he may adjourn them to such Time as he shall think proper; he shall receive Ambassadors and other public Ministers; he shall take Care that the Laws be faithfully executed, and shall Commission all of the Officers of the United States.

Section 4. The President, Vice President and all civil Officers of the United States, shall be removed from Office on Impeachment for, and Conviction of, Treason, Bribery, or other high Crimes and Misdemeanors.

ARTICLE III

Section 1. The judicial Power of the United States shall be vested in one supreme Court, and in such inferior Courts as the Congress may from time to time ordain and establish. The Judges, both of the supreme and inferior Courts, shall hold their offices during good Behaviour, and shall, at stated Times, receive for their Services a Compensation which shall not be diminished during their Continuance in Office.

Section 2. The judicial Power shall extend to all Cases, in Law and Equity, arising under this Constitution, the Laws of the United States and Treaties made, or which shall be made, under their Authority;—to all Cases affecting Ambassadors, other public Ministers and Consuls;—to all Cases of admiralty and maritime Jurisdiction;—to Controversies to which the United States shall be a Party;—to Controversies between two or more States;—between a State and Citizens of another State;[6]—Between Citizens of different States;—between Citizens of the same State claiming Lands under Grants of different States, and between a State, or the Citizens thereof, and foreign States, Citizens or Subjects.

In all Cases affecting Ambassadors, other public Ministers and Consuls, and those in which a State shall be a Party, the supreme Court shall have original Jurisdiction. In all the other Cases before mentioned, the supreme Court shall have appellate Jurisdiction, both as to Law and Fact, with such Exceptions, and under such Regulations as the Congress shall make.

The trial of all Crimes, except in Cases of Impeachment, shall be by Jury, and such Trial shall be held in the State where the said Crimes shall have been committed; but when not committed within any State, the Trial shall be at such Place or Places as the Congress may by Law have directed.

Section 3. Treason against the United States, shall consist only in levying War against them, or in adhering to their Enemies, giving them Aid and Comfort. No Person shall be convicted of Treason unless on the Testimony of two Witnesses to the same overt Act, or on Confession in open Court.

The Congress shall have power to declare the Punishment of Treason, but no Attainder of Treason shall work Corruption of Blood, or Forfeiture except during the Life of the Person attainted.

---

[6] See the Eleventh Amendment.

ARTICLE IV

Section 1. Full Faith and Credit shall be given in each State to the public acts, Records, and judicial Proceedings of every other State. And the Congress may by general Laws prescribe the Manner in which such Acts, Records and Proceedings shall be proved, and the Effect thereof.

Section 2. The Citizens of each State shall be entitled to all Privileges and Immunities of Citizens in the several States.

A Person charged in any State with Treason, Felony, or other Crime, who shall flee from Justice, and be found in another State, shall on demand of the executive Authority of the State from which he fled, be delivered up, to be removed to the State having Jurisdiction of the Crime.

No Person held to Service or Labour in one State, under the Laws thereof, escaping into another, shall in Consequence of any Law or Regulation therein, be discharged from such Service or Labour, but shall be delivered up on Claim of the Party to whom such Service or Labour may be due.[7]

Section 3. New States may be admitted by the Congress into this Union; but no new States shall be formed or erected within the Jurisdiction of any other State; nor any State be formed by the Junction of two or more States, or parts of States, without the Consent of the Legislatures of the States concerned as well as of the Congress.

The Congress shall have Power to dispose of and make all needful Rules and Regulations respecting the Territory or other Property belonging to the United States; and nothing in this Constitution shall be so constructed as to Prejudice any Claims of the United States, or of any particular State.

Section 4. The United States shall guarantee to every State in this Union a Republican Form of Government, and shall protect each of them against Invasion; and on Application of the Legislature, or of the Executive (when the Legislature cannot be convened) against domestic Violence.

---

[7] Obsolete. See the Thirteenth Amendment.

ARTICLE V

The Congress whenever two-thirds of both houses shall deem it necessary, shall propose Amendments to this Constitution, or, on the Application of the Legislatures of two-thirds of the several States, shall call a Convention for proposing Amendments, which, in either Case, shall be valid to all Intents and Purposes, as part of this Constitution, when ratified by the Legislatures of three-fourths of the several States, or by Conventions in three-fourths thereof, as the one or the other Mode of Ratification may be proposed by the Congress; Provided that no Amendment which may be made prior to the Year One thousand eight hundred and eight shall in any Manner affect the first and fourth Clauses in the Ninth Section of the first Article; and that no State, without its Consent, shall be deprived of its equal Suffrage in the Senate.

ARTICLE VI

All Debts contracted and Engagements entered into, before the Adoption of this Constitution, shall be as valid against the United States under this Constitution, as under the Confederation.

This Constitution, and the Laws of the United States which shall be made in Pursuance thereof; and all Treaties made, or which shall be made, under the Authority of the United States, shall be the supreme Law of the Land; and the Judges in every State shall be bound thereby, any Thing in the Constitution or Laws of any State to the Contrary notwithstanding.

The Senators and Representatives before mentioned, and the Members of the several State Legislatures, and all executive and judicial Officers, both of the United States and of the several States, shall be bound by Oath or Affirmation, to support this Constitution; but no religious Test shall ever be required as a Qualification to any Office or public Trust under the United States.

ARTICLE VII

The Ratification of the Conventions of nine States shall be sufficient for the Establishment of this Constitution between the States so ratifying the Same. Done in Convention by the Unanimous Consent of the States Present the Seventeenth Day of September in the Year of our Lord one thousand seven hundred and Eighty seven and of the Independence of the United States of America the Twelfth. In Witness whereof We have hereunto subscribed our Names

Go. Washington
Presid't and deputy from Virginia

Delaware
Geo: Read
John Dickinson
Jaco: Broom
Gunning Bedford jun
Richard Bassett

Maryland
James McHenry
Danl Carroll
Dan: of St. Thos Jenifer

South Carolina
J. Rutledge
Charles Pinckney
Charles Cotesworth Pinckney
Pierce Butler

Georgia
William Few
Abr Baldwin

New York
Alexander Hamilton

New Jersey
Wil: Livingston
David Brearley
Wm. Paterson
Jona: Dayton

New Hampshire
John Langdon
Nicholas Gilman

Massachusetts
Nathaniel Gorham
Rufus King

Connecticut
Wm. Saml Johnson
Roger Sherman
Robt. Morris

Virginia
John Blair
James Madison, Jr.

North Carolina
Wm Blount
Hu Williamson
Richd Dobbs Spaight

Pennsylvania
B. Franklin

Thos. Fitzsimons
James Wilson
Thomas Mifflin
Geo. Clymer
Jared Ingersoll
Gouv Morris

Attest:
William Jackson, Secretary

AMENDMENTS[8]

Amendment I

Congress shall make no law respecting an establishment of religion, or prohibiting the free exercise thereof; or abridging the freedom of speech, or of the press; or the right of the people peaceably to assemble, and to petition the Government for a redress of grievances.

Amendment II

A well regulated Militia, being necessary to the security of a free State, the right of the people to keep and bear Arms, shall not be infringed.

Amendment III

No Soldier shall, in time of peace be quartered in any house, without the consent of the Owner, nor in time of war, but in a manner to be prescribed by law.

---

[8] The first 10 Amendments were adopted in 1791.

Amendment IV

The right of the people to be secure in their persons, houses, papers, and effects, against unreasonable searches and seizures, shall not be violated, and no Warrants shall issue, but upon probable cause, supported by Oath or affirmation, and particularly describing the place to be searched, and the persons or things to be seized.

Amendment V

No person shall be held to answer for a capital, or otherwise infamous crime, unless on a presentment or indictment of a Grand Jury, except in cases arising in the land or naval forces, or in the Militia, when in actual service in time of War or public danger; nor shall any person be subject for the same offense to be twice put in jeopardy of life or limb, nor shall be compelled in any criminal case to be a witness against himself, nor be deprived of life, liberty, or property, without due process of law; nor shall private property be taken for public use, without just compensation.

Amendment VI

In all criminal prosecutions, the accused shall enjoy the right to a speedy and public trial, by an impartial jury of the State and district wherein the crime shall have been committed, which district shall have been previously ascertained by law, and to be informed of the nature and the cause of the accusation; to be confronted with the witnesses against him; to have the compulsory process for obtaining witnesses in his favor, and to have the Assistance of Counsel for his defence.

Amendment VII

In suits at common law, where the value in controversy shall exceed twenty dollars, the right of trial by jury shall be preserved, and no fact tried by a jury, shall be otherwise reexamined in any Court of the United States, than according to the rules of the common law.

Amendment VIII

Excessive bail shall not be required, nor excessive fines imposed, nor cruel and unusual punishments inflicted.

Amendment IX

The enumeration in the Constitution, of certain rights shall not be construed to deny or disparge others retained by the people.

Amendment X

The powers not delegated to the United States by the Constitution, nor prohibited by it to the States, are reserved to the States respectively, or to the people.

Amendment XI[9]

The Judicial power of the United States shall not be construed to extend to any suit in law or equity, commenced or prosecuted against one of the United States by Citizens of another State, or by Citizens or Subjects of any Foreign States.

Amendment XII[10]

The Electors shall meet in their respective states and vote by ballot for President and Vice President, one of whom, at least, shall not be an inhabitant of the same state with themselves; they shall name in their ballots the person voted for as President and in distinct ballots the person voted for as Vice President, and they shall make distinct lists of all per-

---

[9] Adopted in 1798.
[10] Adopted in 1804.

sons voted for as President, and of all persons voted for as Vice President, and of the number of votes for each, which lists they shall sign and certify, and transmit sealed to the seat of the government of the United States, directed to the President of the Senate;—The President of the Senate shall, in the presence of the Senate and House of Representatives, open all the certificates and the votes shall then be counted;— The person having the greatest number of votes for President, shall be the President, if such number be a majority of the whole number of Electors appointed; and if no person have such majority, then from the persons having the highest numbers not exceeding three on the list of those voted for as President, the House of Representatives shall choose immediately, by ballot, the President. But in choosing the President, the votes shall be taken by states, the representation from each state having one vote; a quorum for this purpose shall consist of a member or members from two-thirds of the states, and a majority of all the states shall be necessary to a choice. And if the House of Representatives shall not choose a President whenever the right of choice shall devolve upon them, before the fourth day of March next following, then the Vice President shall act as President, as in the case of the death or other constitutional disability of the President.—The person having the greatest number of votes as Vice President, shall be the Vice President, if such number be a majority of the whole number of Electors appointed, and if no person have a majority, then from the two highest numbers on the list, the Senate shall choose the Vice President; a quorum for the purpose shall consist of two-thirds of the whole number of Senators, and a majority of the whole number shall be necessary to a choice. But no person constitutionally ineligible to the office of President shall be eligible to that of Vice President of the United States.

Amendment XIII[11]

Section 1. Neither slavery nor involuntary servitude, except as a punishment for crime whereof the party shall

---

[11] Adopted in 1865.

have been duly convicted, shall exist within the United States, or any place subject to their jurisdiction.

Section 2. Congress shall have power to enforce this article by appropriate legislation.

Amendment XIV[12]

Section 1. All persons born or naturalized in the United States and subject to the jurisdiction thereof, are citizens of the United States and of the State wherein they reside. No State shall make or enforce any law which shall abridge the privileges or immunities of citizens of the United States; nor shall any State deprive any person of life, liberty, or property, without the due process of law; nor deny to any person within its jurisdiction the equal protection of the laws.

Section 2. Representatives shall be apportioned among the several States according to their respective numbers, counting the whole number of persons in each State, excluding Indians not taxed. But when the right to vote at any election for the choice of electors for President and Vice President of the United States, Representatives in Congress, the Executive and Judicial Officers of a State, or the members of the Legislature thereof, is denied to any of the male inhabitants of such State, being twenty-one years of age, and citizens of the United States, or in any way abridged, except for participation in rebellion, or other crime, the basis of representation therein shall be reduced in the proportion which the number of such male citizens shall bear to the whole number of male citizens twenty-one years of age in such State.

Section 3. No person shall be a Senator or Representative in Congress, or elector of President and Vice President, or hold any office, civil or military, under the United States, or under any State, who, having previously taken an oath, as a member of Congress, or as an officer of the United States, or as a member of any State legislature, or as an executive or judicial officer of any State, to support the Constitution of the United States, shall have engaged in insurrection or rebel-

---

[12] Adopted in 1868.

lion against the same, or given aid or comfort to the enemies thereof. But Congress may by a vote of two-thirds of each House, remove such disability.

Section 4. The validity of the public debt of the United States, authorized by law, including debts incurred for payment of pensions and bounties for services in suppressing insurrection or rebellion, shall not be questioned. But neither the United States nor any State shall assume or pay any debt or obligation incurred in aid of insurrection or rebellion against the United States, or any claim for the loss or emancipation of any slave; but all such debts, obligations and claims shall be held illegal and void.

Section 5. The Congress shall have power to enforce, by appropriate legislation, the provisions of this article.

Amendment XV[13]

Section 1. The right of citizens of the United States to vote shall not be denied or abridged by the United States or by any State on account of race, color, or previous condition of servitude.

Section 2. The Congress shall have power to enforce this article by appropriate legislation.

Amendment XVI[14]

The Congress shall have power to lay and collect taxes on incomes, from whatever source derived, without apportionment among the several States, and without regard to any census or enumeration.

Amendment XVII[15]

The Senate of the United States shall be composed of two Senators from each State, elected by the people thereof, for six years, and each Senator shall have one vote. The electors

---

[13] Adopted in 1870.
[14] Adopted in 1913.
[15] Adopted in 1913.

in each state shall have the qualifications requisite for electors of the most numerous branch of the State legislatures.

When vacancies happen in the representation of any State in the Senate, the executive authority of such State shall issue writs of election to fill such vacancies: Provided, That the legislature of any State may empower the executive thereof to make temporary appointments until the people fill the vacancies by election as the legislature may direct.

This amendment shall not be so construed as to affect the election or term of any Senator chosen before it becomes valid as part of the Constitution.

Amendment XVIII[16]

Section 1.   After one year from the ratification of this article the manufacture, sale, or transportation of intoxicating liquors within, the importation thereof into, or the exportation thereof from the United States and all territory subject to the jurisdiction thereof for beverage purposes is hereby prohibited.

Section 2.   The Congress and the several States shall have concurrent power to enforce this article by appropriate legislation.

Section 3.   This article shall be inoperative unless it shall have been ratified as an amendment to the Constitution by the legislatures of the several States, as provided in the Constitution, within seven years from the date of the submission hereof to the States by the Congress.

Amendment XIX[17]

The right of Citizens of the United States to vote shall not be denied or abridged by the United States or by any State on account of sex.

Congress shall have power to enforce this article by appropriate legislation.

---

[16] Adopted in 1919. Repealed by the Twenty-first Amendment.
[17] Adopted in 1920.

Amendment XX[18]

Section 1. The terms of the President and Vice President shall end at noon on the 20th day of January, and the terms of Senators and Representatives at noon on the 3d day of January, of the years in which such terms would have ended if this article had not been ratified; and the terms of their successors shall then begin.

Section 2. The Congress shall assemble at least once in every year, and such meeting shall begin at noon on the 3d day of January, unless they shall by law appoint a different day.

Section 3. If, at the time fixed for the beginning of the term of the President, the President elect shall have died, the Vice President elect shall become President. If a President shall not have been chosen before the time fixed for the beginning of his term, or if the President elect shall have failed to qualify, then the Vice President elect shall act as President until a President shall have qualified; and the Congress may by law provide for the case wherein neither a President elect nor a Vice President elect shall have qualified, declaring who shall then act as President, or the manner in which one who is to act shall be selected, and such person shall act accordingly until a President or Vice President shall have qualified.

Section 4. The Congress may by law provide for the case of the death of any of the persons from whom the House of Representatives may choose a President whenever the right of choice shall have devolved upon them, and for the case of the death of any of the persons from whom the Senate may choose a Vice President whenever the right of choice shall have devolved upon them.

Section 5. Sections 1 and 2 shall take effect on the 15th day of October following the ratification of this article.

Section 6. This article shall be inoperative unless it shall have been ratified as an amendment to the Constitution by the legislatures of three-fourths of the several States within seven years from the data of its submission.

---

[18] Adopted in 1933.

Amendment XXI[19]

Section 1. The eighteenth article of amendment to the Constitution of the United States is hereby repealed.

Section 2. The transportation or importation into any State, Territory, or possession of the United States for delivery or use therein of intoxicating liquors, in violation of the laws thereof, is hereby prohibited.

Section 3. This article shall be inoperative unless it shall have been ratified as an amendment to the Constitution by conventions in the several States, as provided in the Constitution, within seven years from the date of the submission hereof to the States by the Congress.

Amendment XXII[20]

Section 1. No person shall be elected to the office of the President more than twice, and no person who has held the office of President, or acted as President, for more than two years of a term to which some other person was elected President shall be elected to the office of the President more than once. But this Article shall not apply to any person holding the office of President when this Article was proposed by the Congress, and shall not prevent any person who may be holding the office of President, or acting as President, during the term within which this Article becomes operative from holding the office of President or acting as President during the remainder of such term.

Section 2. This article shall be inoperative unless it shall have been ratified as an amendment to the Constitution by the Legislatures of three-fourths of the several States within seven years from the data of its submission to the States by the Congress.

Amendment XXIII[21]

Section 1. The District constituting the seat of Govern-

---

[19] Adopted in 1933.
[20] Adopted in 1951.
[21] Adopted in 1961.

ment of the United States shall appoint in such manner as the Congress may direct:

A number of electors of President and Vice President equal to the whole number of Senators and Representatives in Congress to which the District would be entitled if it were a State, but in no event more than the least populous State; they shall be in addition to those appointed by the States; but they shall be considered, for the purposes of the election of President and Vice President, to be electors appointed by a State; and they shall meet in the District and perform such duties as provided by the twelfth article of amendment.

Section 2.   The Congress shall have power to enforce this article by appropriate legislation.

Amendment XXIV[22]

Section 1.   The right of citizens of the United States to vote in any primary or other election for the President or Vice President, for electors for President or Vice President, or for Senator or Representative in Congress, shall not be denied or abridged by the United States or any State by reason of failure to pay any poll tax or other tax.

Section 2.   The Congress shall have power to enforce this article by appropriate legislation.

Amendment XXV[23]

Section 1.   In case of the removal of the President from office or his death or resignation, the Vice President shall become President.

Section 2.   Whenever there is a vacancy in the office of the Vice President, the President shall nominate a Vice President who shall take the office upon confirmation by a majority vote of both houses of Congress.

Section 3.   Whenever the President transmits to the President pro tempore of the Senate and the Speaker of the House of Representatives his written declaration that he is unable to

---

[22] Adopted in 1964.
[23] Adopted in 1967.

discharge the powers and duties of his office, and until he transmits to them a written declaration to the contrary, such powers and duties shall be discharged by the Vice President as Acting President.

Section 4. Whenever the Vice President and a majority of either the principal officers of the executive departments or of such other body as Congress may by law provide, transmit to the President pro tempore of the Senate and the Speaker of the House of Representatives their written declaration that the President is unable to discharge the powers and duties of his office, the Vice President shall immediately assume the powers and duties of the office as Acting President.

Thereafter, when the President transmits to the President pro tempore of the Senate and the Speaker of the House of Representatives, his written declaration that no inability exists, he shall resume the powers and duties of his office unless the Vice President and a majority of either the principal officers of the executive department or of such other body as Congress may by law provide, transmit within four days to the President pro tempore of the Senate and the Speaker of the House of Representatives their written declaration that the President is unable to discharge the powers and duties of his office. Thereupon Congress shall decide the issue, assembling within 48 hours for that purpose if not in session. If the Congress, within 21 days after receipt of the latter written declaration, or, if Congress is not in session, within 21 days after Congress is required to assemble, determines by two-thirds vote of both houses that the President is unable to discharge the powers and duties of his office, the Vice President shall continue to discharge the same as Acting President; otherwise, the President shall resume the powers and duties of his office.

Amendment XXVI[24]

Section 1. The Right of Citizens of the United States, who are eighteen years of age or older, to vote shall not be denied

---

[24] Adopted in 1971.

or abridged by the United States or by any State on account of age.

Section 2.   The Congress shall have power to enforce this article by appropriate legislation.

Proposed Amendment XXVII[25]

Section 1.   Equality of rights under the law shall not be denied or abridged by the United States or by any State on account of sex.

Section 2.   The Congress shall have the power to enforce, by appropriate legislation, the provisions of this article.

Section 3.   This amendment shall take effect two years after the date of ratification.

---

[25] Proposed March 22, 1972.

Index I: Subject Matter

Index II: Court Cases